The Secret Story of
POLYGAMY

Kathleen Tracy

SOURCEBOOKS, INC.®
NAPERVILLE, ILLINOIS

Published by Sourcebooks, Inc.
P.O. Box 4410, Naperville, Illinois 60567-4410
(630) 961-3900
FAX: (630) 961-2168
www.sourcebooks.com

Library of Congress Cataloging-in-Publication Data
Tracy Kathleen.
   The secret story of polygamy / Kathleen Tracy.
      p. cm.
Includes bibliographical references and index.
   ISBN 1-57071-723-0 (alk. paper)
   1. Polygamy—United States. 2. Polygamy—United States—
History. 3. Mormon Church—United States—History. 4. Mormon
families—United States—History. I. Title.
   HQ981.T7 2001
   306.84'23—dc21   289.3

                                          2001032765

Printed and bound in the United States of America
VHG 10 9 8 7 6 5 4 3 2 1

TABLE OF CONTENTS

AUTHOR TO READER

In June 1999, John Daniel Kingston, one of Utah's most promi-nent Mormons and one of the state's most notorious polygamists, was sentenced to seven months in jail. He had been convicted at an earlier trial of brutally whipping his sixteen-year-old daughter, Mary Ann, as punishment for fleeing an arranged, polygamous marriage to her father's brother. In July, her uncle, David Ortell Kingston, was sentenced to ten years in prison after a jury found him guilty of incest and unlawful sexual conduct. What is most worth noting is that although polygamy was at the heart of the prosecutions of David and Daniel Kingston, neither was charged as a polygamist. Instead, they faced charges stemming from the obvious physical abuse to Mary Ann.

Perhaps no other single event in recent memory has galvanized both sides of the polygamy question as much as the Kingston trials, which have become lightening rods for all the issues surrounding plural marriages. The sensational details of the case alone made the trial compelling enough, but what turned it into spectacle were the participants. More than merely being defendants in the trial that shone a national spotlight on obscure religious practice, the Kingston clan is pivotal in any discussion of plural marriages. Not only are they one of the wealthiest family empires in Utah, with fif-teen hundred members and interests in everything from casinos to farms, with an estimated worth of $150 million, they are also polygamy hardliners who rule with an iron fist and who have been accused more than once of enforcing their religious code with vio-lence and abuse.

Although polygamy is illegal in the United States, and the Church of Jesus Christ of Latter-Day Saints, as the Mormon Church is for-mally known, renounced polygamous marriages in 1890 as a condition to the Utah territory becoming a state, the practice not only continues with the often-tacit acceptance from religious and state authorities, in many areas it is positively flourishing.

While proponents of plural marriages claim they are being denied religious freedom as guaranteed by the United States Constitution, opponents say that in addition to rampant welfare fraud, polygamy fosters horrible physical and sexual abuse of minor girls and is resulting in an alarming number of birth defects, the product of generational inbreeding. In the wake of the shocking trials of the Kingston brothers in 1999, many in Utah—including those in the Mormon mainstream—are beginning to openly question why state authorities are not more aggressively enforcing the laws against polygamy, particularly since many of the women involved in the illegal marriages are underage. And that is the crux for many opponents who argue that the concept of religious freedom was never intended to be a legal loophole for child abuse, sexual molestation, and statutory rape.

Obviously, nobody in law enforcement or any elected official condones the victimization of young girls. However, prosecution is complicated. Part of the problem, say officials, is that the ceremonies are conducted in secret, far from prying eyes and within clans that obsessively—and, according to defectors, menacingly—guard their privacy. Some officials have noted that plural marriage is so common that Utah would not have the means, money, or facilities to house the number of polygamists, which are estimated to number as high as sixty thousand in Utah and other parts of the West. However, because of the secretive nature of plural marriages, it's impossible to know for sure the exact number or the proportion of male to female polygamists.

And Utah Governor Mike Leavitt, whose own family engaged in polygamy four generations ago, has defended the lack of prosecutions on the grounds that there is a freedom of religion concern. But to the women who claim to have been beaten, forced into unwanted marriages, sexually molested, and virtually held prisoner, the issue isn't about religious freedom but civil rights; about abuse hiding behind the smoke screen of religion.

And with the eyes of the world turning on Utah as polygamy cases grab media attention, these opponents of polygamy are turning up the heat on state law enforcement officials and politicians to confront the issue of plural marriages by going public with their fight. Among those pushing the issue most passionately are women who, having escaped from arranged plural marriages, are coming forward with tales of abuse, terror, and treatment usually associated with more fundamentalist third world cultures than our own.

Connie Rugg, a half-sister of John and David Kingston who fled the family in 1977, is one survivor who believes that even if authorities did go on the offensive, they would be fighting an uphill battle to enforce current polygamy laws, in large part because of the social structure within plural marriages. "The men control everything, from how much money the women may have, to what car they can drive," Rugg says. "Polygamy is a state of mind. It's like waking up and finding yourself in a different country where women have lost any free will. It will take a long time to change that."

Much of what officials are learning of the plural marriage lifestyle comes from women like Rugg, who together have formed an alliance called Tapestry Against Polygamy, a self-help group of former polygamous wives who have set up a network of "safe houses" with the goal of freeing women and children from what they assert are the horrors of these male-dominated colonies. The group was formed as a grass-roots effort to help those wanting to flee plural marriages, founded by women who shared the common experience of having lived the lifestyle themselves.

Among other revelations, these women paint a picture of endless servitude, a culture where women are treated like brood mares, expected to bear a child each year and mark down their "fertile dates" on their husbands' calendars. All property and land are held in the husband's name, and, while sons are often given a college education, daughters rarely receive an education beyond high school. Defectors also claim that child and sexual abuse are rampant, that incest is common, and that women and children are trapped in a system resembling slavery where resisters are threatened with "blood atonement," or death.

"Polygamy is about power. It's about the control of women," said Rowenna Erickson, fifty-eight, who grew up in the Kingston group and spent more than three decades in a plural marriage before leaving in 1994.

Equally passionate are those who believe polygamy is a God-given directive and who see the campaign against their way of life as no less than religious persecution. To these fundamentalists, both men and women, their lifestyle is protected by divine right and by the Constitution. They claim media-fueled tales of forced marriages and criminality are merely sensational attempts to discredit their beliefs. "It's quite healthy for women," says Mary Potter, a founder of the Women's Religious Liberties Union, formed to promote the legalization of polygamy. "It's honorable and fulfilling just like any other family structure."

What's interesting is that for as isolated and secretive as polygamists are, the history of polygamy within the Mormon Church is readily available to anyone who visits Salt Lake City or who owns a computer with access to the Internet. The written history of the Latter-Day Saints is an integral part of the Mormon faith and since it's very beginnings, every meeting, every sermon, and every important event has been carefully and painstakingly written and recorded, including personal "affidavits" that are as compelling as they are revealing. In addition to library research, many of the documents referenced or referred to in this book were obtained through Internet research.

However, the heart and soul of *The Secret Story of Polygamy* lies in the people who populate it. Among those interviewed include Erickson, one of the Tapestry Against Polygamy founders, and Detective Scott Cosgrove, who took on the Kingston family when many of his superiors told him he'd never succeed in getting a conviction. It is through their words and others' that the reader will get a vibrant sense of the polygamous world depicted in the book.

As with any complex issue, there are no clear-cut, easy answers when religious freedom and societal mores collide, when the rights of children and the right to practice one's beliefs unencumbered are at odds, when an increasingly vocal constituency challenges the perceived ineffectiveness of authorities. In an effort to more clearly define the issues, both sides of the polygamy quandary will be presented in these pages, including interviews with women who have lived in plural marriages and, in their words, "escaped," as well as some proponents of polygamy, who paint pictures of domestic and spiritual completion.

Against this backdrop of the complex and conflicting religious, social, and cultural issues surrounding plural marriages and all its ramifications, it will be left for the reader to decide whether polygamy is God's will, the devil's work, or a religious artifact trying to coexist in a new millennium.

ical, now called Morton-Thiokol, opened operations in Brigham City, signaling the start of the area's close ties to the defense and aerospace industries. After buying eleven thousand acres of land and building a $3 million plant to developed and manufacture huge rocket motors, in 1958 Thiokol was awarded a contract to build the first stage for the Air Force's revolutionary Minuteman ICDB, which was the largest solid rocket motor built to date. In addition, the company also built the Poseidon and Trident submarine-launched missiles as well as the Peacekeeper missile. Later, they would also work on space shuttle booster rockets. Even so, by 1997, the per capita earnings of the local residents was below $20,000, and despite a few wealthy families, the majority of those living in the county are of modest means at best. And unlike urban centers on the country's east and west coasts, the population density throughout Utah is low, with the county having a population under forty-five thousand, and Brigham City, the largest town in the county, having fewer than twenty thousand residents.

Currently, local officials tout Box Elder County as both a tourist destination and a place that offers "a casual lifestyle, a strong sense of community, and a firmly ingrained work ethic that have fashioned the county into an appealing place for families to live, work, and play. Box Elder County's far-flung communities project a small town atmosphere combined with easy urban access. Most of the County's communities are located within an hour's drive of Salt Lake City."

That said, for however close in minutes the county towns may be to Salt Lake City's cultural arts and city life, in many ways Box Elder County is hovering in a time warp of days and mores past. Certainly, Mary Ann Kingston's life bore little resemblance to that of the typical American teenager's. From the moment of her birth, her life and destiny was already determined for her—in the Kingston clan the only roles for women are as childbearer and obedient participant in maintaining the legacy of polygamy.

The Death of Andrea Johnson

Long before Mary Ann filed an official complaint against her father, the Kingston's were well known to local authorities. In addition to numerous civil suits, there was one particular criminal investigation that cast the first significant spotlight on the family's inner workings. In 1992, the Salt Lake County sheriff's office investigated the death of a fifteen-year-old girl named Andrea Johnson. A Box Elder County sheriff's detective, Scott Cosgrove, contends his department raised a red flag about the girl's death shortly after she died in a local hospital. Johnson was born on July 19, 1976. According to her death certificate, Andrea was the eleventh of thirteen children born to Isabell Johnson. Although the death certificate names a fictitious truck driver named Steven Joseph Johnson as the father, according to both a relative and the findings of a 1983 state investigation, the real father is John Ortell Kingston, the now-deceased leader who built the fifteen hundred–member Latter-Day Church of Christ, a splinter sect that adheres to polygamy as a cornerstone of their faith.

"Somebody sent us a program from the funeral, and John Daniel Kingston was listed as a pallbearer," Cosgrove recalled. "That was enough for us to notify the sheriff's office in Salt Lake and tell them they ought to look at it." Simultaneous to that, detectives working in the juvenile division received information from a confidential informant that raised questions about the circumstances of Johnson's death.

Specifically, Andrea died from complications due to her pregnancy. Her condition, preeclampsia, commonly called toxemia, is an easily treatable condition many women experience during pregnancy. However, Andrea Johnson's symptoms were not treated and some claimed the reason for that was that getting her the medical attention she needed would have exposed that Andrea was involved in a polygamous marriage with one of the Kingstons. According to Johnson's sister, Connie Rugg, Andrea had secretly married Jason Kingston, the youngest brother of Paul Kingston, who now headed the Latter-Day Church of Christ.

Rugg is in a position to know. When she was seventeen, Connie ran off and eloped with a boy who was from the Kingston clan. However, when the two later divorced, she fell out of contact with most of that group. Through her mother and a few siblings, she learned that Andrea had married her teenage half-brother, Jason Kingston, in a secret Mormon ceremony. Another former member of the clan, Elaine Jenkins, also confirmed the marriage had taken place. There would not be any official record because the marriages are not reported to the state. Even in Utah, it's illegal to marry a half-sibling, with incest being a third-degree felony.

Eventually, Andrea's condition worsened to the point where she was brought to the University of Utah Health Sciences Center. According to one of Andrea's sisters, by the time doctors diagnosed her, the toxemia had progressed to a critical stage. She was suffering from such advanced edema, or swelling, that she had become blind. Three days after Andrea arrived at the hospital, doctors performed an emergency Cesarean section, delivering a one-pound, eleven-ounce boy. Eleven days later, Andrea died. The baby survived, but was diagnosed with cerebral palsy. The official cause listed on the death certificate was brain hemorrhage. But on Andrea's death certificate, attending physician James B. Burns wrote that Andrea must have exhibited signs of hypertension "at least two weeks" before her death. He noted that the underlying cause of death, eclampsia, had persisted for an "unknown duration," and that the brain hemorrhage had been developing for twelve days.

Isabell Johnson was quoted in an interview with Salt Lake City's *Tribune* that her daughter was not sick until the day Isabell traveled 170 miles from Ibapah, Utah, to Salt Lake City to take Andrea to the hospital. Johnson said she thought Andrea had come down with the flu. Whatever the cause, Rugg, who is now an advocate against polygamy, believes her sister died needlessly.

"This doesn't happen that quick," Rugg says. "I had that same condition and I was sick for a good two months before I went to the hospital. Andrea had to be delirious for at least a week for her to be in that condition. She was way beyond the point that I was. She had two blood clots the size of lemons. They actually had to cut into her skull to release the pressure. It was completely unnecessary. Nobody dies from an illness like that. It's like dying from a broken leg because it's not set. It's easily treated."

Rugg feels her sister was left to suffer without medical help only because Jason, then just sixteen himself, and his mother, LaDonna

Kingston, were afraid it would reveal their family's polygamist lifestyle if doctors and authorities started to ask questions about Andrea's condition. "When they got there she was swollen beyond recognition," Rugg said. "She was in bed screaming, 'Why won't anybody help me?' They worried people at the hospital would ask them who the father was, why a fifteen-year-old girl was pregnant, and where her mother was. They were waiting for a responsible party, and they did not want to be that party."

If they indeed were reticent, it was grounded in past experience. In 1983, a state investigation resulted in Jason's father being charged with welfare fraud after he was linked to four wives who had claimed they were single mothers needing state assistance for their twenty-nine children. Isabell Johnson, Andrea's mother, was one of those women. Also, had Andrea revealed the alleged paternity of the child, Jason would be open to incest charges.

However unusual it was for a fifteen-year-old to die from toxemia, her death almost went unnoticed by authorities. It wasn't until the Kingston connection was revealed and confidential tips were placed that authorities took another look into the possibility that Andrea's death was due to criminal negligence. "It was brought to our attention after her death that her death might have been due to neglect," says Lake County sheriff's spokeswoman Peggy Faulkner.

Interestingly, hospital records and Andrea's death certificate do not list her as having a husband. In death, her only official link to the Kingston clan is the name listed on cemetery records as owner of her burial plot, "J.O. Kingston."

But the investigation came to an abrupt and, to some eyes, premature halt when hospital officials informed detectives working the case that Andrea Johnson's medical records had been lost. Sheriff Lt. Leslee Collins, who worked the juvenile division then, recalled, "I was able to get enough information to get an investigative subpoena for the medical records." When they disappeared, "That struck me as odd because that was a pretty powerful subpoena. Everything in that case pretty much hinged on the medical records."

The missing file seemed more conspiratorial than coincidental to many investigating the case. And there were some in the sheriff's office who pressed to bring obstruction of justice charges against the hospital, which in the end never came to fruition. Instead, the case was shelved and authorities reluctantly let the matter drop. In a final footnote, Medicaid paid for Johnson's $48,000 hospital bill.

Currently, the exact whereabouts of Andrea's baby are unknown. His father, Jason, works for the state auditor's office and had repeatedly ignored requests for interviews. A sworn deposition given by Jason's sister, Ruth Kingston Brown, to the state Attorney General's office in 1994 indicates he is now married to his niece.

While Connie Rugg may have bitterly felt the Kingstons had dodged a bullet in having their lifestyle publicly exposed, others saw the investigative dead-end in the Johnson case as business as usual in Utah. When it came to polygamy issues, it was as if the judicial system had gone into suspended animation. Despite the laws on the books, the last polygamy cases to be prosecuted occurred in the 1950s when authorities attempted a crackdown on the town of Short Creek, perched on the Utah-Arizona border.

Short Creek

Short Creek, located just inside Arizona, was originally settled by Mormons during the 1860s and got its name from the nearby stream that was absorbed into the sand before it had traveled very far. The town existed in relative obscurity until around the turn of the twentieth century. By that time, the Mormon Church had outlawed polygamy—a decree ignored by many of the more fundamentalist members. Those unwilling to abide by the law left their homes and went in search of a place they could practice their belief freely. Short Creek, along with the nearby town of Hilldale, Utah, suddenly became the top destination for these suddenly disenfranchised church-goers, who lived there in plural-marriage peace for the next half century.

Then, in 1953, the political climate changed. The governor of Arizona, John Howard Pyle, felt the two communities were blatantly flaunting the violation of several laws, including tax fraud and polygamy. More importantly, officials also believed the two hundred and sixty-three children of the community were at physical and spiritual risk and felt morally and legally it was time to crack down. With Pyle's consent, several hundred Arizona state officials and police officers raided the town in the early morning hours of July 26, 1953, serving warrants on thirty-six men and eighty-six women. Although bloodless, it was a brutal coup. More than two hundred children were taken from their family homes and placed with foster families in Phoenix. Twenty-seven people were arrested and received a symbolic one-year probationary sentence.

Although Pyle and his advisors felt the raid had been a success, the public apparently felt otherwise, particularly over tales of children screaming as they were forcibly taken away from hysterical mothers and overpowered fathers. Protests erupted across the state, forcing authorities to do an about-face. Eventually, all of the families were reunited, but the Pyle administration had suffered an irreparable public relations disaster. Outrage simmered and Governor Pyle lost in his bid for reelection a year later. Haunted by the memory of the raid and the attention it brought, Short Creek officially changed its name Colorado City in 1963.

The Abuse of Mary Ann Kingston

Ever since the Short Creek debacle, authorities had turned a blind eye to polygamous clans, adopting a live-and-let-live stance based on the credo that what consenting adults do together is their business alone. However, Mary Ann Kingston rocked that long-standing complacency and forced authorities to confront the very real possibility that there were other young girls out there being physically and sexually abused.

Up until October 1997, fifteen-year-old Mary Ann Kingston would have passed for a typical teenager. She was attending high school and found herself seriously attracted to a boy four years older than herself. Her adolescent heart fell hard and Mary Ann daydreamed of marrying the boy. But Mary Ann wasn't your typical teenager and the schoolgirl object of her desire stood little chance in actually winning her hand. In the Kingston family, women ultimately had very little say in whom they would marry, and in Mary Ann's case her father wouldn't hear of Mary Ann marrying the young man of her choice.

Even though she recalls her father telling her when she had been about thirteen to "start preparing for marriage and who I should marry," the tacit understanding was that the ultimate decision wouldn't be hers. Instead, girls her age in "the order," as she refers to the polygamous sect her family belongs to, are married to whomever clan leader Paul Kingston, her father's brother, approves of. And her boyfriend wasn't on the list. While Paul Kingston does not directly arrange marriages, she said he has to approve them.

A few months after her sixteenth birthday, Mary Ann had a meeting with her father, John; her mother Susan Nelson—who also happens to be John's half-sister—and her uncle David, who told her that one of his other wives had dreamed "about me coming into their family and that it was a good thing." Inside her heart and mind, Mary Ann bristled and didn't want to marry David. But she was powerless to do anything to stop it. Rather than argue, all she said was, "Sounds like this is supposed to happen." Although she left the church without a set date, there was no doubt she was now officially betrothed. In whatever ways she could, Mary Ann found herself trying to stall. "I wasn't ready. I didn't want it to happen so fast," she says then adds pointedly, "I just didn't want to get married"—at least, not to her uncle. It would later be revealed that Mary Ann had so set her heart on marrying her boyfriend that she had secretly bought a wedding dress; but any hopes she may have had were soon destroyed.

On October 13, 1997, David called Mary Ann to tell her they were getting married two days later. "I was kind of in shock because it was in two days and I needed more time." But the decision was entirely out of her hands. After her mother Susan gave her consent, David Kingston said he would call Paul Kingston to obtain his approval. The date of the arranged marriage, October 15, 1997, was not happenstance. Her uncle, David Kingston, picked the date because she was going to be his fifteenth wife. He would also buy her a ring with fifteen diamonds, further highlighting the significance of the number.

It's unclear why Mary Ann was given such short notice about the decision that she was to marry her uncle. Whether because there was concern over her emotions for the boy she was in love with or whether it was simply part of a prearranged timing, Mary Ann had only two days to adjust emotionally and mentally to the idea that life as she had known it was ending. The teenager spent the next day cleaning and decorating the church where she'd be married—alone. On the morning of her wedding, Mary Ann helped her mother prepare some food, then put on her wedding dress and drove the church where the ceremony would take place—the same west Salt Lake City church where she had first learned she would be David's next wife. At two in the afternoon, John Kingston walked her down the aisle and steered her into a front pew, where she sat with David Kingston's fourteen other wives.

The self-described "secret" ceremony between Mary Ann and her uncle David, then thirty-two years old, was presided over by her father and was attended only by her family—mother Susan, Mary Ann's six sisters, and two of her three brothers—who watched as Mary Ann exchanged vows with her uncle. To her recollection, the wedding lasted several hours and, at 7:30 P.M., she and David left the church to spend their honeymoon night together. David drove Mary Ann to the Olympus Park Hotel in Park City, Utah, where they would spend the evening. However, David's plans to consummate the marriage were thwarted when Mary Ann told him she was having her period.

After their aborted honeymoon, Mary Ann returned home to the Salt Lake City suburb of Sandy, Utah, and somewhat naïvely hoped to resume her normal, high school life. And for a while, she might have actually believed she was succeeding. She went to class, had fun with friends, and even managed to go on dates. But her idyll was shortlived. In late January 1998, three months after her wedding, David Kingston came calling. Mary Ann says he had called her earlier that day to ask if he could come over, and he arrived about 9 P.M., just as she was getting ready for bed. With the consent and knowledge of her mother, David and Mary Ann had sex for the first time in her room. "I guess it was my night," she would say later. "I didn't say anything. I didn't want it to happen, but I didn't stop him." The reason she chose not to resist was out of fear of what would happen if she did. "I didn't dare to. I didn't know what he'd do if I pushed him away." And it wasn't as if she could turn to her family for protection and support. All she could do was submit and wait for it to be over. "After he fell asleep, I grabbed a blanket and a pillow and went to sleep on the floor."

Mary Ann continued living in her mother's house for the next couple of months until March 1998, when David brought her into an apartment at a Kingston family–owned coal yard located in Murray, Utah. The apartment was located behind the home of David's second wife, Maryann Isaacson, and she would share it with her uncle's half-sister. Mary Ann says the reason he had insisted she changed the place where she lived was "to keep close tabs on me," and to monitor her every move, which he accomplished by having one of his other wives stay with her at all times.

The move itself had come after Mary Ann had stood David up on an arranged conjugal visit to her mother's house. As a result, she was beginning to be seen as someone needing watching. In addition to feeling imprisoned, the move also dashed any hopes Mary Ann clung to of going back to school. She says she hadn't been allowed to extend her education beyond the ninth grade at Mount Jordan Middle School because, for girls in "the order," education is not considered a priority or even a necessity. "Girls didn't go to school much. It wasn't part of the plan, I guess, for other girls my age, like me. Wives."

Once she was living in the apartment, David was able to arrange a regular visitation schedule to have sex with Mary Ann, although he would never spend the night. The first encounter occurred on the night when she moved in. He returned in April, and then again in May. "I always knew when he would be there," she says. "Tuesday was my night."

During his last visit in May, he finally gave her the fifteen-stone wedding ring, apparently feeling she was now truly in the familial fold. But it was merely an act. Mary Ann didn't feel part of the group; she was terrified at the thought of her uncle touching her again, and felt trapped by the prying eyes surrounding her. It was a feeling very familiar to the members of Tapestry Against Polygamy, a support group of former polygamist wives.

"Through all the sex acts you never heard her say he kissed her," notes Rena Mackert, formerly with a LeBaron polygamist group.

Another, Laura Chapman, a great niece of former polygamist leader Rulon Allred, says bluntly, "He treated her like a prostitute." She goes on to add that, "They never had to slap us; we were beat up by the scriptures daily. We're told it was our role. It was enculturated [sic]. And the first thing they do is get you pregnant so you have a bunch of kids that'll keep you from leaving."

The primary job of watching Mary Ann fell on Christine Gustafson, who had known the teen all her life and, according to Mary Ann, was one of David Kingston's wives. "She was married to David, and she was a cousin of mine," the girl said. "I think it was to watch over me; kind of just baby-sit me." Gustafson would tell authorities she and David Kingston were also related. "I think we are fourth cousins. We're related, somewhere, but it goes kind of way back."

Gustafson says Kingston asked her to live in the apartment on South and she agreed, moving in on March 3, 1998, one day after Mary Ann arrived. "I was there to kind of help her to kind of break the ties with some of her other friends. I figured, if I was there, she wouldn't go out and find alternate entertainment." Not that she had much freedom to do much of anything. According to Mary Ann, she wasn't allowed to go anywhere, not even to the store. However, she resisted being insulated and isolated. Even though she and Christine shared the same bedroom, Mary Ann would brazenly sneak out in the middle of the night and not come back until the next day. Dutifully, Gustafson reported Mary Ann's indiscretions to David Kingston, claiming her motivation was in the teen's best interests. She says both Mary Ann's husband and parents were worried about "the associations that she had and some of the things that she was doing at the time."

But all Mary Ann was trying to do was desperately hold on to some part of her individuality. Feeling ever more trapped, Mary Ann made her first bold bid for freedom when she ran away from the apartment, only to have her father return her to her uncle. Then in May, shortly after David's conjugal visit, Mary Ann took off again. When she didn't come home on May 21, Gustafson notified Susan Nelson, not knowing that after spending the night at a party with friends outside the clan who had been drinking, Mary Ann had then gone to her mother's house hoping for shelter. Instead, Nelson telephoned John Kingston on the evening of May 22, and told him their daughter was there.

Kingston arrived at the house around 11:00 that evening, furious. He ordered Mary Ann to get into his truck, where two other relatives sat. They drove north, dropping the relatives off in Salt Lake City, then got on I-15 and headed towards the group's Washakie Salers ranch in Plymouth near the Idaho border, a huge Kingston property where, according to that former members, wayward wives and children are taken to be punished and disciplined. "I didn't know where we were going, but I kind of figured it out when we passed Ogden," Mary Ann told authorities. The drive to the ranch was terrifying and brutal, with Kingston grabbing his daughter's hair and yanking her head, where he punched her in the mouth and forehead. "I could taste blood from my nose," Mary Ann recalled. She also remembers him saying, "I don't want you to leave, but if you do, you can never come back."

By the time they drove the eighty miles to the ranch, it was in the middle of the night, and Mary Ann's isolation was complete. John ordered her into the barn, and as he turned on the lights, instructed her to take off her jacket and lift up her shirt. He took off his belt and "said he was going to give me ten licks for every wrongdoing. He said there were three," meaning the times she had tried to run away. "I remember him telling me that before the night was over, I'd think twice before I ran away," she added. During the beating, Mary Ann remembers that the barn lights turned off for some reason. Her father coolly turned them back on then resumed the whipping. But before John could finish, after enduring twenty-eight lashes with the belt, his daughter mercifully passed out.

Mary Ann says she has no memory of ever leaving the barn and doesn't know if she walked out or was carried out. She woke up the following morning on a living room couch in the nearby house of Margaret Larsen, who former members say is one of John Kingston's more than twenty wives. Once awake and able to move, Mary Ann fled. It took her two hours to walk six miles on a dirt road to Tri Valley Chevron, where she used a pay phone to dial 911. At one in the afternoon, a Box Elder sheriff's deputy pulled into the station and helped Mary Ann into his car. Initially, she was reluctant to tell the deputy what had happened, saying over and over she didn't want to get anyone in trouble and only wanted a place to stay. Finally, after her safety was guaranteed, she broke down and confided to a detective how she didn't want to be married to her father's brother and just wanted to be able to finish high school.

Detective Scott Cosgrove notes, "This is one of the more serious child abuse cases I've worked on. When we went to the Brigham Hospital to meet her, she had bruises all on her backside beginning at the top of her shoulder blades all the way down her back and the backside of her legs.

"This girl knew she had to pay a price to leave the family because her father was very violent at times, but she decided she needed to leave to go get the life that she desired. She just wanted a normal life. All she wanted was to go back and finish high school," Cosgrove says. "But she knew she'd never be able to do that unless she got away." Then he adds, "You can't explain it. I think that's the highest form of abuse for a child, especially that age, wanting a decent life and then be told who to marry, how to live. That's the highest form of abuse to me."

Mary Ann's injuries as a result of the beating were substantial and shockingly apparent. Her face appeared bloodied and she suffered a swollen nose, cut lip, and deep bruises and welts on her arms, back, buttocks, and legs. The detectives carefully photographed her wounds and had her examined by doctors who took X rays to make sure her nose wasn't broken. Detective Cosgrove recalls the doctor saying her beating was "consistent with a leather strap and that this took great force to cause this extent of the bruising." But more than the beating, Mary Ann's charges opened the door to a second prosecution—this one against her polygamous uncle. Once her statement was signed and prepared, the Box Elder County Sheriff's Office forwarded her allegations against David Kingston to the Salt Lake County Sheriff's Office.

Predictably, David Kingston denied all charges, claiming that he was never married, secret ceremony or otherwise, to his niece, nor had he ever had sex with her. Kingston's defense attorney, Steve McCaughey, accused Mary Ann of being a troubled teenager who was lying to get out of the Kingston clan. As the legal maneuverings started to grind into action, Mary Ann was put under temporary custody with the state Division of Child and Family Services and sent out into foster care. Even so, at the time, Detective Cosgrove noted Mary Ann was "still scared her family would find her. She just wants to go to high school and have a normal life. She is a brave girl. She's willing to testify and go through the whole mess."

A friend of Mary Ann, whose identity was hidden, appeared in an A&E documentary to say, "If David were to say she wasn't his wife by law to the government, it would be truth because there are no papers. Nothing shows they were ever married. But to him, it would be a lie because they were sealed by the leader of the church and they were married. She wasn't allowed to leave her room to go off the property where she was living unless it was with him or another sister-wife."

In August, David Ortell Kingston was arrested and formally charged. After a two-and-half-hour preliminary hearing in 3rd District Court on December 10, 1998, during which a now seventeen-year-old Mary Ann testified about her life as David's fifteenth wife, Judge Leon A. Dever ordered Kingston to stand trial on three counts of incest and one count of unlawful sexual conduct with a minor, all third-degree felonies punishable by up to five years in prison. The trial was set for June 1999.

John Daniel Kingston was charged with second-degree felony child abuse and was scheduled to stand trial beginning March 3, 1999, before Brigham City's 1st District Judge Ben Hadfield. Veteran Salt Lake defense attorney Ron Yengich would represent him. In addition, John was also still under investigation for his part in arranging Mary Ann's marriage to his brother. Besides the trial, there was also a custody hearing scheduled whereby John could be stripped of parental rights. However, attorneys agreed to postpone the juvenile court proceedings before 1st District Juvenile Judge Jeff Burbank until after the criminal trial had concluded.

Amidst all the sensational testimony at David Kingston's preliminary trial, an interesting sidebar was brought to light. While on the stand, Mary Ann admitted that initially she didn't mind the idea of moving out of her mother's house into the apartment David offered because she had been sexually abused at Nelson's residence when she was a child. Prosecutors looked up the case and discovered that detectives had investigated charges Mary Ann, then nine years old, had been raped by another uncle. The investigation was dropped, however, when the girl refused to cooperate—a result of the order's code of silence that had frustrated law enforcement for years when trying to investigate crimes within the Kingston family.

Sgt. Grant Hodgson of Bountiful, Utah, where the family owned some businesses, notes that the local police have repeatedly received complaints of child abuse and other alleged crimes in the family for years. But the cases almost always go nowhere because victims refuse to talk, or worse. "When we get wind of anything, people disappear," Hodgson said in an interview. "How many atrocities are occurring?"

Hodgson gave an example of the difficulty in investigating allegations when he discussed another incident of alleged child sexual abuse involving two cousins in 1987. When officers tried to talk to the children, they had disappeared, only to turn up later at a Kingston-owned farm in Idaho, outside the department's jurisdiction. The police believe the Kingstons have a number of places designated for out-of-line or unruly family members where they can be punished and kept out of the public eye.

While Mary Ann Kingston's allegations would receive the majority of press coverage, her case seemed to ignite a flurry of other investigations. Coincidentally or not, shortly after her story broke, the Salt Lake County Sheriff's Office confirmed it had reopened their investigation into the death of Andrea Johnson, which investigators now believed was caused by her family's refusal to obtain medical help out of fear it would be revealed that Andrea's baby was sired by her half-brother.

"We're on it. In fact, we're pushing it a bit," sheriff's spokesman Jim Potter said in a statement. He also noted that the investigation would likely be given to the same detective who handled the David O. Kingston incest investigation. The break in the case came when Johnson's long-missing medical records mysteriously appeared at

University Hospital. Sheriff's spokeswoman Peggy Faulkner observed that, "Having those records, we can investigate fully to see if she died due to neglect. That's homicide, or at the very least it's manslaughter."

Then, in June 1999, state child welfare officials took seven children from a Sandy, Utah, home after they were found unsupervised and living in garbage-strewn squalor and filth, police reported. Sandy police officer Al Nortz said authorities found food stuck to counters and plates and mold growing in the home's two kitchens. "The kids themselves looked unkempt but not really dirty." The children were discovered alone when officials from the Division and Child of Family Services went to the home on a routine welfare check, and to look for a fifteen-year-old girl who had been reportedly removed from school against her will a year earlier. A hearing was quickly scheduled to determine if the children would be returned to their parents or remain in state custody. Salt Lake County records showed the home was owned by Ellery Kingston, a cousin of John Daniel Kingston. Former Kingston clan member Rowena Erickson gave an interview revealing the children were the offspring of Ellery Kingston and his second wife Maurine Gustafson, with whom he has over a dozen children.

Everywhere authorities turned, it seems a Kingston was there. Shortly after the preliminary trial, Box Elder County Sheriff Detective Scott Cosgrove, who first investigated Mary Ann's case, acknowledged her allegations had led Salt Lake County investigators to other Kingstons allegedly involved in incest. "I can't say what was discussed and what is ahead, but I can say this is not over," Cosgrove commented. At the same time, he was well aware of the challenges involved in pressing incest charges when victims are willing to testify. Still, he said, "My hope is other victims, once these two cases are over, will jump ship; that they will have confidence in the police that they can climb over the wall to escape."

Beyond the problem of hesitant witnesses, there were also fiscal and political issues to overcome. In early 1999, Utah lawmakers rejected a $750,000 appropriation to investigate incest, fraud, and child abuse in "secret societies." Attorneys in Salt Lake and Davis counties said that while they would be willing to prosecute incest cases, they didn't simply didn't have the money to spearhead investigations. "They should be prosecuted, and we have the technology now where we can go out and pursue, through a court order, blood testing, and we can determine without a doubt what's going on," said Davis County Attorney Melvin C. Wilson. However, Wilson also acknowledged prosecuting married couples can be tricky and should be handled on a case by case basis. "As a county attorney you have to use your discretion and take into account the interests of law and justice to pursue that prosecution."

However, prosecutors in other states showed more resolve on the issue. "A good analogy would be cases of drunk driving," says Jeff Klingfuss, Mississippi's special assistant attorney general. "If someone is caught, even though they are good law-abiding citizens in all other areas of their lives, society should prosecute because the potential is there that society will be damaged."

But prosecuting a polygamous clan like the Kingstons could not only pose special challenges, but special dangers as well. Cosgrove revealed that he had received two anonymous death threats and a warning that his life might be in danger because of his investigation into the Kingston family. "I received a few phone calls starting about a week into the investigation, basically telling me not to look at the Kingstons or I could be killed. I received one letter from an inmate at the prison who claims to be a polygamist but not in this family and he basically told me to watch my back if I knew what was good for me." Cosgrove seemed nonplussed by the potential danger. "It's probably just some nut responding to the news," he said. "But the family is feeling the pressure, no doubt. Every day it seems like somebody turns over a rock and finds something else."

Chapter Two
GOD'S WILL

For many on the outside looking in, modern polygamy can be the stuff of one-liners; an oddity that seems blatantly out of step with the new millennium. Jay Leno once did a comedic riff on the concept of plural marriage during his opening monologue on *The Tonight Show.* "Think of it," he said, his voice steeped in sardonic wonder. "Can you imagine having five wives? You'd have to see *Bridges of Madison County* five times; you'd have to see *Hope Floats* five times…"

Ever since the Kingston case attracted the attention of the national media, Utah's long-standing polygamist culture has come under ever-increasing scrutiny, from the public, from ex-members of polygamous clans, from women's groups, and from children's advocates. More than the issue of consenting adults cohabitating within the context of a perceived religious dictum, it's the reports of child abuse, welfare fraud, and other criminal acts that have fueled questions over why state authorities are so reluctant to prosecute. But to understand how polygamy evolved into the divisive and contentious practice it did, resulting in insulated, secret sects officially outcast from the Mormon mainstream which denounces plural marriages, it's important to understand the role polygamy—and early persecution of it—has played, and continues to play, within the history of the Church of Latter-Day Saints.

A Prophet of God

The Mormon faith is based on the belief that founder Joseph Smith was a true prophet of God. Even those who view Smith in less divine terms, such as a charismatic charlatan or possible paranoid schizophrenic, cannot discount his impact on social, political, and spiritual history of this country. He was very much a product of his times and used the alienation felt by his followers at the dramatic social changes occurring around them to establish his own brave new world.

Joseph Smith was born 1805 in Sharon, Vermont, to a poor and transient family that moved repeatedly across New England. If there was a notable bright spot for the young Smith, it was his mother's storytelling ability that offered much needed diversion and entertainment for the family. But when the boy was just a teen, he had an experience that would forever change his life. Sometime during 1820, Smith experienced the First Vision:

> The Lord heard me cry in the wilderness and while in the attitude of calling upon the Lord in the 16th year of my age a pillar of light above the brightness of the sun at noon day come down from above and rested upon me. I was filled with the spirit of God and the Lord opened the heavens upon me and I saw the Lord.
>
> He spake unto me saying, Joseph my son thy sins are forgiven thee. Go thy way, walk in my statutes and keep my commandments. Behold I am the Lord of Glory. I was crucifyed for the world that all those who believe on my name may have Eternal life. Behold the world lieth in sin at this time and none doeth good, no not one. They have turned aside from the gospel and keep not my commandments. They draw near to me with their lips while their hearts are far from me and mine anger is kindling against the inhabitants of earth to visit them according to their ungodliness and to bring to pass that which hath been spoken by the mouth of the prophets and Apostles. Behold and lo, I come quickly as it is written of me, in the cloud clothed in the glory of my Father.

Smith would experience another vision the following year:

> And it came to pass when I was seventeen years of age, I called again upon the Lord and he shewed unto me a heavenly vision. For behold an angel of the Lord came and stood before me. It was by night and he called me by name and he

said the Lord had forgiven me my sins. He revealed unto me that in the Town of Manchester, Ontario County, New York, there was plates of gold upon which there was engravings which was engraven by Moroni and his fathers, the servants of the living God in Ancient days, deposited by the commandments of God and kept by the power thereof and that I should go and get them. He revealed unto me many things concerning the inhabitants of the earth which since have been revealed in commandments and revelations.

Later, Smith would reveal in his writings that the angel Moroni had told him that the gold plates contained the history of the divine origins of the first Americans. In addition, with the plates were two special stones, the Urim and Thummin. According to the angel, the stones held the power through which Smith would be able to translate the plates. However, Joseph claimed it took him three years before he could retrieve the plates because Moroni had deemed him unworthy:

You have not kept the commandments of the Lord which I gave you…And in his own due time thou shalt obtain them.

At this time in America, folk magic was widely practiced and taken quite seriously. According to some biographies, prior to his reported First Vision, the young boy had found a "seerstone," which was alleged to have magical powers that enabled the holder of the stone to locate lost objects as well as precious metals buried in the earth. Perhaps not-so-coincidentally, Smith and his father were called treasure hunters and "money-diggers" by others where they lived. Later, many of his followers believed he would have never found the golden plates of Moroni if he hadn't possessed the seerstone.

Around 1827, Joseph met Emma Hale while he was working in Pennsylvania, and although he was smitten, her family had reservations about their daughter becoming involved with someone they saw as a zealot. Smith would later write that after they were married, "Owing to my continuing to assert that I had seen a vision, persecution still followed me, and my wife's father's family were very much opposed to our being married. I was therefore under the necessity of taking her elsewhere." They eloped and were married in New York, then went to stay with his family.

After Joseph finally retrieved the plates in Ontario County, New York, in 1928, Smith began translating them, a process that took three months. Smith was positioned behind a curtain while having others write down the story he said the plates told. Five hundred pages later the result was the Book of Mormon. According to Smith, in the ancient times of the Old Testament, the family of Lehi came to America to escape falling prey to the bondage that had enslaved Jews following the Babylonian attacks of 587 B.C. Lehi was descended from Abraham and arrived in what would millennia later be known as the New World. After crossing the ocean, Lehi arrived in the future America bringing along his family's genealogy, the Torah, and prophesies of the Holy Prophets.

Once in their new land, the family of Lehi split into two branches—the Nephites and the Lamanites—after the sons turned against one another. For the next six centuries, two factions feuded, until Christ appeared in America and brought peace. But the truce lasted only two hundred years, after which the Nephites and the Lamanites starting warring again. This time, all the Nephites perished except Moroni, who was able to bury the records kept by his father, Mormon. The Lamanites won a Pyhrric victory because in the process of winning the war, they literally lost themselves when they lost the records of their history as the sons of Israel. According to Smith's translations, the Lamanites are the ancestors of the American Indian.

In many ways and for many people, Smith was the right man with the right story at the right time. At the time Smith produced the Book of Mormon, America was in an emotional transition as its citizens tried to figure out their place in the world. Those who embraced Smith felt a spiritual sense of place and a kind of moral validation in making what they saw as a direct historical and divine connection between the Old Testament and America based on the belief the golden plates were authentic.

It's also worth noting the Manifest Destiny zeitgeist that was prevalent at this point in America's history. The story of Lehi complemented the overall sense of Americans being a chosen people, as it were. According to Smith, Lehi's family had been sent to "a land of promise, which was choice above all other lands, which the Lord God had preserved for a righteous people...and whatsoever nation shall possess it, shall be so free from bondage, and from captivity, and from all other nations under heaven, if they but serve the God of the land, who is Jesus Christ." Plus, it was the time of the so-called Great Awakening, when religious fervor was already at a fever pitch.

It's long been said that more crimes have been committed in the name of religion than anything. By embracing a belief that identified a righteous chosen people—and branding the indigenous Native Americans as a fallen people who turned their backs on the true God—it validated the persecution of the Indians in the settlement of the West, which for Mormons became a hold quest to reclaim the land from the hands of the descendents of the Lamanite.

Smith officially established his church in Fayette, New York, on April 6, 1830, and proved himself to be a dynamic, hands-on leader. He worked tirelessly to convert new members and personally led his followers on the first leg of their move west, ending up in Kirtland, Ohio. Later, the congregation would advance to Illinois, and while there, Smith faced the first wave of overt intolerance. For as his Mormon church grew, so did the antagonism of many outsiders, who viewed the new religion as a blasphemous travesty. But it wasn't just religion fanning concerns. There were also concerns that Smith and his followers could influence economic and political issues through their unity as a voting block. Emotions ran so high that Smith and his followers became victims of violence from locals and were harassed by law enforcement, who would arrest members on a variety of often-suspect charges.

One such incident of mob rule occurred on the night of March 24, 1832, when a dozen men raided the Hiram, Ohio, home where Joseph and his wife Emma were staying. With the Smiths were their two young twins, who they had adopted shortly after the post-natal death of Emma and Joseph's own twins. At the time of the attack, Emma was sitting up with the babies and her husband was asleep. According to an account by Smith, the men dragged Joseph from the house and proceeded to strip his clothes off, beat him, and tar and feather him. Somehow, Smith made his way back to the house and spent the rest of the night having tar scraped off his battered and bruised body by friends and followers.

"By morning I was ready to be clothed again," Smith would write. "This being the Sabbath morning, the people assembled for meeting at the usual hour of worship, and among them came also the mobbers. With my flesh all scarified and defaced, I preached to the congregation as usual, and in the afternoon of the same day baptized three individuals." Compounding the Smiths' suffering, one of his twins died the following Friday.

As Smith's power base grew in size and scope, so did the number of his enemies, and, according to some reports, so did his authoritarian and dictatorial rule. But if any one thing truly set Smith apart, it was his private embrace of polygyny, which is popularly, although not completely accurately, called polygamy. Although the practice was a carefully guarded internal secret for many years, eventually Smith would publicly acknowledge its place in the Latter-Day Saint community. And there are some writings that indicate some of the trouble Smith encountered had less to do with religion per se than they did with Smith's pursuit of polygamy, which some apparently contributed to simple carnal lust.

According to a 1920 paper written by former Mormon Bishop R.C. Evans, Smith was known as a bit of a womanizer. Evans claims a man named Levi Lewis testified that, "while Smith was pretending to translate the plates, he tried to seduce Eliza Winters, declaring that adultery was no sin." He also indicated an irate Eli Johnson "led a mob against Smith for being intimate with his sister, Marinda, who afterwards married Orson Hyde. Brigham Young twitted Hyde with this fact, and Hyde put away his wife." Another witness, Fanny Brewer, indicated that some of Smith's problems in Kirtland had arisen "from his seducing an orphan girl."

The Principle of Plural Marriage

When the Book of Mormon was written, its position on the subject of polygamy seemed unequivocal—it was not allowed.

However, at some point after the book's publication in 1830, Smith capitulated. At first, he mentioned his latest revelation about the principle of plural marriage only to his inner circle. According to the May 20, 1886, issue of the *Deseret News*, "The great and glorious principle of plural marriage was first revealed to Joseph Smith in 1831, but being forbidden to make it public, or to teach it as a doctrine of the Gospel, at that time, he confided the facts to only a very few of his intimate associates." In other words, the official party line said that even though Smith was given the revelation on polygamy, he had been commanded by God to keep it secret until the time was right to preach it as doctrine. So, when the first edition of the Book of Commandments was published in 1833, the practice was still condemned.

> And again, I say unto you, that whoso forbiddeth to marry, is not ordained of God, for marriage is ordained of God unto man: 17 Wherefore it is lawful that he should have one wife, and they twain shall be one flesh, and all this that the earth might answer the end of its creation; and that it might be filled with the measure of man, according to his creation before the world was made.

Because Joseph had been receiving new revelations in the intervening years, it was decided to publish a new edition of the Book of Commandments, which would now be called Doctrine and Covenants because of the changes in content. But again, polygamy is denounced.

> All legal contracts of marriage made before a person is baptized into this church, should be held sacred and fulfilled. In as much as this church of Christ has been reproached with the crime of fornication, and polygamy: we declare that we believe, that one man should have one wife; and one woman, but one husband, except in case of death, when either is at liberty to marry again.

It wouldn't be until later that a different view would be stated, specifically:

But the climax in doctrine as in moral daring is reached in this volume by the Prophet committing to writing the revelation on the eternity of the marriage covenant, and, under special circumstances and divine sanction the rightfulness, of a plurality of wives.

Although Smith would be a practicing polygamist for at least a decade before putting his revelation on celestial marriage in writing, it's important to understand the concept of "celestial marriage." When he published his revelation in 1944, it contained sixty-six paragraphs pertaining to "polygamy and concubinage," declaring that a man is not guilty of adultery even if he were to have ten women at once as his wives. More than that, it threatened those who rejected the principal with the loss of heaven.

Smith would say the revelation came after he questioned the issue of why "Abraham, Isaac and Jacob" had more than one wife and concubines. The answer included the following admonitions:

For behold I reveal unto you a new and everlasting covenant; and if ye abide not that covenant then are ye damned, for no one can reject this covenant and be permitted to enter into my glory…

God commanded Abraham, and Sarah gave Hagar to Abraham to wife, and why did she do it? Because this was the law and from Hagar sprang many people. This, therefore, was fulfilling among things, the promises…

Was Abraham, therefore, under condemnation? Verily, I say unto you, Nay, for I, the Lord, commanded it…

Abraham received concubines, and they bear him children, and it was accounted unto him for righteousness—as Isaac also and Jacob did none other things than that which they were commanded. They have entered into their exaltation and sit upon thrones and are not Angels, but are Gods…

And let mine handmaid Emma Smith receive all those that have been given unto my servant Joseph, who are virtuous and pure before me…

And again, Verily, verily I say unto you, if any man have a wife, who holds the keys of this power, and he reaches unto her the law of my priesthood, as pertaining to these things, then shall she believe and administer unto him, or she shall be destroyed, saith the Lord our God, for I will destroy her, for I will magnify my name upon all those who receive and abide in my law.

In other words, polygamy and concubinage was now the official spiritual law of the land. Those who took plural wives—a minimum of three was required—would "pass by the Angels" and become Gods and rule over their own kingdoms. Those men who didn't take more than one wife could never be angels and would serve the others who had become Gods. Those women who refused to enter into polygamy would be damned. It's interesting to note that on their own, women were incapable of reaching the highest level of exaltation—they could only do that through their husbands.

The way it was presented, polygamous marriage was essential for eternal salvation. Mormon doctrine states that God was once a human man, and, "He is now a glorified, resurrected Personage having a tangible body of flesh and bones." It goes on to say, "All gods first existed as spirits, came to an earth to receive bodies, and then, after having passed through a period of probation on the aforesaid earth, were advanced to the exalted position they now enjoy." After dying, a Mormon man will be catapulted to this same status as long as he is "married for eternity." This eternal marriage is called celestial marriage and it was particularly essential for a Mormon woman because unless she was celestially married to a holder of the priesthood, she couldn't be saved. So whether or not she lived with him under the same roof on Earth, all that mattered was that they were celestially married so she could get into heaven.

Because a woman was incapable of reaching heaven on her own, it gave her husband incredible power over her. If she displeased him or was not as compliant as he wanted, he could go get another wife. Brigham Young went on record saying that if a man wasn't content with his wife, to take one or two more, "since this was a sure cure for a shrewish and recalcitrant female." Even though technically the first wife was supposed to approve any additional wives, in practice there weren't many women tough enough to exert that authority. The risk of facing the ire of her husband or church elders was far too intimidating.

Smith spoke of this revelation as early as 1831 to a few close, trusted church confidants and began practicing it shortly thereafter. It would take a decade before he'd put it to paper. So for the time being, polygamy was destined to become the Mormon's dirty little secret. Any public pronouncement aside, what seems most pertinent is that by 1833, it is believed Smith had taken his first plural wife, named Fanny Alger. And by two years later, he and the Mormons had settled in Kirtland, Ohio, and from there they migrated to Nauvoo, Illinois.

Within a decade, Nauvoo would be second only to Chicago as an urban center in Illinois. For a while, Smith thrived, serving as mayor, commander of the Nauvoo Legion state militia, justice of the peace, and university chancellor. Predictably, his powerbase inflamed more fears among the non-Mormon citizens, who joined forced with former church members to destroy Smith. But while nonbelievers might have worried about Smith's political power, for the former Church members, the issues were more personal.

Descent

Doctor John C. Bennett, for example, had received his patriarchal blessing from Smith's brother Hyrum and for a while was included in the inner circle. But then Bennett had a change of heart and publicly accused Smith of adultery, claiming he had seduced a number of single and married females, including a woman named Nancy Rigdon. After she turned down Smith's advances, Nancy told her parents, brother, and Bennett of the incident. Her brother, John W. Rigdon, would later sign a sworn statement detailing his confrontation with Smith over the matter. It's important to note that Rigdon had been Joseph Smith's first counselor. He would also later write that, "Joseph Smith departed from the living God, and like David and Solomon he contracted a whoring spirit and that the Lord smote him off from the earth." He says he loved Joseph, but when he found that he was teaching the unholy spiritual wife doctrine secretly and denying it openly, he was compelled to lose faith in him and denounce him.

More damning was the following from the second volume of the *Messenger and Advocate:* "This system of polygamy was introduced by the Smiths some time before their death, and was the thing which put them in the power of their enemies and was the immediate cause of their death."

In the end, it appears it was indeed polygamy that caused the internal fissure that would eventually result in Smith's death. William Law had been baptized into the Mormon Church near Toronto and soon went to Nauvoo where Joseph made Law his counselor in the first presidency of the church. However, after a time, Law was disillusioned and began to view Smith as an imposter in light of his obsession with taking plural wives. Law would give sworn statements that Hyrum Smith read the revelation on polygamy before the high council, and then gave it to him to take home and read to his wife, which he did.

Through it all, Smith continued accumulating wives. Emily Dow Partridge testified that she and her sister were married to Joseph without Emma's consent:

> The Prophet Joseph and his wife Emma offered us a home in their family. We had been there about a year when the principle of plural marriage was made known to us, and I was married to Joseph Smith on the 4th of March 1843, Elder Heber C. Kimball performing the ceremony. My sister Eliza was also married to Joseph a few days later. This was done without the knowledge of Emma Smith. Two months afterward she consented to give her husband two wives, providing he would give her the privilege of choosing them. She accordingly chose my sister Eliza and myself, and to save family trouble Brother Joseph thought it best to have another ceremony performed. Accordingly on the 11th of May, 1843, we were sealed to Joseph Smith a second time, in Emma's presence. From that very hour, however, Emma was

our bitter enemy. We remained in the family several months after this, but things went from bad to worse until we were obligated to leave the house and find another home.

It was stories such as this that troubled some of Smith's followers. Even though Joseph asserted it was a revelation from God, some like William Law couldn't accept it. Neither could others, including Mormon followers Charles Irvins, F. M. Higbee, C. L. Higbee, Robert Foster, and his brother Charles. And it was this group that got together and bought a weekly paper called the *Nauvoo Expositor*. The first issue, dated June 7, 1844, was a series of sensational accusations hurled at Smith through which exposed the revelation regarding polygamy.

Inevitably, the situation became explosive. Not only was Smith the leader of the Church, he also happened to be the mayor. So after a town meeting, during which he declared the *Nauvoo Expositor* a public nuisance, he ordered the city marshal to destroy the opposition newspaper. The press and type were dismantled and thrown into the streets, with some carried to the river. The rebel members who had put out the paper escaped, but the incident failed to intimidate them. Smith's adversaries struck back by bringing criminal charges against him and his brother Hyrum for inciting a riot. They were later exonerated, but the issue wouldn't go away.

In response to the uproar caused by the *Nauvoo Expositor*, which had become a sensation throughout the country, Smith called the city council together to discuss what the paper had referred to as "the revelation of polygamy." According to published council minutes, "Councillor [sic] H. Smith referred to the revelation read to the High Council of the church, which has caused so much talk about a MULTIPLICITY OF WIVES, that said revelation was in answer to a question concerning things which transpired in former days, and had no reference to the present time."

Then Smith was recorded in the local newspaper as saying, "They make a criminality for a man to have a wife on the earth while he has one in heaven, according to the keys of the Holy Priesthood." He also said that he had never preached the revelation in private nor had he privately taught it to the anointed in the church. And in answer to a prayerful question, "he received for answer: Men in this life must marry in view of eternity, otherwise they must remain as angels, or be single in heaven, which was the amount of the revelation referred to, and the Mayor spoke at considerable length in explanation of this principle."

But it was impossible to put the genie back in the bottle. Illinois Governor Thomas Ford ordered the two Church leaders to stand trial again on the same charges, only this time in Carthage, located in the western part of the state. Joseph and Hyrum considered a number of options, including an appeal to then-President John Tyler. But perhaps feeling the pressure, the Smiths fled, heading west. However, Smith's departure led to discontentment among the members of the Church, who saw his leaving as being completely inconsistent with the invincible image he had so carefully cultivated. Bowing to pressure from others, the brothers agreed to return to Nauvoo and surrender. However, Smith did so with the prophesy that he would be going "like a lamb to the slaughter" and would be "murdered in cold blood."

Governor Ford had promised the Smiths both protection and a fair trial. He also allowed them to be jailed in Carthage without bail and to face the additional charge of treason for having previously declared martial law in Nauvoo. On June 27, after the governor left town, a large mob of armed men stormed the jail.

They met little resistance from the guards left behind to protect the Smiths and easily made their way to where the brothers were being held, where they opened fire. Hyrum was the first to be shot and died instantly. One of Smith's followers, John Taylor, was shot five times but would miraculously survive. (And he would go on to become the Church's third president.) Willard Richards, another apostle, escaped unharmed. As he was trying to climb out the window, Joseph was shot twice in the chest, then two more times, dying where he fell.

According to some accounts, during the gun battle Smith shot and killed two men and "shot the arm off another and would have killed more but his six-shooter missed fire three times, when he jumped out of the window, and in trying to escape was shot dead." Whatever the actual sequence of events, the shocking and violent death of Smith at the age of thirty-eight signaled an abrupt turning point in the history of the Church of Latter-Day Saints.

The Rise of Brigham Young

The transition of power after Smith's killing was not smooth. Emma Smith felt strongly that her husband's authority should be handed down to their son, Joseph Smith III. But Brigham Young, who had been Smith's functional number two, felt that he should be named the Church's next president and prophet, and enough agreed so that indeed, Young was Smith's successor. For the first time since the church's founding, a new leader would guide the members and determine their direction. The man who became the second president of the Church would also be its most pivotal leader. It had long been Smith's plan to keep moving west and establish a permanent base somewhere far from the persecutions and harassment, but it would be Brigham Young who would finally fulfill that dream.

Chapter Three
BRIGHAM YOUNG

Young was born in Whitingham, Vermont, on June 1, 1801, the ninth of eleven children. His parents, John Young and Abigail Howe, were poor farmers who struggled to get by and feed their large brood. When Brigham was three, they moved to New York, and as he grew older he assumed an ever-greater workload, learning to clear land, trap animals for their fur pelts, and help maintain the farm by assisting with the planting, cultivating, and harvesting of the crops. His hardest task was caring for his mother who was suffering from tuberculosis.

After Abigail died in 1815, John married a widow named Hannah Brown, who had several children of her own. Whether because he couldn't adjust to his father's new family or because he simply felt it was time to go, Brigham left home. After staying with one of his sisters, he finally struck out on his own, working variously as an apprentice carpenter, painter, farmer, handyman, and glazier. For several years, Young was gainfully employed working on the construction of Auburn's first marketplace, a prison, and a seminary. By this time a master carpenter, Brigham did ornate and intricate work on many homes in the area, some of which are still standing today.

Brigham left Auburn in the spring of 1823 and moved to Port Byron, New York, where he found work repairing furniture and painting canal boats. When he was twenty-three, Young met Miriam Works and they married on October 5, 1824. Less than a year after the wedding, the couple became parents to a daughter, Elizabeth.

Four years after getting married, Brigham and Miriam moved to Mendon, New York, near where his father and other relatives were living—and not far from where Joseph Smith was preparing to publish the Book of Mormon. After the move, Miriam gave birth to another daughter named Vilate. However, the joy of the occasion was tempered. Miriam contracted tuberculosis and, just like his mother had, became a semi-invalid. Undaunted, Young took up the slack, caring for both the children and his wife, who he would gently carry to a rocking chair so she could sit in front of the fire and stay warm. In addition to his responsibilities at home, Brigham also ran his own shop in town where he built and repaired furniture.

Early in 1830, one of Joseph Smith's brothers passed through Mendon and left a copy of the Book of Mormon with Brigham's oldest brother, Phineas, who in turn passed it to other members of the family. Eventually, it landed with Brigham, who initially adopted a wait-and-see attitude about it. Although a practicing Methodist, from the moment he first picked up the Book of Mormon in 1830, Brigham found himself drawn to Smith and his Church of Jesus Christ of Latter-Day Saints, and for the next two years, Young studied the book and spoke with other members of the Church. Finally, Young was convinced and in the spring of 1832, along with all of his immediate family, he was baptized into the Mormon Church. In September of that same year, Miriam died.

Once he was baptized, Young was compelled to begin preaching. About a week after he joined the Church, Brigham gave his first sermon, saying after his baptism, "I wanted to thunder and roar out the Gospel to the nations. It burned in my bones like fire pent up…Nothing would satisfy me but to cry abroad in the world, what the Lord was doing in the latter days." So deeply felt were his convictions that Brigham gave up his business, found people to care for his daughters, and set out to devote himself to helping build the "kingdom of God."

After working in Canada as a missionary, in 1933 he traveled to Kirtland, Ohio, where he finally met the then twenty-six-year-old Smith and where, during a prayer session at Smith's house, he first spoke in tongues. From that point on, Brigham's stature within the Church grew. He worked as a missionary, would travel to communities facing hostility and harassment, and helped organize the Church's move to Nauvoo, Illinois. Young also took the Mormon message to other countries, traveling to England in 1840 and converting between seven and eight thousand working-class people.

When he returned from abroad in 1841, his devotion was rewarded when Smith appointed Brigham President of the Quorum of Twelve Apostles, the governing body of the Church, second in authority only to Smith himself. As president, Young was responsible for directing the Twelve in their supervision of missionary work, purchase of lands, construction projects, and the settling of immigrants.

While in Kirtland, Brigham met Mary Ann Angell, a native of Seneca, New York, who had worked in a factory in Providence, Rhode Island, prior to her conversion. She and Young were married on February 18, 1834. In addition to caring for Brigham's two daughters from his marriage to Miriam, she and Young would eventually have six children of their own.

After Smith's murder in 1844, it was Brigham who was instrumental in keeping the shell-shocked Church from dismantling. He organized what almost amounted to an evacuation of the Saints and led the group west, first to Winter Quarters, Nebraska, in 1846. Worried about possible interference from the government, he ordered the migration to begin in the inhospitable month of February. By late spring, an estimated sixteen thousand Mormons had traveled to the Winter Quarters on the Missouri River, a spot where Florence, Nebraska, now sits.

However, not every one of the Mormon faithful decided to follow Young. About one thousand stayed behind, and in an interesting historical footnote, a few years later, Joseph Smith III—Emma and Joseph's son who had been passed over in favor of Young—would come to lead an offshoot of the Church that called itself the Reorganized Church of Jesus Christ of Latter-Day Saints. The most obvious differences between the two groups were that the reorganized Church never condoned polygamy and it denounced Brigham Young's later practice of "blood atonement," which decreed that Mormons who leave the Church should be killed and their blood spilled in order to save their eternal souls. Nor do they call themselves Mormons because of the word's association with polygamy.

But Young spent little time worrying about those who chose to stay behind. In April 1847, Brigham and an advance party of 143 men, three women, and two children left Nebraska to scout out possible settlement locations. Then, on July 24, 1847, Young arrived in Utah's Salt Lake Valley and decreed they had found their home. It was here, far from the persecuting crowds and far from the jurisdiction of the government, where Brigham believed the Latter-Day Saints would be able to find peace and freedom to worship and live as they were intended. He named the new settlement Great Salt Lake City, Great Basin, North America. Although he had been the de facto leader of the Church since Smith's death, his authority was made official later that year when Brigham was named president and prophet of the Church, thereby inheriting the authority of Joseph Smith.

Deseret

In 1849, the Mormons established the provisional state of Deseret, with Young as governor. But their petition to be recognized by Congress was rejected because the state boundaries were too small and most of the included area was uninhabited. It was a minor setback. In some ways, Brigham almost set out to establish the Mormons their own country within their Utah sanctuary. The Church became more than just a spiritual entity under his direction, it also oversaw the local economic development, ran the law enforcement, shaped cultural affairs, and oversaw education. In short, it was its own government, a theocracy intent on expanding its authority whenever it could. To that end, Young appreciated that there was strength in numbers. So he offered assistance to any convert willing to make the grueling trip to Salt Lake and stressed the importance of establishing satellite colonies throughout the nearby western territories of Arizona and Idaho.

He also did whatever he could to discourage nonmembers from immigrating to the area by urging members of the Church to become materially and economically self-sufficient—if there was no demand, there would be no need for outsiders to show up with supplies. Not only did Young establish a permanent community for the Mormons, he also finally succeeded in 1850 of having the geographically smaller area of Utah officially recognized as a territory, and in 1851 he was appointed its governor and the superintendent of Indian Affairs by then President Millard Fillmore.

However, that led to some unexpected problems, brought on by Young now having to deal with non-Mormon federal appointees, some of whom were blatantly opposed to the Church of Latter-Day Saints, in large part because they practiced polygamy. Beyond that, Young came under scrutiny because Mormons refused to use federal judges to preside over civil cases and because of issues over federal expenditures. So even though Young and the Church were operating out of sight, far from the seat of government in Washington, D.C., they weren't out of mind. As had happened before, many within the government were uncomfortable with the Mormons, even more so now that they seemed to be thriving in their own insulated corner of the country. One rallying point for opponents was that the U.S. Constitution expressly insisted on the separation of church and state, meaning that a theocracy of any kind where those lines were unclear would be illegal and unconstitutional.

But it was the 1852 acknowledgement that polygamy, or plural marriage, was a basic tenet of the Church that precipitated the biggest public outcry against the Mormons. In a predominantly Christian nation, which had been founded by the ultra-conservative Puritans, the idea of sanctioned adultery was simply intolerable. Even those without strong moral feelings on the issue saw the practice as blatantly illegal, since bigamy was expressly against the law.

The Roots of Mormon Polygamy

Although rumors had flourished about Mormon men taking more than one wife, few outside could have suspected the scope it had reached. As Young became a member of Smith's inner sanctum, he was schooled in the principal of plural marriage, which had to be authorized and could only be performed through the sealing power controlled by the presiding authority of the Church. Simply put, the more wives you had, the higher your place would be in heaven. According to several historical accounts, Brigham was at first reluctant to accept the concept of polygamy, and spent considerable time praying over Smith's revelation. In the end, as was his wont to do, he embraced it with his typical fervor. With Mary Ann's consent, he married Lucy Ann Decker Seeley in June 1842.

Though Smith did not reveal the principle until 1842, it is believed that he already had long been immersed in polygamy—having kept the 1831 revelation mostly to himself and a few select inner circle members. Joseph F. Smith, a relative of the Church leader and a high-ranking official in his own right, notes in his writings, "This, however, was not the time this principle was first known to the Prophet Joseph Smith, for as early as 1831 the Lord revealed the principle of celestial and plural marriage to him, and he taught it to others."

Because of the early secrecy of the practice, it is only from coalescing bits and pieces of historical data that a picture of the beginnings of polygamy in the Mormon Church can be seen. Not surprisingly, if there was anyone who had a hard time reconciling plural marriage, it was Emma Smith, Joseph's first wife, who apparently vacillated from strained acceptance to bitterness throughout her time with Smith. She was not amused when she once found Joseph in a locked bedroom with a young woman.

Apparently, this wasn't a totally unique experience for Emma. A 1920 paper written by a former Church bishop named C.R. Evans noted, "Mr. Moreton told his daughter and her husband that Emma Smith detected Joseph in adultery with a girl by the name of Knight, and that Joseph confessed the crime to the officers of the church."

Confessions or not, Joseph Smith remained resolute. "The object with me is to obey and teach others to obey God in just what he tells us to do," he said. "It mattereth not whether the principle is popular or unpopular. I will always maintain a true principle even if I stand alone in it."

That said, when Smith was finally ready to reveal the principle, he knew it was not going to sit well with his wife. William Clayton, the man who transcribed the revelation as Smith dictated it to him, gave a sworn statement to John T. Caine, a notary public in Salt Lake City, on February 16, 1874, in which he describes Joseph's hesitancy to tell his wife:

> On the morning of the 12th of July, 1843; Joseph and Hyrum Smith came into the office in the upper story of the brick store, on the bank of the Mississippi river. They were

talking on the subject of plural marriage. Hyrum said to Joseph,

If you will write the revelation on celestial marriage, I will take it and read it to Emma, and I believe I can convince her of its truth, and you will hereafter have peace. Joseph smiled and remarked, You do not know Emma as well as I do.

Hyrum repeated his opinion, and further remarked,

The doctrine is so plain, I can convince any reasonable man or woman of its truth, purity and heavenly origin, or words to that effect. Joseph then said, Well, I will write the revelation and we will see.

He then requested me to get paper and prepare to write…

Joseph and Hyrum then sat down and Joseph commenced to dictate the revelation on celestial marriage, and I wrote it, sentence by sentence, as he dictated…Hyrum then took the revelation to read to Emma. Joseph remained with me in the office until Hyrum returned. When he came back, Joseph asked him how he had succeeded. Hyrum replied that he had never received a more severe talking to in his life, that Emma was very bitter and full of resentment and anger.

In other accounts, it describes how Emma did more than give Hyrum a tongue-lashing; she ended up kicking him out of the house in a fit of fury. Clayton goes on to recall that once Hyrum returned:

Joseph quietly remarked, I told you you did not know Emma as well as I did. Joseph then put the revelation in his pocket, and they both left the office.

The revelation was read to several of the authorities during the day. Towards evening Bishop Newel K. Whitney asked Joseph if he had any objections to his taking a copy of the revelation; Joseph replied that he had not, and handed it to him. It was carefully copied the following day by Joseph C. Kingsbury. Two or three days after the revelation was written Joseph related to me and several others that Emma had so teased, and urgently entreated him for the privilege of destroying it, that he became so weary of her teasing, and to get rid of her annoyance, he told her she might destroy it and she had done so, but he had consented to her wish in this matter to pacify her, realizing that he knew the revelation perfectly, and could rewrite it at any time if necessary.

Emma destroyed her copy of the revelation by throwing it into a burning fireplace while Joseph looked on.

To some of Joseph's detractors, the revelation of celestial marriage was just the latest in a series of suspect writings. In fact, even his original publication of the Book of Mormon came under intense scrutiny by those who would charge that he had plagiarized a significant portion of the work from the Solomon Spaulding work, *Manuscript Found*. To this day, the "Spaulding theory" can elicit heated debate from pro- and anti-Smith corners alike.

Spaulding was born in 1761, and after leaving Dartmouth University he worked as a minister before leaving preaching behind. In his later years, he dabbled in writing, including an historical novel on the early inhabitants of America called *Manuscript Found*. (He had also penned another fictional work, *Manuscript Story*, the similarity of title causing some confusion among those rushing to defend Smith against plagiarism.) According to his widow, Matilda, after Solomon's health started to fail, they moved to Ohio.

In the town of New Salem there are numerous mounds and forts, supposed by many to be the dilapidated dwellings and fortifications of a race now extinct. Numerous implements were found and other articles, evincing great skill in the arts. Mr. Spaulding being an educated man and passionately fond of history, took a lively interest in these developments of antiquity; and in order to beguile the hours of retirement, and furnish employment for his lively imagination, he conceived the idea of giving a historical sketch of this long lost race.

Spaulding's brother John added that the book was:

a historical romance of the first settlers of America, and endeavored to show that the American Indians are the descendants of the Jews, or the Ten Lost Tribes. It gave a detailed account of their journey from Jerusalem, by land and sea until they arrived in America under the command of

Lehi and Nephi. They afterwards had quarrels and contentions and separated into two distinct nations, one of which he denominated Nephites, the other Lamanites. Cruel and bloody wars ensued, in which great multitudes were slain. They buried their dead in large heaps, which caused the mounds so common in this country. Their arts, sciences and civilization were all brought into view, in order to account for all the curious antiquities found in various parts of Northern and Southern America. I well remember that he wrote in the old style, and commenced almost every sentence with, And it came to pass or Now it came to pass.

Although Spaulding died in 1816, before his novel could be published, there appears to be intriguing circumstantial evidence linking him to Smith via Sydney Rigdon. After spending time in Ohio, the Spauldings moved again, this time to Pittsburg, where Solomon Spaulding submitted *Manuscript Found* to a newspaper editor named Patterson. According to a declaration by Rev. John Winter, "In 1822–3 Rigdon took out of his desk in his study a large manuscript stating that it was a Bible romance purporting to be a history of the American Indians. That it was written by one Spaulding, a Presbyterian preacher whose health had failed and who had taken it to the printers to see if it would pay to publish it. And that he (Rigdon) had borrowed it from the printer as a curiosity."

James Jeffries, a St. Louis businessman who had dealing with the Mormon in Nauvoo, Illinois, went on record saying:

> I knew Sydney Rigdon, he acted as general manager of the business of the Mormons (with me). Rigdon told me several times, in his conversation with me, that there was in the printing office with which he was connected in Ohio, a manuscript of the Rev. Spaulding, tracing the origin of the Indians from the lost tribes of Israel. This manuscript was in the office several years. He was familiar with it. Spaulding wanted it published but had not the means to pay for printing. He and Joseph Smith used to look over the manuscript and read it on Sundays.

Those most critical of Smith said there was a reason he stayed hidden behind a blanket as he translated the plates to Oliver Cowdery—because he was actually reading from Spaulding's manuscript. But whether or not the similarities between *Manuscript Found* and the Book of Mormon are merely exaggerated, coincidental—including the usage of the names Mormon, Moroni, Lamanite, and Nephi—the result of the zeitgeist of the times, or plagiarism, be it deliberate or unconscious, the mere perception of scandal only served to inflame anti-Mormon passions among those already suspicious of the Church of Latter-Day Saints. If the very creation and inspiration of the Book of Mormon was suddenly suspect, then how could the public possibly accept the tenets of polygamy as being a divine directive?

Scholarly estimates as to the actual number of wives to whom Joseph Smith was sealed to in his life vary from as high as forty-eight to the more widely accepted thirty-three. According to Dr. Tom Compton, a Mormon writer who has exhaustively researched Smith, the Church leader might have married more often but he "proposed to at least five more women who turned him down." Compton also reported that in 1841, "Smith cautiously added three wives in the first eight months of the year." Then in the first six months of 1843, he "married fourteen more wives, including five in May." Obviously, Smith had already been engaged in polygamy by the time he had the revelation written down and shown to Emma, thus her reaction seems borne out of pent-up frustration.

Among the women who were sealed to Smith was Lucy Walker Smith Kimbel, who says in an affidavit, "I was a plural wife of the prophet Joseph Smith and was married for time and eternity in Nauvoo, State of Illinois, on the first day of May, 1843, by Elder William Clayton. The prophet was then living with his first wife, Emma Smith, and I know that she gave her consent to the marriage of at least four women to her husband as plural wives, and she was well aware that he associated and cohabitated with them as plural wives. The names of these women are Eliza and Emily Partridge and Mary and Sarah Lawrence."

Melissa Lot Willes swore "that on the twentieth day of September 1843, at the city of Nauvoo," she was married to Smith in the presence of her parents, Cornelius Lott and Parmelia Lott. Bishop Evans had something to say about Lott:

> Melissa Lott told me that when a girl she sewed for Emma Smith and took care of the children. Joseph had to pass through her room to go to Emma's room. She said Joseph never had sexual intercourse with her but once and that was in the daytime saying he desired her to have a child by him. She was barefooted and ironing when Joseph came in, and the ceremony was performed in the presence of her parents.

Although the majority of Smith's wives were of legal age, he did also establish the Mormon precedent for underage couplings when he married fourteen-year-old Helen Mar Kimball. But that was only one of his dealings with the Kimball family. According to Compton, Smith had shocked his longtime friend Heber Kimball earlier by telling Heber it had been revealed to him that Heber's own wife, Vilate, should be sealed to Smith in marriage. Later, Helen's son Orson would write a biography of Heber, in which he claimed that it was in early 1842 that Smith first approached Heber. "It was no less than a requirement for him to surrender his wife, his beloved Vilate, and give her to Joseph in marriage!"

Although a believer, Heber had trouble swallowing this demand and spent several anguished days struggling between his love for his wife and his faith. In the end, he bowed to Smith. "Then, with a broken and bleeding heart, but with soul-mastered for the sacrifice, he led his darling wife to the Prophet's house and presented her to Joseph. Joseph wept at this proof of devotion, and embracing Heber, told him that was all that the Lord required. It had been a test, said Joseph, to see if Heber would give up everything he possessed." However, now Heber was given another task—Smith required him to take another wife, a woman Joseph had already selected. According to Orson, "Heber was told by Joseph Smith that if he did not do this he would lose his apostleship and be damned." In other words, polygamy wasn't a choice; it was a requirement for not losing one's eternal soul.

There was one more trial Smith would impose on Heber and Vilate, and that was sealing her "in the holy bonds of celestial marriage" with him. In Orson's account, Helen related how she learned of her upcoming marriage in the summer of 1843. "Without any preliminaries [my father] asked me if I would believe him if he told me that it was right for married men to take other wives...My sensibilities were painfully touched. I felt such a sense of personal injury and displeasure; for to mention such a thing to me I thought altogether unworthy of my father, and as quick as he spoke, I replied to him short and emphatically, No I wouldn't! This was the first time that I ever openly manifested anger towards him." But her emotions would hold little sway and eventually, she would become one more of Smith's wives.

Less talked about than the obvious polygamy involved in these unions was the fact that several of the women both Young and Smith took as wives happened to already be married. Technically, it is called polyandry when a woman has more than one husband, but this wasn't a proactive choice on the women's part; they were merely pawns in what they were told was a divine big picture being played out by the men in their lives.

As Dr. Todd Compton notes in his book, *In Sacred Loneliness*:

> A common misconception concerning Joseph Smith's polyandry is that he participated in only one or two such unusual unions. In fact, fully one-third of his plural wives, eleven of them, were married civilly to other men when he married them. If one superimposes a chronological perspective, one sees that of Smith's first twelve wives, nine were polyandrous. So in this early period polyandry was the norm, not the anomaly...
>
> these marriages to Smith as a sort of de facto divorce with the first husband. However, none of these women divorced their 'first husbands' while Smith was alive and all of them continued to live with their civil spouses while married to Smith. In the eleven certain polyandrous marriages, only three of the husbands were non-Mormon and only one was disaffected. All other husbands were in good standing in the church at the time Joseph married their wives. Many were

prominent church leaders and close friends of Smith. These data suggest that Joseph may have married these women, often, not because they were married to non-members but because they were married to faithful Latter-Day Saints who were his devoted friends. This again suggests that the men knew about the marriages and permitted them.

While Smith would leave the married plural wives to live with their husbands, Brigham Young was more possessive. Zina Huntington Jacobs was married to Smith in 1841 after being married to Henry Jacobs for just seven months. After Smith's murder, Zina—then seven months pregnant with her and Henry's second child—was then sealed to Young. Later, Young would send Henry to England on a mission after which Zina would go to live with Young and the rest of his family.

It's interesting to note how Smith's death affected his otherwise unmarried plural wives. The majority of the women were considerably younger than Smith, a good third of them ranging in age from fourteen to twenty. For all the spiritual benefits Smith promised they would receive, the reality was, being a plural wife was an emotionally difficult, isolating existence fraught with frustrations, both mental and sexual.

Dr. Compton notes, "Often plural wives who experienced loneliness also reported feelings of depression, despair, anxiety, helplessness, abandonment, anger, psychosomatic symptoms, and low self-esteem. Certainly polygamous marriage was accepted by nineteenth-century Mormons as thoroughly sacred—it almost defined what was most holy to them—but its practical result, for the woman, was solitude."

After his death, Smith's wives suffered even greater desolation. One allegedly even joined a convent. The majority of the women were taken in or "appropriated" by Smith's successors, a practice based on the Old Testament law of the Levirate. Others chose to stay in the Midwest and eventually remarry. But for the most part, records indicate few if any felt happy with their lives. Smith's first wife, Emma, left the Church after his death but would steadfastly deny he had ever engaged in polygamy, even though he was believed to have been married to twenty-seven wives at the time of his death.

The Need to Go Public

By that time, polygamy was being openly practiced within the Church and was accepted as an integral part of the faith. Outsiders who passed through the settlement in Salt Lake would return home and comment on the practice, although Church leaders continued to deny the tenet of polygamy in any official public forum.

But it was an issue that wouldn't die. Shortly after Young was appointed governor, four out of the five federal officials appointed to serve in the Utah Territory resigned and left. Afterwards, they complained to President Fillmore that Young refused to cooperate and that the "plurality of wives" was openly avowed and practiced in the territory. "So universal is this practice that very few, if any, leading men in that community can be found who have not more than one wife each...and some of them...as many as twenty or thirty."

It seemed that going public had become the lesser of two evils, as it were. If they remained in denial, there was a greater chance of the practice being misrepresented by opponents. If they acknowledged the principle, they could do so within the framework and context of the divine revelation that Smith had expressed it to be. So on Sunday, August 29, 1852, Young directed Elder Orson Pratt to make the official proclamation on the revelation on celestial marriage during a specially convened conference.

It is clear that Pratt was treading the new ground carefully. "I have not been in the habit of publicly speaking upon this subject and it is rather new ground to the inhabitants of the United States, not only to them, but to a portion of the inhabitants of Europe," he said. "It is well known, however, to the congregation before me, that the Latter-Day Saints have embraced the doctrine of a plurality of wives, as part of their religious faith." He went on to defend the practice with references to the biblical precedents set by Abraham, Jacob, David, and others. But, he emphasized, "It is not, as many have supposed, a doctrine embraced by them to gratify the carnal lusts and feelings of men; that is not the object of the doctrine."

Hoping to make a legal point to opponents, Pratt noted, "I think, if I am not mistaken, that the Constitution gives the privilege to all inhabitants of this country, the free exercise of their religious notions, and the freedom of their faith, and the practice of it. Then if it can be proven that the Latter-Day Saints have actually embraced, as a part and portion of their religion, the doctrine of a plurality of wives, it is constitutional."

Pratt spent approximately two hours explaining Smith's revelation, then finally closed the discussion, saying, "What does the Lord intend to do with this people? He intends to make them a kingdom of Kings and Priests, a kingdom unto himself, or in other words a kingdom of Gods, if they will hearken to his law. There will be many who will not hearken, there will be the foolish among the wise who will not receive the new and everlasting covenant [plural marriage] in its fullness, and they never will attain to their exaltation, they never will be counted worthy to hold the scepter of power over a numerous progeny, that shall multiply themselves without end, like the sand upon the seashore."

Interestingly, among the average Mormon males who practiced polygamy, two or three wives were the norm. Unimaginably large families like those of Smith or Young were the rare exception in general, but seemed to be the rule when it came to the Church hierarchy. Although the faithful struggled to comply with the principals that would lead them to heaven and exaltation, the day-to-day reality of polygamy for the average Mormon was frequently less than a divine experience.

Chapter Four
THE CULTURE OF POLYGAMY

For those men in the upper echelon of Church hierarchy, the taking on of many wives seemed proportional to just how important they were. And in fact, it was understood that to be a plural wife of Brigham Young or John Taylor, another high-ranking apostle in the Church, was in itself an honor that was equivalent to a free pass to heaven. But for the common Mormon, as it were, the logistics of polygamy could be tricky with daunting financial realities. The majority of men only had two or three wives because that was as much family as they could afford.

Rather than publicly try to coerce women into accepting polygamy, the Church leaders took the opposite tact of urging men to do their religious duty by taking a plural wife and the resulting additional children. Though some were reluctant to accept such responsibility, many responded and dutifully sought other wives. The logistics of plural families fell into one or two general patterns. In some cases, the wives lived in the same house, each having her own bedroom. In other cases, the arrangement involved the house being divided into a duplex-type apartment, where each wife had her own half. The latter arrangement obviously offered more privacy, since the wives didn't have to navigate around each other in the same living space—and didn't have to hear her husband having sex with another woman. For those of greater means, the wives might each have her own house, sometimes in different towns. In all cases, the husband would orbit from marital bed to martial bed on some pre-arranged schedule.

Looking through the mountain of affidavits left by women at the time, the most common complaint of second and third wives was that they felt they weren't being treated equally; that the first wife and her children were somehow given greater standing. These other wives insinuated that their husbands were not sensitive to their feelings and sometime were guilty of neglecting them. And in some cases, the women were so unhappy they chose to leave the plural family altogether. According to Church history, Brigham Young disliked divorce and actively discouraged it. However, if a woman felt strongly enough, as a rule he was said to have granted it so that she could have the opportunity to find a better situation—presumably in another polygamous marriage. In contrast, men were not given as much leeway because being a provider was considered the man's duty. Young was said to counsel against divorce in the strongest terms to those who wanted to use it to lighten their burden.

Although their circumstances were far from typical within the context of nineteenth century American society, polygamous families from the outside could look very average, as far as the number of children, how the homes were kept, and the general dress and work habits of family members. However, over time as the national birth rate dropped, Mormon family fertility rates started skewing heavily outside the norm. As one might imagine, although many "sisters," as the wives were called, claimed they have developed close, familial bonds, animosity, anger, and hostility was also a fact of life for many of the women involved in polygamous relationships. Likewise, it was not unheard of for a wife to take the lead and insist that her husband take another wife; yet, in other cases, many a first marriage fell apart after the husband insisted on taking another wife.

Polygamy across Religions

In the case of the Latter-Day Saints, the culture of plural marriage was strikingly outside the accepted social norm. That has not been the case in other cultures and societies. As noted earlier, the term for a man having more than one wife is polygyny, while the practice of a woman having more than one husband is called polyandry. Polygamy is an umbrella term covering both customs and means having more than one spouse, although in popular culture it's come to be a generic description for the taking of many wives. Historically, polygamy has been a widely accepted practice in disparate cultures on nearly every continent, and was common among Native

American tribes, although European settlers opposed the practice. Currently, it is estimated that one-third of the world's population belongs to a culture that allows polygamy. It is openly practiced in Jordan, Israel, Syria, Yemen, Iraq, Iran, Egypt, Morocco, and Algeria.

In a way, since the Book of Mormon was purported to tell the story of how an ancient lost tribe of Israel ended up in the America, it's probably not all that surprising that polygamy was incorporated in the faith. That said, what is surprising is how much more of an emphasis Smith and Young placed on the practice than was ever implied in the Old Testament. Through the stories of Abraham, Jacob, David, and others, it's obvious that polygamy was not unknown among the ancient Hebrews, and was common enough that there were some regulations attached to the practice. Among the admonitions was that if a man chose to marry a second wife, it couldn't adversely affect the economic standing and security of the first wife and her children. Also, no child born of any subsequent wife could have a higher standing than any child born of the first wife when it came to family inheritance. In some circumstances, it did appear as if polygamy was indirectly encouraged. In Deuteronomy, it's noted that if a woman's husband died, her brother-in-law was supposed to take her as his wife—regardless of whether or not he was already married. However, marrying sisters is the only aspect of polygamy specifically forbidden in both Islamic law and the Bible. (Although early patriarchs such as Jacob married sisters, it was outlawed after the Mosaic law was established.)

The Hebrew high priests were restricted to one wife and it was even written that any king of Israel should refrain from taking too many wives—a rule to which Solomon and David, at least, took some license when deciphering how many "too many" meant. According to scholars, King Solomon is believed to have had seven hundred wives and three hundred concubines, while King David had ninety-nine wives.

In the Bible, the term "concubine" is apparently synonymous with "wife," although it is only applied to plural wives. Many experts agree that the term was specifically used to describe "second class" wives, which referred to their standing in the inheritance hierarchy. Children of wives were entitled to full inheritances from their fathers, whereas children of concubines received no inheritances. As is noted in a passage from Genesis, "And Abraham gave all that he had unto Isaac. But unto the sons of the concubines, which Abraham had, Abraham gave gifts, and sent them away from Isaac his son, while he yet lived, eastward, unto the east country."

Despite the apparent acceptance of the practice among the biblical Jews, polygamy was not promoted and encouraged the way it was among the Mormons. Rather than an ideology that distinguished their faith, it was more a relic from ancient times past that had filtered down through the ages. And as Jewish civilization evolved, as the great prophets refined and redefined morality and religious consciousness, polygamy gradually faded from the culture, even though it didn't die out completely among the mainstream until well after the time of Christ.

The New Testament offers nothing on the subject. In the Bible, Jesus doesn't address the issue of polygamy. That absence of a recorded dictum prompted Martin Luther to express his own ambivalence on the subject over fifteen hundred years later so that there instances of polygamy among Christian bluebloods. Although Luther tolerated polygamy under special circumstances as a political necessity to "ensure the success of the Reformation," he did not want it to become a common practice among his followers. On the other hand, the practice had already completely disappeared among Jewish families throughout Europe. Around 950 A.D., a powerful rabbi named Gershom of Mayence, influenced by Christians who embraced monogamy, banned polygamy among Northern European Jews.

When Israel was established in 1949, the new government prohibited polygamy. While those who already had several wives could bring them into the country, no new polygamous marriages could be formed. However, it is still common among the 180,000 or so Bedouin living in Israel, and there are known cases among some Sephardic Jews of the Mediterranean region, whose culture has been heavily influences by Islam.

For Muslims, the Koran defines very specific rules for polygamy: "If you fear that you will not act justly towards the orphans, marry such women as seem good to you, two, three, four. But if you fear you will not be equitable, then only one."

In addition to setting a limit of four wives, the wife or wives must agree to the new marriage. And each wife must be well provided for and given her own place to live. If a man tries to sneak in a fifth wife, it gives the first wife grounds for divorce. Unlike Joseph Smith, the Muslim prophet Mohammed was married monogamously to his wife Khadijah for twenty years. But after her death, he married several women, some the widows of friends in order to support their children, and in other cases, to forge political alliances. Over all, Mohammed married ten women—none of whom apparently were concerned that he had exceeded the four-wife limit—and had two concubines, but he never had children with any of them.

There are a number of practical reasons that polygamy was an acceptable option for Muslim men and women, none of which are directly related to religion. First, because adultery is sternly frowned upon, it was an acceptable way for a man to have a mistress, the trade-off being that he had to take legal responsibility for her and any children they might have. Also, if a woman becomes ill or cannot bear children, it gives the man an opportunity to marry another. Even so, the first wife retains her status as first wife. It also makes sense that instances of polygamy increase during times of war, when many women find themselves widowed. Ironically, although there seems to be a general attitude of acceptance among Muslims, in reality it was relatively rare in Islamic societies, restricted primarily among the socially elite, such as wealthy landowners. And as the populations of many traditional Muslim countries are becoming more urban, the practice is declining even more.

"When I was growing up in Bangladesh, my grandfather had two wives," said Iqbal Hossain, president of the Islamic Society of Greater Salt Lake City. "But now it is fast becoming a thing of the past."

In an interesting historical footnote, prior to the great oil shortage of 1973, when the OPEC nations quadrupled oil prices, the older patriarchs in the Gulf States were all polygamous. However, the staggering wealth brought by the oil had a significant effect on their children who embraced modern, more western values, which in turn caused many to reject the social practices, including polygamy, of their parents.

Polygamy around the World

However, polygamy continues to flourish in parts of Africa, a continent with a high number of Muslims combined with a more agricultural way of life, particularly in East Africa. Here, the sexual aspect is acknowledged. Whereas the Latter-Day Saints deny that polygamy is intended to at all serve sexual gratification, in East Africa no such distinction is made. More wives mean more sex, more children, which in turn leads to more family labor and a greater social standing.

There are other practical concerns, too, which cause many women to accept her husband having multiple wives. Considering the harsh agrarian lifestyle many in East Africa live, having more wives in the family means more help with domestic responsibilities and chores. And in some cases the current wife or wives may assist in finding their husband's next spouse because it's in their vested interest to find a woman who is hard-working and willing to carry her share of the work-load. Of course, because the women have a say over who joins the family, sometimes the man gets the brunt of it when the wives join forces against him over an issue.

That is one of the few disadvantages men face. When compared to the advantages, it seemed a small price to pay. Because not only did one's social standing improve as a man amassed more wives and children, it also meant he had to do less work himself. Also, says Rev. Patrick Gaffney, an Islamicist at the University of Notre Dame, the number of wives is "related to the amount of agricultural production a man can oversee. The more wives you have, the more productive the farm is."

It's taboo in some societies for couples to have sexual intercourse if the woman is menstruating or pregnant, so having more than one wife prevented men from having to abstain. While there is no social stigma attached to polygamy in areas in Africa, there are potential medical ones. Ever since the outbreak of AIDS, plural marriages have become a risk factor for contracting the disease. By definition, polygamists are obviously not monogamous, and part of the reason for more wives is to have more children, so condoms aren't exactly popular, either.

Some modern tales of polygamy seem to be the result of pragmatism—and almost biblical in scope. In 1999, seventy-two-year-old Vietnamese bricklayer Tran Chu was reported to have fathered at least sixty-four children, with 109 grandchildren and great-grandchildren. However, trying to do an accurate census proved difficult. "We don't know the age of the youngest child because he still keeps impregnating women," Nguyen Thao, a planning official with Hai Lang district told Deutsche Presse-Agentu. Tran Chu sired his first child when he was seventeen. Nine of his ten "wives" were scattered throughout central Vietnam and one lived in the United States. Although Vietnamese men are not allowed to legally marry more than one woman, Chu somehow still provides for the women to whom he is unofficially married.

According to Thao, Chu was once famous for going on trips, just to get his wives pregnant, but, "Now he is old and he stays at home but many women still come to ask him to impregnate them. They come and stay with him for two months or so and then go away."

The situation is not actually as bizarre as it may seem at first glance, and in some ways is one of the many far-flung affects of the Vietnam war. So many North Vietnamese lost their lives in the conflict, many of them teenagers and even younger, that many women in their late thirties and early forties have a hard time finding husbands or partners their own age. "Most of Chu's wives are spinsters, who can't find a husband," explains Thao. "They are between thirty-five and forty-five years of age when they come to him and they come voluntarily." And according to Vietnamese law, unmarried women over thirty are entitled to have a child. The policy was adopted particularly to compensate the thousands of young Vietnamese women volunteers who gave their youth to the war effort and then found, after the conflict ended in 1975, that they could not find husbands.

Polygamy in Indonesia has a much different history. Prior to the introduction of Islam to the region, under Jawanese law Indonesian women were frequently subjected to clitoral circumcision, forced marriage for underage girls, and the repudiation of childless women. Although the Islamic influence was a distinct improvement, women in the culture did not support the practice. Today, it's estimated that only 5 percent of all Indonesian households still practice polygamy because of raised feminist consciousness and because polygamy is simply seen as old-fashioned.

In fact, in Indonesia and elsewhere, there have been some Islamic women's organizations lobbying for a "reinterpretation" of the Koran, with the specific hope of repealing the right for a man to have more than one wife. One of the primary arguments is that only someone as sublime as Mohammed is realistically capable of truly treating all wives equally.

In China, Confucianism held polygamy to be legal, in large part because of the belief that to die without an heir is a mortal sin. During the fifth and sixth centuries, it was customary for a feudal chief to marry his daughter to another chief along with other relatives who worked as servants. But should the first wife die, then the chief would have a group of other wives from which to pick her replacement. The practice of making concubines wives was almost universal throughout ancient China, and for over two millennia the practice was taken for granted until Li Kui, one of the infamous Legalists who helped shape China, declared polygamy a crime punishable by death. What was particularly significant about this was up until Kui, the law had never taken precedence over the tenets of Confucianism.

Although polygamy is not usually associated with Western European cultures, in large part because of the heavy Christian influences in the area, references to the practice do exist. Although many of the stories come within the context of local mythologies, there remains an element of historical truth. Dr. Fergus Kelly says that polygamy was probably widespread in Celtic culture, for example., "The large number of sons begotten by kings indicates widespread polygyny among royalty."

Peter Ellis, who wrote the book *Celtic Women*, adds, "In pre-Christian Celtic society, and indeed for a while after Ireland converted to Christianity, marriage was a polygamous institution. Men and women could engage in various sexual unions." Ellis also notes that since the Old Testament seemed to justify the practice, it made it harder to denounce it outright.

As in many other cultures, the viability of polygamy among Celtic people was conditional on both the financial status of those involved and on family approval. And unlike in Muslim societies, the first wife was seen as superior to subsequent wives. In fact, there were three classes of wife: secondary mates, by contract, were held to be in an inferior position to the primary mate: a chief wife, who is entitled to half her husband's honor price; a second wife, who is entitled to one-third; and any other wife, who is entitled to one-quarter. Concubines were in a less authoritative position than even a third wife.

Being pragmatic, the Celts even wrote into law how much misery a first wife could inflict on secondary spouses. "They may but satirize them without punishment, and physically may go so far as to pull hair and scratch them with their nails." And although the first wife could not prevent her husband from taking a second wife, she could opt for divorce and was allowed to take whatever property she brought to the marriage. Needless to say, that was powerful leverage and frequently put an end to a husband's polygamous fantasies.

Those who did take more than one wife were usually able to afford it; not just providing homes for each wife (it would be an insult of the highest order to expect a first wife to share her house), but being able to pay the required dowries of the day. However, it was also prevalent among the "farmer caste." As opposed to prestige, polygamy in these circles was an effort to increase the work pool. But even the lower classes had traditions regarding polygamy. In Ireland, the Lughnasadh Fair—a combination of county fair, harvest feast, and athletic games—was the time when contracts were made for additional mates using the system of "handfasting," a pagan term for a wedding in which two people agreed to stay together for a year and a day after which if they each agreed, they would officially marry. Not surprisingly, as Christianity took root, polygamy became a source of contention, and as such, would eventually fall into disfavor.

In North America, many Native Americans practiced polygamy. According to Patricia Albers, chairman of American Indian studies at the University of Minneapolis, there were plural marriages among the Dakota of Southern Minnesota, Ojibway of northern Wisconsin, and the Mesquakia of Iowa. Further west, the Shoshone, Paiute, Utes, and Navajos also practiced polygamy. "I don't know any tribal nation in this general region that didn't have it or disallowed it," Albers says.

As the West became settled, economics played a big part in the continuing appeal of polygamy. Early in the nineteenth century, the Blackfoot Indians of the Dakotas, Wyoming, and Montana were increasingly involved in buffalo-hide trade, and "families were more successful when they had more women engaged in processing of buffalo hides," Albers notes. Also important was that among most tribes, women were not considered subordinate to men but their equals, putting a different social spin on the practice.

Many tribes expected women to have responsibility, not only for her own children, but for those of her sisters as well. As a result, the type of polygamy most commonly practiced among American Indians was sororal polygamy, meaning two sisters married to the same man. This usually happened after one of the sisters was widowed; she would then marry her sister's husband. Two sisters being married to the same man was also common among nineteenth-century Mormons.

Another similarity between the Mormons and Native Americans was for a man to marry a widow or divorced woman who had a daughter by her first marriage. Then when the daughter was older, the man would wed her also. However, neither of these practices was allowed among Jews or Muslims. "Even though the daughter is not the man's biological child, it is considered incest in the Bible and in Islamic law and is prohibited," explains Israeli anthropologist Joseph Ginat.

Officially, the Catholic Church forbids more than one spouse. And it's interesting to note that neither the Greeks nor the Romans, the ruling civilization in which Catholicism first flourished, permitted polygamy either. And considering that Jesus didn't seem to lay down any specific words on the subject, it is quite conceivable that Roman law might have influenced some of the Catholic Church's stance against the practice of polygamy.

Despite its official position, occasionally, throughout its history, exceptions were made for certain royalty. For the most part, though, the Church stood firm against allowing polygamy to become the accepted norm, even in royal circles. Moreover, anyone wishing to convert to Catholicism is required to only have one wife—a rule that created obstacles for missionaries working in cultures where polygamy was permitted. In Colorado, for example, the Franciscan Friars who first mapped the region spent as much time lecturing the Ute Indians on the evils of polygamy as they did exploring.

In fact, polygamy was perhaps the biggest obstacle for the various missionaries who worked in cultures that permitted the practice, including the Jesuits in their efforts with Mexican Aztecs. Very few adults were willing to sacrifice such a long-held custom, especially if they were already part of a plural marriage. But some did, and over time more followed. Obvious problems arose when one-time polygamists did convert. Since the Church didn't recognize the additional marriages as valid in the first place, those relationships were expected to end. It was left to the man to provide for whatever offspring came of the unions.

Perhaps one reason why polygamy in Europe was less pervasive than in other parts of the world was due to the force sometimes exerted by the Roman Catholic Church to enforce its rules, such as when Pope Gregory III instituted the Inquisition in 1231. Originally, the Pontiff explained the reason for this religious tribunal was to understand those whose beliefs differed from the mainstream church. The "inquisitors," or judges of this medieval Inquisition were almost exclusively from the Franciscan and Dominican orders. To put it nicely, with some prodding, "heretics" would see the error of their beliefs and return to the Church. However, if such individuals refused to denounce their ill-advised thinking or actions, they would be handed over to local authorities, because Church law was civil law. Pope Gregory justified his edict as a way of protecting the rest of the Catholic community. The penalty for being deemed such a threat could be severe—at the time, one punishment for civil disobedience was to be burned at the stake.

However, the Church no longer wields that kind of civil control. In fact, today in the United States a new but still small movement of Christian polygamy has taken root. Ironically, these Christian polygamists are wary of and suspect the Mormon fundamentalists. It should be mentioned that Mormonism is not considered a Christian faith, a fact that has resulted in tension and animosity between the Church of Latter-Day Saints and its offshoots and certain Christian denominations, particularly Baptists.

Unlike the fundamentalist Mormons who believe Joseph Smith received a revelation from God, Christian polygamists believe their mandate comes straight from the Old Testament. Steven Butt, who heads the Worldwide Church of Christian Polygamists, says, "We believe that plural marriage is allowed for in the Bible to meet practical, real needs, and this should be acknowledged by the Christian Church. Obviously polygamy can't be something that's immoral if God allowed it with these people whom he showed so much favor."

To spread the word of Christian polygamy, Butt moved to the heart of plural-marriage land, settling in Circleville, Utah. His stated idea is to convert cultural polygamists to Christianity, as opposed to trying to convert mainstream Christians to polygamy. Butt says there are striking differences between his brand of polygamy, which he says is all about freedom, not oppression, and that of clans such as the Kingstons. He says the institutional incest and alleged abuses within the Kingston group is appalling and ungodly. While Butt, like the patriarchal fundamentalists, does believe that the husband should be the family leader, he says it's the husband's job to see that his wives reach their full potential. And in Butt's crowd, children know who their father is and everyone lives under one roof.

Polyandry

Ask Steven Butt, or any male polygamist for that matter, about polyandry—the practice of a woman having more than one husband—and it's clear the concept is akin to outright blasphemy. The idea, they say, is "unnatural." And, at least quantitatively, for as common as polygamy has been since almost the beginning of recorded history, polyandry occurs much less frequently. Considering political and social norms regarding female/male relationships, it's not too surprising to find that this form of polygamy is not only rare, but specifically outlawed in most countries. In a survey of 849 societies around the world, 16 percent were monogamous, and the rest were polygynous to some degree. Only four of them—0.5 percent—were polyandrous. Today, polyandry is found in select pockets of the world such as rural regions of India, Sri Lanka, Nepal, and Tibet. In general, in most cultures there's not much to be gained from polyandry. For example, a woman will not be able to have children faster, as a man with many wives could. So it takes a unique set of circumstances for the practice to flourish.

The typical polyandrous arrangement has a woman marrying a man plus his brothers, who then share her as their wife. An interesting result is that because she has sex with all the brothers, nobody can be sure who the father is when she becomes pregnant. So all the husbands treat the children as if they were their own, since nobody is really sure to whom the child belongs.

If there is a polyandry stronghold, it's in the region where Nepal and Tibet meet. Anthropologists who have studied Tibetan polyandry have puzzled over its cause, but it seems to boil down, again, to economics. The area in Nepal where polyandry is practiced is inhospitable in terms of its landscape. It's a harsh environment with little arable land. However, in that society, a father is required to divide the land equally among his sons, rather than the eldest being sole heir apparent. About the only way to accommodate the law is for the father to give the land to all the sons as a unit. Plus, practically speaking, only having one wife who can only bear one child a year limits the number of offspring and people to provide for. Beyond that, since many families have to depend on herding in addition to farming to make ends meet, it means those men would be away from home for long periods. With more than one husband, the wife and children are always being looked after and there are still enough people to work the farm while one of the husbands is off herding.

One reason why polyandry is so rare is that while with polygamy, there's never a doubt who the mother is, with polyandry, men never know for sure if they are the father. And even those who practice polyandry cite that as a distinct disadvantage. In fact, it appears that had the men involved in the polyandrous relationship had a choice, they would not freely choose to participate in it. But because of the unique difficulties in earning a living in these remote areas, it is the lesser of evils for the men. And women, too, for that matter, complain that their husbands are constantly jealous of one another and argue over paternity. Plus, being the only woman means being required to provide sex almost constantly.

Another consequence of a polyandrous society is that there will be a shortage of men, which is why in these areas of Tibet and Nepal many women turn to religion, becoming celibate Buddhist nuns. Although instead of leaving the community to live in a monastery, they stay at home to help work the farms. For those women who neither want to lead a religious life or have multiple husbands, some can—and do—become single mothers running their own households.

Among the Nair people, who are found along the Malabar Coast of India, a woman is permitted to marry several men as long as they are of equal or superior social standing. What's different from the other polyandrous societies is that the Nair are a matriarchy in which the children are considered part of the mother's family rank and heirs are determined by the female line. But the same economic factors are at work as in Nepal in that it keeps family farms from having to be split up, and gives men the freedom to work away from home for long periods knowing there are others to take care of the wife and children. And should one husband die, there are others who will provide for the family. The down side, and it's a dark one, is the disturbing rate of infanticide for baby girls, because of the high priority these societies have on women bearing sons. Because of that, men outnumber women, so polyandry is a "practical" solution for husbands wanting a wife, even if on a time-share basis.

But as elements of modern society filter through, these polygamous societies seem to be in danger of becoming antiquated. Anthropologists have noted that in more recent times, the Western concept of "romantic love," as opposed to practical unions, have made couples want more exclusive relationships, with men in particular not wanting to share a woman.

Polyamory

In recent years, a new wrinkle has been added to the mix, a decidedly new millennium approach to love called polyamory, which means "many loves" and which encompasses relationships and sexual intimacy between a number of people—married, not married, or a combination of both—without exclusivity but where all parties involved are aware of the others. In other words, having more than one lover and/or partner in your life. Nor is polyamory related to any religion or particular belief system. There are support groups from California to Kansas. Participants do not consider themselves swingers because more opportunities for sex isn't their point—relationships are. In fact, polyamorists believe what they engage in is "responsible nonmonogamy." While the movement's roots might lie in the ghost of Haight-Ashbury past, its descendents approach polyamory with a raised new age consciousness that is more about intimacy than free love.

One of the more prominent proponents of polyamory is Dr. Sasha Lessin. In a recent commentary, Lessin outlined the rationale behind polyamory:

> The monogamous tradition—sexual loving with only one mate your whole life—may, for some people, be constricting and hurting you and those you cherish. And people hardly ever live up to the monogamy ideal; they have affairs and divorce. Global censuses show 70 percent of men and 50 percent of women have extramarital affairs...
>
> Your loving feelings flow naturally to people who each can uniquely contribute to your development and you to theirs. So don't criticize yourself when you experience attraction to more than one person. Instead, consider the perspective of polyamory.
>
> Polyamory—loving more than one person—offers an alternate perspective to monogamy. Polyamory provides other valid ways of sharing intimacy, family, and community. Polyamory includes all forms of multi-partner relating, such as open relationships, intimate networks, and various forms of polyfidelity (commitment to more than one).

It's more common than one might expect. "Ten years ago, there were maybe three support groups for polies," says Brett Hill, who helps run a magazine, a website, and two annual conferences for an organization called Loving More. Currently, though, there are an estimated 250 polyamory support groups, mostly on the Internet. "If you are married, but you meet someone in the office you fall in love with, what do you do?" Hill asks rhetorically. "Most of us have to give up someone. But that's so painful. People destroy themselves, destroy their families over that. All I'm saying is, we have choices."

According to Lessin and others, the fundamental ingredient in polyamorous couples is honesty and trust. Those who accept the practice claim it's an inclusive rather than exclusive arrangement where everyone gets the attention, companionship, and sexual sharing they need. To those who believe polyamory flies in the face of any religious or social convention, it is nothing short of perversion.

Loving More leader Ryam Nearing takes a scientific tact, saying, "People are biologically poly." Her comment seems to be backed up by the research Rutgers University anthropologist Helen Fisher, who wrote the book *Anatomy of Love*. Fisher claims less than one-fifth of recognized cultures embrace monogamy. Although she herself is not a polyamorist, Fisher notes, "These polyamory people are fascinating. They are trying to be realistic." That said, Fisher adds pointedly that while "polyamory is extremely mature, it is also extremely naïve."

In a sense, the Mormon settlers who put down roots in Utah during the nineteenth century were also naïve to think that the United States government would allow the Church of Latter-Day Saints to carve out a theocracy in the West. But Brigham Young and other leaders would soon find out the kind of hardball government officials could play once they realized what exactly was at stake.

Chapter Five
THE EVOLUTION OF MODERN MORMON POLYGAMY

It's hard to know exactly how many or what percentage of Mormons in the Utah territory participated in polygamy. Some studies claim that only 20 to 25 percent of the adult population were part of a plural family, with no more than a third of women who were of marriageable age. Ironically, as previously noted, Mormons in high leadership positions with many wives were not only a decided minority within the Mormon faith, but the exception among polygamous families. However, in one regard, the 20 percent figure seems low for no other reason than to hear Brigham Young preach—it wasn't an option, it was mandatory:

> "Now if any of you will deny the plurality of wives and continue to do so, I promise that you will be damned," Young warned. "And I will go still further, and say that this revelation, or any other revelation that the Lord had given, and deny it in your feelings, and I promise that you will be damned."

Now that the gauntlet had been thrown via Orson Pratt's public acknowledgment, it almost forced the government to respond, because it had become evident that the Utah territory was a fully functioning theocracy flying directly in the face of the Constitutional separation of church and state mandate; a theocracy that was also encouraging the practice of polygamy.

The Utah War

In 1856, James Buchanan was elected U.S. President and he decided the reports coming in regarding the situation in Utah required some kind of prompt action. He dispatched troops to escort new federal appointees to Utah, where Young would be replaced as governor in a pointed show of governmental authority. The troops were there to enforce the transition and establish federal order. Although President Buchanan had neglected to inform Young he was being replaced as governor by Alfred Cummings, a non-Mormon, the Department of the Army dispatched an assistant quartermaster to Utah to inform Young of the expedition's mission and to establish some camps for the Army. When Brigham found out, he took military action of his own, which he felt was his divine right.

"We have got a territorial government, and I am and will be the governor," he had said. "And no power can hinder it until the Lord Almighty says, Brigham, you need not be governor any longer, and then I am willing to yield to another."

He wasn't willing yet. Young deemed the incoming troops a mob of a similar sort that had attacked Mormons back in Missouri, and as such, declared martial law on September 15, 1957, announcing, "Citizens of Utah, we are invaded by a hostile force." Brigham called people home from the outlying colonies in order to defend their land and homes. But Young wasn't truly eager to engage in armed confrontation. Although Mormon militia, called the Nauvoo Legion, conducted raids against the encamped government troops throughout the winter of 1857–58, for the most part the Utah War, or Mormon War, as it has been called, was waged on the food lines, not on the battle lines.

Young's chosen method of warfare was to cut off the troops' supply lines. Under Young's direction, three supply trains were burned and government cattle were captured, which forced both the troops and the officials they were escorting into winter quarters at Camp Scott, located about one hundred miles east of Salt Lake City. The result was a miserable encampment for the government troops, the freezing weather killing scores of animals and leaving the humans to battle frostbite and hunger.

Back in Washington, two additional volunteer regiments were assembled and sent to back up the forces in Utah, which in turn caused more Mormon men to prepare for war. The escalating tensions could have led to true tragedy. At the very least, it strengthened the Latter-Day Saints' suspicion and mistrust of the United States government and reinforced feelings of persecution.

One reason for the strong presidential response was that much of the country was still in shock and outrage over an incident that occurred in September 1857, shortly after Young's proclamation of martial law, which would taint the Church leader for the remainder of his life. The pivotal event is called the Mountain Meadows Massacre, in which a group of more than one hundred pioneers coming west from Arkansas were murdered in a Mormon–Paiute Indian conspiracy.

In April 1857, the caravan of covered wagons accompanied by cattle and horses set out for California. In their pockets was a mini-fortune of gold coins, and in the wagons their worldly possessions. The group was comprised of several families, mostly children and teenagers. They reached Utah in August just as the storm of anger was building over the impending presidential appointment of a new territorial governor and the belief they were about to be invaded by the U.S. Army.

Will Bagley, author of the book *Blood of the Prophets*, notes, "There was a phenomenal war hysteria. I believe that the emigrant train became a target of opportunity, and a sense that they could extract some revenge on America, specifically by attacking this wagon train."

Adding to the tension was the fact that this particular wagon train emanated from Arkansas, where a Mormon apostle had recently been murdered. So, inhabitants on the wagon road included people who vowed to avenge the blood of their prophets. However, it would turn out that the carnage at Mountain Meadows wasn't simply the work of overly passionate Mormon colonists.

As the Arkansas contingent approached Great Salt Lake City in the summer of 1857, they passed various groups of Mormons preparing for war against the United States, which made for some awkward moments. Because of the belief they were being "invaded by a hostile force," few Mormons were feeling particularly generous to any gentile, as non-Mormons are called. The Arkansas settlers were warned to remove their livestock from Mormon pastures. When the caravan passed through Provo, locals refused to sell them fresh vegetables or other provisions.

As some of the group camped in Mountain Meadows to rest its animal, Isaac C. Haight, a high-ranking Mormon elder, riled Church members during a meeting by claiming, "The gentiles will not leave us alone. They have followed us and hounded us…and now they are sending an army to exterminate us. So far as I am concerned I have been driven from my home for the last time."

Apparently, he meant it. Later John D. Lee, one of Brigham Young's personal body guards and a member of the Mormon militia, would divulge in written testimony that Haight played an instrumental part in what happened next. On the morning of September 7, Indians opened fire on the settlers' camp, initially killing a dozen settlers. The others quickly circled the wagons, beginning a four-day siege. However, time was not on the side of the settlers because they were cut off from the nearby spring. In the summer heat, thirst became unbearable.

The standoff raised tensions between the Mormons and the Paiutes, who had seen two of their chiefs wounded by sniping settlers. The Indian leaders insisted their Mormon counterparts find a way to finish what they had asked the Paiutes to join them in doing. John Lee, who worked with the Indians, was summoned while Haight, along with William H. Dame, organized the Iron County militia to put the immigrants "out of the way," according to historian Jaunita Brooks.

The solution was effective and brutal. Along with William Bateman, John Lee approached the wagon trains waving a white flag signifying truce. After meeting with a couple of settlers who met them halfway, Lee went to the camp and convinced the exhausted and frightened settlers that the way to safety was to lay down their weapons and allow the Mormons to escort them out of the meadow. Not really having a lot of options, the settlers agreed to trust the Mormons who had three of their own wagons brought over. In one of the wagons they placed all the youngest children, in the second all the weapons and in the third, the settlers who had been wounded during the siege.

On Friday, September 11, 1857, the women and older children left the camp first, walking behind the first two wagons. After a while, the men started to walk, each accompanied by a member of the Mormon militia, ostensibly there to offer protection against the Indians. The man in charge of the evacuation was Maj. John Higbee of the Iron

Militia. The settlers had walked perhaps a mile when Higbee suddenly shouted, "Halt! Do your duty." At the command, each of the militiamen turned to the male settler they walked beside and shot him. At the same time, according to Lee's later testimony and the recounts of Mormons present, the Indians then rushed the women and children, slaughtering them with tomahawks. Of the wagon train families, only seventeen children under the age of six survived, because it was believed they would not be able to remember details of the attack if asked. After the bloodbath, the Mormons said they left while the Indians plundered the dead bodies, then returned the next day to bury the brutalized corpses. The surviving children were initially placed in Mormon homes, but were eventually returned to relatives in Arkansas: According to Lee's written testimony, he claims:

> The immediate orders for the killing of the emigrants came from those in authority at Cedar City. At the time of the massacre, I and those with me, acted by virtue of positive orders from Isaac C. Haight and his associates at Cedar City. Before I started on my mission to the Mountain Meadows, I was told by Isaac C. Haight that his orders to me were the result of full consultatation [sic] with Colonel William H. Dame and all in authority. It is a new thing to me, if the massacre was not decided on by the head men of the Church, and it is a new thing for Mormons to condemn those who committed the deed.

Although the Mormon leaders who had authorized the attack—whether directly or tacitly—thought it would be possible to keep the truth of the massacre buried with the dead settlers, word of what happened at Mountain Meadows soon began to appear. As it spread through the country, outrage and shock rippled in its wake. For Brigham Young, the incident was particularly problematic. Young was a micromanager. For years, nothing had happened within the Church he inherited from Smith without his knowledge. So it seemed somewhat unbelievable that Young would have absolutely no knowledge of the murders of one hundred Arkansas settlers as he claimed, raising a cloud of suspicion that would hang over his head.

In March 2000, a University of Utah forensic anthropologist named Shannon Novak rekindled the embers of controversy when he reported that after examining the remains of massacre victims, he concluded that among the women and children killed, there is evidence some were shot in the head and not slaughtered by Indian weapons. The inference being that the Mormon militia had murdered women and children. "Typically with history, the winning side writes the story," Novak noted. "This is giving the dead a chance to speak."

Not everyone was interested in hearing what the remains had to say. In fact, Novak accused Utah Governor Michael Leavitt of ordering the remains immediately reburied before her examinations were completed in an effort to avoid further embarrassment to the state. Ironically, a contractor working for the Mormon Church had accidentally uncovered the remains. In a message to state antiquities officials, Leavitt wrote that he did not want controversy to highlight "this sad moment in our state's history and the rather good-spirited attempt to put it behind us."

Back in 1858, Young was also anxious to bury the incident as he tried to guide the Church through the crisis at hand. As the additional troops made their way to Utah, historians believe Brigham had decided that an all-out war would be suicidal. Instead, he apparently preferred to abandon and burn Mormon settlements rather than be occupied by the enemy—the government. The memories of the persecutions in Missouri and Illinois were still raw and fresh in his mind.

The impasse remained until the intervention of Thomas L. Kane. Although not a Mormon himself, Kane had previously gained the trust of Young and other Latter-Day Saints by speaking out against what he saw as the religious persecution against the Mormons. Kane, who would later reach the rank of general after the Civil War, was also a friend of President Buchanan, but it was Young who approached him. Kane received presidential approval to go to Utah as an unofficial mediator in early 1858. When Kane arrived in Salt Lake City, the situation became so tense that when rumors filtered back that Kane's first meetings with the general leading the Army troops hadn't resulted in much progress, Young ordered what became known as the Move South. In March 1858, Brigham decreed that all settlements in northern Utah should be evacuated and prepared to be burnt to the ground should the U.S. Army advance.

Although most of the Mormons thought they were leaving their homes for good, again, it seems more likely it was just a tactic on Young's part. Whatever the motivation, Kane was able to convince in-coming Governor Cummings to travel to Salt Lake City with him in April, without military escort. Once in Salt Lake, an agreement was worked out relatively quickly. In June, two statesmen appointed by President Buchanan arrived in Utah carrying a Proclamation of Pardon dated April 6, 1858, which coincidentally happened to be the twenty-eighth anniversary of the founding of the Latter-Day Saints' Church. The document offered amnesty to all who "would submit to the authority of the federal government." So, in exchange for accepting Cummings as the new governor and agreeing to a permanent army garrison, Church leaders would be pardoned for alleged offenses and, at least for the time being, Mormons would be left to practice their religion unimpeded.

On June 26, 1858, Army troops passed through Salt Lake City and found their permanent settlement about forty miles away, where they built Camp Floyd. At the same time, the Mormons who had been evacuated returned to their homes. The Utah War that never was, was over. The aftermath was somewhat anticlimatic. Ironically, Cummings proved to be more acceptable to the Mormons. As a result, Camp Floyd and the nearby town of Fairfield that sprang up in its shadow became the first non-Mormon residents in Utah of note. Although the mere presence of the Army troops remained a thorn in the psyche of Mormons, Young refused to let it impede his goal of continued expansion. He and his advisors would avow that while Cummings might be governor of the territory for the present, Young remained governor of the people. Although the Army left Utah at the outbreak of the Civil War in 1861, their presence had served the Mormons pointed notice; any dreams Young may have had of establishing an independent Zion state had been effectively dashed. Even so, Young remained defiant.

On June 3, 1866, Brigham Young declared:

> We are told that if we would give up polygamy—which we know to be a doctrine revealed from heaven, and it is of God and the world for it—but suppose this Church should give up this holy order of marriage, then would the devil, and all who are in league with him against the cause of God, rejoice that they had prevailed upon the Saints to refuse to obey one of the revelations and commandments of God to them…Will the Latter-Day Saints do this? No; they will not to please anybody.

Two months later, he reiterated his stance:

> The only men who become Gods, even the sons of God, are those who enter into polygamy. I heard the revelation on polygamy, and I believed it with all my heart. Do you think that we shall ever be admitted as a State into the Union without denying the principle of polygamy? If we are not admitted until then, we shall never be admitted.

For once, it was more than rabble-rousing. Polygamy had indeed become the sticking point for Utah's admittance into the Union as a state. By the time Buchanan had replaced Young with Cummings, there had already been two petitions for Statehood for the State of Deseret and both had been rejected. The growing anti-Mormon sentiment among the rest of the nation was one reason for the rejections. Also, government officials were worried about sanctioning a theocracy because, even if Cummings was the official state governor, the laws of the land still apparently emanated from the Mormon Church.

In 1862, the 3rd State of Deseret constitution was written as a bid for Statehood. Young and others had anticipated the Civil War would dissolve the Union. However, the government of Abraham Lincoln would prove resolute in its determination not to let the country divide. Moreover, on July 8, 1862, Lincoln signed into law the Morrill Anti-Bigamy Law, the first federal legislation designed "to punish and prevent the practice of polygamy in the Territories of the

United States." In addition to making bigamy punishable by a $500 fine and imprisonment up to five years, it also stated all acts passed by the Legislative Assembly of the Territory of Utah "pertaining to polygamy and spiritual marriage" were annulled and no longer valid. Most important, the Morrill Act held that religious or charitable organizations were limited to $50,000 of real property holdings. Any amount exceeding the $50,000 limit was to be forfeited to the United States. Although no money was allotted for enforcement, the mere existence of the provision was a foundation for future action.

In 1871, Young was tried under Morrill Act. At the time, Young had more than twenty wives and forty-seven children. But then, as now, the prosecution's case was difficult to prove because his wives were unwilling to bare witness against their husband. Young was acquitted. The real point of the prosecution was a renewed effort by officials in Washington to cleave Church and State in Utah, an endeavor that would continue.

Despite the legal troubles, Young pressed on, and both the Church and the economy flourished, helped immensely by the completion of the transcontinental railroad at Promontory Point, Utah. But the railroad also brought a downside; suddenly there was a fresh flow of gentiles into the area that threatened the economic monopoly of Mormon merchants. Young countered by creating a network of church-financed cooperative stores that effectively shut out competition from non-Mormon merchants. He also saw to it that women won the right to vote, thereby increasing the Church's political block.

Every step Young took to preserve Mormon strength also served to further ingrain the insular mindset of the Mormons. It made for fresh tensions with the gentile settlers, as well as for some of the more liberal-minded Mormons. In a case of history repeating itself, in 1870, a group of dissatisfied Mormons who baulked at Young's micromanagement started a newspaper that would later become the *Salt Lake Tribune*. The conservative core of Church officials complained, "The *Nauvoo Expositor* was holy writ compared to the *Salt Lake Tribune*."

Almost twenty years after the Mountain Meadows Massacre, the memory of the slayings provided the government with more ammunition against Young. In 1877, prosecutors attempted to prove Young's complicity in the crime by pressing murder charges against conspirator John D. Lee. But at the trial, Lee refused to implicate Young. His first trial ended in acquittal, but after claims that the outcome was influenced by Young, Lee was tried again. This time, Young stayed in the background and Lee was found guilty and condemned to die by firing squad. On March 23, 1877, John Lee was executed at Mountain Meadows where the slaughter had occurred twenty years earlier. The question of Young's culpability in the massacre has never been determined. Young died a few months later, on August 29, 1877, of peritonitis, the result of a ruptured appendix.

Blood Atonement

But the Meadows Mountain Massacre and John Lee's participation would bring to the fore another issue that added to the wariness many felt towards Mormons: the principal of blood atonement. Although it has never been proved, it has long been believed that Brigham Young employed an ultra-secret band of avengers who would carry out "righteous" killings against "enemies of the Saints."

Like polygamy, the principal of blood atonement has been a source of contention and controversy. The doctrine was taught by Brigham Young, later repudiated by the Church and church leaders, but still remains a part of Mormon history and lore. On September 21, 1856, Brigham Young gave a seminal sermon about blood atonement, explaining:

> There are sins that men commit for which they cannot receive forgiveness in this world, or in that which is to come, and if they had their eyes open to see their true condition, they would be perfectly willing to have their blood spilt upon the ground...
>
> I know, when you hear my brethren telling about cutting people off from the earth, that you consider it is strong doctrine; but it is to save them, not to destroy them....
>
> There are sins that can be atoned for by an offering upon an altar, as in ancient days; and there are sins that the blood

of a lamb, or a calf, or of turtle dove, cannot remit, but they must be atoned for by the blood of the man.

In another sermon, he expanded on the theme:

Will you love your brothers and sisters likewise, when they have committed a sin that cannot be atoned for without the shedding of their blood? Will you love that man or woman well enough to shed their blood? That is what Jesus Christ meant....

If you have sinned a sin requiring the shedding of blood, except the sin unto death, would not be satisfied nor rest until your blood should be spilled, that you might gain that salvation you desire. That is the way to love mankind.

To carry out his blood atonement ministry, some believe Young had at his disposal a secret band of avengers, as it were; Mormon "Destroying Angels" whose mission was to defend the Church against their antagonists, and as a result, allegedly conducted a number of blood atonements for Young and other Church leaders. Moreover, they were said to act against dissenters within the Church or ex-members. Some has speculated Young was referring to this covert group, known as the Danites, when he said:

And if the Gentiles wish to see a few tricks, we have Mormons that can perform them. We have the meanest devils on the earth in our midst, and we intend to keep them for we have use for them; and if the Devil does not look sharp, we will cheat him out of them at the last, for they will reform and go to heaven with us.

Among those who have been identified as Danites are William Hickman, Orrin Porter Rockwell, and John Lee, all of whom participated in the Mountain Meadows Massacre. Hickman and Rockwell in their own way were as colorful as Smith and Young. Orrin Porter Rockwell was described in newspapers and journals of the day as a notorious gunman and religious zealot. He was also one of Joseph Smith's first converts and was said to have become a Danite prior to Smith's death.

After Young took over, Rockwell became his personal bodyguard. In 1857, he was involved in an attack on a half-dozen Californians known as the Aiken party, who were attempting to reach U.S. troops wintering at Fort Bridger. Twenty years later, he was indicted on two counts of first-degree murder in the deaths of John and William Aiken. Orrin died of natural causes in June 1878 while awaiting trial on the Aiken murder charges. In his obituary, the *Salt Lake Tribune* wrote that he had "participated in at least a hundred murders."

In his dotage, William Hickman would write a book titled, *Brigham's Destroying Angel: Being the Life, Confession, and Startling Disclosures of the Notorious Bill Hickman, The Danite Chief of Utah.* In it, Hickman claimed he had committed murders by the orders of Brigham Young and Apostle Orson Hyde.

In modern times, there have been instances of blood atonement among the more extreme fundamentalists, such as Ervil LeBaron's the Church of the Lamb of God sect, as well as occasional isolated cases. And although the Church of Latter-Day Saints officially disavows blood atonement, the principle behind it is why Utah still allows death by firing squad as an option for state executions—unlike electrocution or injection, being shot literally "spills" the murderer's blood.

However, after Young's death, there were greater concerns than enemies of the Saints. Brigham's death would prove to be another turning point for the Mormons.

Polygamy and the Courts

In the decade after Young's death, the government increased legal pressure on the Mormons in its quest to strip the Church of its political power and force the end of polygamy as an institutionally approved practice. The way Young had been able to protect the practice had been to insulate members of the Church from the outside influence and control of the United States government. But by the 1880s, the Mormons were under intense scrutiny. The Church of Latter-Day Saints fought the government attempts to dictate polygamy in the courts, claiming it was a constitutionally protected right.

In 1878, Joseph F. Smith reaffirmed the Church's stance, saying,

"I understand the law of celestial marriage to mean that every man in this Church, who has the ability to obey and practice it in righteousness and will not, shall be damned, I say I understand it to mean this and nothing less, and I testify in the name of Jesus that it does mean that."

The case of *Reynolds v. the United States* went to the Supreme Court, which ruled in 1879 that polygamy could not be protected by freedom of religion because it was "subversive of the public order," a reference to the disturbances that arose from anti-Mormon sentiments. The court also stated that while laws "cannot interfere with mere religious belief and opinions…they may with practices."

The Supreme Court decision had a dramatic effect. It gave federal authorities the ammunition they needed to continue their efforts to cleave Utah's ingrained theocratic mindset. In 1882, the Edmunds Act was passed making "bigamous cohabitation" a misdemeanor. The Edmunds Act also prevented polygamists from serving on juries, holding public office, or voting. The fact was, prosecuting bigamy itself was difficult because documentation was hard to come by and wives protected their husband. Still using whatever laws they could, authorities sought to enforce anti-polygamy statutes, forcing many plural families into hiding. Over one thousand Mormons were arrested, convicted, and sentenced to jail terms. The first man prosecuted under the new law was named Rudger Clawson, who was sentenced to three years and six months in the penitentiary and fined $500. The severity of the sentence was intended to send a message that this time, the government was serious.

Less than a month after the Edmunds Act was approved, Mormon officials made their fifth bid for statehood. The proposal was opposed by the newly formed Liberal Party, comprised mostly of gentiles, who made up about 10 percent of the territory's population and who still feared the idea of living under a theocratic state government. Again, statehood was denied.

Then, in 1887, Congress passed the Edmunds-Tucker Act as a supplement the Edmunds Act, and it included provisions that forced wives to testify against their husbands, required all marriages to be recorded with a probate court with the probate judges to be appointed by the president of the United States, and, most crucial, authorized seizure of Church real estate not directly used for religious purposes and acquired in excess of the $50,000 limitation instituted by the Morrill Act. Again, the Church waged legal war in the courts only to again lose.

The concern and paranoia proved so great that Brigham Young's successor, John Taylor, went underground and ran the Church for nearly three years from seclusion. A staunch polygamist, he refused to bend to the will of the United States government and rallied his people to remain resolute. But age and strain took its toll, and he died in July 1887 from congestive heart failure. He in turn was succeeded by Wilford Woodruff, who inherited a Church on the verge of collapse.

In 1890, the Supreme Court upheld the seizure of Church property under the Edmunds-Tucker Act in *The Late Corporation of the Mormon Church v. United States*. In part, the Court held that, "Congress may not only abrogate laws of the Territorial Legislature but it may itself legislate directly for the local government. Congress had a full and perfect right to repeal its [LDS] charter and abrogate its corporate existence." It was quickly becoming clear that the Church of Latter-Day Saints was in danger of being completely dismantled if its members clung to polygamy.

Whether by divine intervention or pragmatism, shortly after the decision was handed down, Woodruff was said to have a revelation that adhering to the practice of polygamy would result in the ruin of the Church, endangering their fundamental mission, not to mention any hope they had of being granted statehood. So on September 26, 1890, Woodruff issued his manifesto in which he announced the official end of Church-sanctioned polygamy and formally charged Latter-Day Saints to abide by the anti-bigamy laws. Woodruff announced, "I now publicly declare that my advice to the Latter-Day Saints is to refrain from contracting any marriage forbidden by the law of the land." And in keeping with its adversarial, the *Salt Lake Tribune* noted that the "manifesto was not intended to be accepted as a command by the President of the Church, but as a little bit of harmless dodging to deceive the people of the East."

On one hand, it's hard to argue with that assessment, considering that although plural marriages had been banned publicly, privately they were still being condoned by certain Church elders who now secretly performed ceremonies. Wanting to ensure conformity, federal officials wanted the ratified manifesto to include specific language dealing with sexual cohabitation. In October 1891, Woodruff went on record saying that any person entering into plural marriage after the date of the September announcement could be excommunicated from the Church. He also made clear the ban applied everywhere in the world, not just in America.

As an exclamation point, Congress passed one last federal anti-bigamy statute in 1892, in which excluded polygamists from immigration into the United States, a law that remains part of the U.S. Immigration and Naturalization Code today.

With polygamy at least officially dealt with, the primary obstacle to statehood was removed. In 1896, the territory of Utah was admitted into the union as the forty-fifth state, with the following provision, called Section 3, written into the state constitution:

> The following ordinance shall be irrevocable without the consent of the United States and the people of this State: [Religious toleration—Polygamy forbidden.] First:—Perfect toleration of religious sentiment is guaranteed. No inhabitant of this State shall ever be molested in person or property on account of his or her mode of religious worship; but polygamous or plural marriages are forever prohibited.

Mormon Fundamentalism

In recent years, the Mormon Church has gone out of its way to distance itself from polygamy. Although Joseph Smith's revelation concerning plural marriage remains in the Doctrine and Covenants, it is extremely difficult for any non-Mormon to obtain a copy of the book. In some ways, the Latter-Day Saints Church is caught between a rock and a hard place. On the one hand, they have to address polygamy as a righteous principle because of Smith's revelation, but on the other, they have to discourage members of the Church from

actually entering into its practice. Brigham Young is another compli-
cation, since he so wholeheartedly embraced polygamy. So in 1997,
the First Presidency of the Mormon Church and the Quorum of the
Twelve Apostles published *Teachings of Presidents of the Church:
Brigham Young* that completely fails to mention his many plural
wives, leaving the impression he was monogamous. Needless to say,
the manual generated a good deal of controversy, leaving the Church
open to the criticism it was trying to deny the issue of polygamy
completely, perhaps hoping the issue would go away.

It wouldn't. If federal officials thought they had effectively ended
polygamy at the turn of the twentieth century, they too were mistaken, although the evolution of polygamy as it is practiced today has
since followed a sometimes-winding road. Because it was estimated
that only a minority of Mormons ever practiced polygamy to begin
with, the manifesto outlawing it didn't really affect the daily lives of
the majority of Mormons. Most affected would have been the church
elders who had embraced plural wives in a great manner and those
others who had taken an additional wife or two. It should be noted
that those who felt strongly about polygamy did so because they felt
they were the true keepers of the faith. Hence, this minority became
known as fundamentalists, which in general refers to any group of
individuals—in any religion—who feel the central Church has
moved away from its basic, fundamental doctrines. Within the Latter-Day Saints, polygamists began referring to themselves as fundamentalists around the 1940s. They adhere to the belief that after
death, they will become godlike and move on to heaven where their
plural wives and children will constitute their kingdoms.

Even though, in the years following Woodruff's manifestos, many
church leaders tacitly condoned polygamy, by the time the fundamentalists began attracting a following, Latter-Day Saints officials
adopted a stricter attitude against plural marriage. The Church began
requiring Mormon men to sign loyalty oaths stating that they
denounced "the advocacy and practice of plural marriage," and that
they themselves were not in polygamous relationships. Those who
refused to sign were excommunicated. Tabs were kept on who
attended fundamentalist meetings, the Salt Lake City librarian was

asked to remove all fundamentalist literature from the library, and the Church actively encouraged authorities to prosecute the fundamentalists.

Modern polygamy's revival began in the 1930s with members gathering at informal meetings, during which they would discuss issues, including their disenchantment with the manifesto. Interest in polygamy got another boost following published claims made by Lorin C. Woolley, who said that in1886, then-President John Taylor had a vision in which Joseph Smith told him to uphold plural marriages. Later, according to Woolley, Taylor ordained five men, including Woolley and his father, with the mission to make sure not a year passed that a child wasn't born from a union that adhered to the principal of plural marriage.

Woolley's claims generated attention and interest, and he appointed a seven-member Priesthood Council given the authority to govern the Church. Woolley died in 1934 and was succeeded by J. Leslie Broadbent, who himself died a short time later. Stepping up to assume a leadership role was John Y. Barlow, who founded a polygamist colony at Short Creek, Arizona, near the Utah border, which is now known as Colorado City. Although officials raided the community in 1935, it survived, and a decade later was populated by thirty-six men, eighty-six women, and 263 children. Also playing a prominent role was Joseph W. Musser, who had been excommunicated from the Church for being a polygamist. The community established a corporation called the Union Trust through which they purchased land and holdings.

The splinter group was fairly stable until Barlow's death in 1951, which led to a significant split. When Musser succeeded Barlow, some in the group objected because Musser had been left partially disabled from a stroke. His popularity diminished even more when he singularly appointed Rulon C. Allred as his successor, seeking to bypass the authority of the Priesthood Council. While some remained with Musser, his loyalty to Allred caused others to split off into their own group.

Those who split from Musser remained in control of the United Trust and, under the leadership of LeRoy Johnson, prospered. They also became the most conservative arm of the Fundamentalist Movement, believing sex is to be engaged in only for procreation and is prohibited during pregnancy or when a woman is nursing or menstruating. After Johnson's death in 1986, Rulon Jeffs took over leadership.

Generally speaking, polygamists today fall into two broad categories. The first includes groups whose claims to priesthood authority have passed down through a direct line from Lorin Woolley. They include the Allreds' Apostolic United Brethren, the Fundamentalist Church of Jesus Christ of Colorado City, and the Kingstonites. The other category consists of "independent" polygamists, who don't affiliate themselves with any particular group. While the mainstream Mormon Church does not recognize these fundamentalist offshoots, it is these splinter groups than have become most associated with the Church, largely because of some infamous run-ins with the law, such as the one involving Rulon Allred of the Apostolic United Brethren (AUB).

After John Barlow's death, about one thousand of his followers remained loyal to Joseph Musser. After Musser passed away in 1954, Rulon Allred took over leadership. He had first made a name for himself in 1944 after being arrested during an anti-polygamy raid. He was paroled on the condition he would not participate in or promote polygamy. In short order, he violated terms of his parole and fled to Mexico. He eventually returned to Utah and wound up having to serve only a short time in jail. A year after he took over the AUB, one of group's members, Joel LeBaron, broke away to form his own group, called the Church of the First Born of the Fullness of Time. In the 1970s, Joel's brother Ervil LeBaron broke away from Church of the First Born and formed his own Church of the Lamb of God. Moreover, Ervil claimed authority over all of the polygamous groups and the right to execute any who defied him. To prove his point, in 1972 he had Joel killed.

Three years later, in April 1975, Ervil sent Allred a pamphlet titled, "A Response to an Act of War," along with a handwritten note. Allred promptly ignored it. On May 10, 1977, two female members of the Church of the Lamb of God murdered Rulon Allred. After a long pursuit, Ervil was finally apprehended by authorities. He and his two accomplices were convicted and sent to prison, where LeBaron died in 1981. However, prior to his death he wrote a book which listed the names of renegade members who should be killed, and over the course of the decade, several of LeBaron's children carried out his post-mortem wishes, murdering several former church members in Dallas, Houston, Utah, and Mexico.

Another group that has received its share of headlines is The True and Living Church of Jesus Christ of Saints of the Last Days, run by James Harmston, who claims to be the reincarnation of Joseph Smith. Harmston, who has been excommunicated from the Mormon Church for advocating polygamy, is married to several former members of Arvin Shreeve's infamous Zion Society. Shreeve and other leaders of his sect were convicted of sexually abusing four girls under the age of fourteen in Northern Utah in 1991.

Modern Polygamy

Because of the inherent secrecy exhibited by the fundamentalist groups, it's hard to estimate the number of polygamists practicing today. In late 1965, the *New York Times* reported that as "many as thirty thousand men, women, and children live in families in which polygamy is practiced."

In 1967, William M. Rogers, former special assistant to the Utah State Attorney, told Ben Merson of *Ladies Home Journal*, "There are more polygamous families than in the days of Brigham Young. At least thirty thousand men, women, and children in this state are now living in plural households—and the number is rapidly increasing."

On June 7, 1998, Maxine Hanks wrote an article in the *Salt Lake Tribune* noting, "Utah usually ignores polygamy, hoping it will go away. But its scope and problems have grown and 'festered like cancer,' according to an ex-wife....Today, there are a dozen major clans consisting of hundreds of families. And there are small independent groups....Estimates vary widely, but insiders claim that Mormon fundamentalism may involve 60,000 people scattered from Canada to Mexico across seven Western states. Most of them are practicing some form of polygamy."

Lt. Mike King of the attorney general's criminal division says modern polygamists groups fall into two types: generational and convert groups. The generational groups are of longer standing, have an older leader, and do not actively recruit new members; convert groups, however, are typically led by a younger man who has been excommunicated from a generational group. In both cases, many modern polygamist clans require members to turn over their wealth and possessions to holding companies, which in turn enjoy non-profit status as a religious group. And that practice is just one of many that has come under ever-increasing scrutiny from the public and law enforcement alike.

Former Utah Attorney General Jan Graham advised state lawyers to crack down on crimes that might surround polygamy, such as child abuse, statutory rape, welfare fraud, and incest, while sidestepping the actual prosecution of polygamy itself. However, most law enforcement officials agree that prosecuting polygamy is difficult—and expensive.

While prosecuting consenting adults who enter into a plural marriage may not be a popular way to spend taxpayer money, when the wife is a minor, the stakes of the issue change dramatically. Previously, proof that young girls were forcibly married off into plural families was the stuff of rumor. But Mary Ann Kingston changed all that and shone an unwanted spotlight on one of the wealthiest and most secretive fundamentalist polygamy clans in America.

Chapter Six
THE KINGSTONS

Though not the largest polygamous grouping in America, by all accounts the Kingstons are the wealthiest, with assets estimated anywhere between $170 million to $300 million. Their financial mother lode comes from a variety of business interests, from real estate holdings to mining to gaming. In addition to their money and power, the charges against John Daniel Kingston and David Ortell Kingston have ignited an emotional and extraordinary debate over the practice of polygamy because if any family symbolizes to opponents all that is wrong with plural marriage, it is the Kingstons.

The Kingston family first embraced polygamy around 1931 when Charles W. Kingston helped produce a pamphlet detailing a revelation given to Lorin Woolley, a Mormon fundamentalist who believed polygamy was the word of God. Woolley revealed that former Church president John Taylor had set aside a select group of men to carry on polygamy, with Woolley being one of them. Wooley's eldest son, Charles Elden Kingston, immediately embraced Woolley as a prophet and began practicing polygamy. After Woolley died, and as John Y. Barlow was taking over, Charles Elden broke away to form his own fundamentalist group, officially known as the Latter-Day Church of Christ, or the Davis County Cooperative. Kingston said he established the group after seeing a vision while praying in a cave. The revelation instructed Charles to base the new order on fundamentalist Mormon principles, including polygamy, and emphasized the importance of prayer, clean living, and supporting the group.

In 1941, the Latter-Day Church of Christ incorporated the Davis County Cooperative Society, which would become the umbrella organization for all Kingston enterprises. Those who belonged to the clan lived communally and were expected to contribute as much as they could to the general Society, which was controlled by Kingston.

All members of the Society were requited to sign a release which said: "I voluntarily transfer all claim and title to all my possessions to said society as a Gift. I also agree to turn the results of my labor, together with the results of my wife and family's labor, to the society, as long as we are members. In case I or we ever withdraw from the society, I or we claim no equity whatsoever in the society." Today, members are expected to consecrate any valuable holdings to the organization. In turn, the Church will see to their basic needs. That structure is why it's next to impossible to find any property records in the Kingston name.

Like the other fundamentalist polygamy groups, from the beginning the Kingston clan lived insular lives, which cut members off from the outside world and created an "us versus them" mindset. Members of the Church frequently worked at firms owned by the Cooperative Society and were paid in script that were useless anywhere but co-op–owned businesses. According to Brooke Adams of *The Observer*, it is standard practice to pay wives and children a starting salary of ten cents an hour, then slowly increase it to minimum wage. "They're pretty clever," Adams' source is quoted as saying. "Everybody in the organization works for really low wages."

Moreover, the houses people lived in and the churches they worshiped in were also owned by the Kingston collective. Kingston not only controlled money and work, but some of the most basic daily activities. By the late 1940s, members were required to adhere to a strict diet in which sugar, caffeine, white flour, and alcohol were forbidden.

Because these groups are frequently bonded by the will, personality and belief of the clan leader, transition can be troubling or unsettling for fundamentalist groups and the Kingstons were no exception. When Charles died in 1948, his brother John Ortell Kingston succeeded him. Where Charles concentrated on an all-for-one philosophy, John was fixated with making and saving money, but certainly not spending it. While it would later be learned that Kingston had a net value in the $70 million range by the mid 1980s, he lived in borderline squalor, as did his progeny.

Most of John's twenty-six children survived on welfare, a fact that eventually caught the attention of authorities. John Ortell Kingston's wives had claimed on the assistance forms that the children's fathers had all left and so they had no way of collecting child support. But state officials were tipped off that all the children actually belonged to John Ortell, and eventually the state sued Kingston for welfare fraud. At first, he denied the children were his, but after a judge ordered DNA tests to be taken to unequivocally determine paternity, John Ortell agreed to an out-of-court settlement and repaid the state a reported $250,000. Judgments entered for more than $100,000 against ten other Kingston clan members were also made on behalf of more than forty children, although recovery services believed it to be a fraction of the money involved. Two other members were convicted and served short prison terms in connection with the case.

However, not much has changed in the Kingston modus operandi when it comes to acknowledging progeny. According to a former Kingston clan member, David Ortell is a chip off the old block: "Even though he's got countless children, he doesn't pretend to support any of them. He doesn't support them financially, he doesn't act the father with the children, he doesn't help in the raising of the children. The only thing he's contributed to these children lives was the sperm to impregnate their mothers."

Senator Scott Howell of the Utah State Legislature says that the abuse of the government welfare system is ironically integral to clans such as the Kingstons:

> What we heard through intelligence, through people who have been in the polygamist environment, is that they're taught that government is evil. That it's an evil thing—but that the welfare system was instituted by God for polygamists. So they could take advantage and continue to feed their large families. That's food stamps; that's giving them allowances for the basics. Those are the abuses and those are the frauds that we put millions and millions of dollars out there to pay for their extreme habits. The Kingstons have taken the principal to authoritarian extremes.

While the John Ortell case may have been a feather in the state's hat, at the same time, it also spotlighted the authorities' hesitancy to go after Kingston on polygamy charges. Randall Skeen, the former assistant Salt Lake County attorney who represented the state in the case, said officials were reluctant to pursue the civil suit and then backed off any criminal charges altogether against John Ortell. "After we got the money back, they kind of dropped the whole thing," says Skeen, who is now in private practice. "If I had been calling the shots, I would have prosecuted every one ·of them." That said, Skeen also admits, "The problem was we didn't have strong ties to the men, just the women." He also acknowledged the only reason they could prosecute John Ortell was because "someone in the group ratted him out."

The Science of Inbreeding

Some have speculated that John Ortell Kingston was more worried about investigators discovering just how closely related those children were than paying the civil fine. Had authorities pursued the matter, they would have made a startling discovery of massive inbreeding. Not coincidentally, besides hording money, Kingston had another obsession with a particularly personal passion—genetics. He had developed some theories about the subject while working on the rundown Kingston dairy farm, located north of Salt Lake City in Woods Cross, where he bred Holstein cows for the best milk production. In what is perhaps the most macabre allegation against Kingston, according to former clan members, John Ortell decided to put what he had learned about in-line breeding dairy cows to practice in his own lineage.

"My father experimented inbreeding with his cattle and then he turned to his children," says Connie Rugg, who is one of John Ortell's estimated sixty-five children. She is also a former Kingston clan member who escaped rather than enter into a forced marriage with an uncle. "All my life, my family told me I had to marry a Kingston," Rugg recalls. "I could choose, but it had to be a brother, uncle, or cousin."

In short, what Kingston had incorporated was a fascination with eugenics, "the science of controlling the traits of future populations through selective breeding" or "the self-direction of human evolution." The eugenics movement in America had its beginnings after the Civil War when the burst of industrialism and immigration made cities overpopulated, often teeming with non-white, non-Americans. Although to the more high-minded, eugenics was an attempt at solving social problems by weeding out undesirable behaviors and characteristics; others saw it as a way of keeping ethnic and racial "purity." The idea was to breed in desirable traits—whether it be intelligence and honor or blue eyes and blonde hair—and breed out undesirable traits such as criminality or dark skin. Modern science now has the means to control these attributes on a cellular level, but when John Ortell was breeding his dairy cows, he was driven by a less exact science and more by his own personal agenda.

John Ortell's goal was to purify or perfect his bloodline using a method that is still a secret shared only by the clan leaders. As one clan member noted, "Brothers marry sisters in an effort to build up a royal priesthood." However, it is believed that the most important blood comes from the sons born of the first wife; these offspring are always held in higher esteem and enjoy greater in-clan status than other male children. And within the Kingstons, those descended directly from John Ortell and LaDonna Peterson, the second of his thirteen wives, are considered to have the better blood, as it were.

Dennis Green, a professor of beef cattle genetics at Colorado State University, told the *Salt Lake Tribune*, "It would have been unusual if he wasn't using artificial insemination in his herd, and by virtue of that, was probably using semen from some bulls that had been inbred. My guess is this man had used some of these inbreeding practices in his herd so he was probably in the camp that believed superior genetics could be propagated in a particular line."

However, there is a definite downside. Adds the professor, "If you don't start with good genetics, and if there is baggage in the genes of the individual, inbreeding will uncover that baggage. When you pair up those undesirable genes, something strange will pop out."

It is this singular trait, the Kingston inbreeding, that truly sets this particular clan apart from many of the others. Throughout the world, most polygamy is exogamous, meaning the plural partners come from outside the bloodline. Inbreeding within, also called endogamous polygamy, is virtually never practiced for reasons to be discussed. While inbreeding can be an accidental by-product of some fundamentalist groups because the inherent population of polygamists is relatively small, within the Kingstons it is intentional and desired. John Ortell began the incest practice by marrying two half-sisters and two nieces.

"My father manipulated and controlled people," Rugg says. "He wanted to control his children and grandchildren through genetics. He believed he had superior bloodlines." The issue of incest was touched upon in court records when the Utah Department of Social Services filed an order declaring John Ortell had fathered three children by his niece, Mary Gustafson, and as a result, wanted back $15,679 in welfare payments.

His other brother, Merlin, also embraced John Ortell's pure-line genetics and the effects of these incestuous couplings quickly became apparent. According to former clan member Rowenna Erickson, when Merlin's children married their own half-siblings, some of the children from these unions were born with deformities caused by inbreeding.

According to an article in the *Salt Lake Tribune* by Greg Burton, "six sons and two daughters of John Ortell and his second wife LaDonna have married at least twenty half-sisters, nieces and first cousins, giving birth to a family tree that twists and tangles, and, at times, withers with children born of genetic deficiencies." Interestingly, it is the disclosure of incest that worries polygamists more than the plural marriage itself. While the public at large might not have strong feelings about consenting adults forming a plural marriage, the very idea of incest goes against what to many people is a primal law of nature. As a result, law enforcement officials are much more apt to prosecute over incest than polygamy. According to Utah's statute, incest is defined as sexual intercourse with an "ancestor, descendant, brother, sister, uncle, aunt, nephew, niece, or first cousin." In addition, it is also considered incest to have intercourse with a stepchild while the marriage is in force, or for sex to occur between a half-sister and half-brother. In thirty-seven states, including Utah, first-cousin marriage is illegal. (However, in 1996, the Utah State Legislature approved first-cousin marriages, but only after the age of sixty-five; the age is lowered to fifty-five if the couple is unable to conceive children.)

Usually, authorities are notified of incest through relatives or close family friends. "But in the polygamist clans, they don't have friends outside, they have no contacts, no way to get the word out," explains Sgt. Don Bell, who heads the sex-crimes unit for the Salt Lake City police force. "We never, ever hear a word about incest within these groups because the children are sheltered."

According to Katy Larsen, northern regional director of the Division of Child and Family Services, "The reason we get involved is protection issues," Larsen says. "Incest is a prevalent problem, one that doesn't get the exposure because investigators and the media, out of kindness, want to protect the parties involved."

On the other hand, that kindness can offer an unintended carte blanche to some chronic abusers, such as the Kingstons are alleged to be, and can keep the general public in the dark as to how widespread a problem incest is in Utah. Again, while a significant part of the population may believe polygamy is a religious belief, few would argue that any religion should be protected to practice institutional incest and child abuse in the name of God's will.

Some cases are harrowing. Rena Mackert was one of seventeen daughters born to her father between four wives. She tells how her father ritually molested his daughters once they turned sixteen by initiating them in his "sex course," a personal instruction on how to please their future husbands. She says on her sixteenth birthday, her father took her to dinner then a movie and on the way home, explained the sex course to her. "He said it would put me on the same level as my mothers, make me like a sister wife," Rena recalls. "But of course I wasn't to talk to any of the sister-wives about this because sister-wives didn't talk about sex."

Her father eventually molested her one night, but was interrupted by the arrival of one of Rena's brothers. Even so, she was shattered. "This man robbed me of my God-given right to be safe and loved and protected and unmolested in my own home. The man who was supposed to protect me from the evils of the world is the one who subjected me to them, all the while vilifying the gentiles as wicked, evil people—a horrifying way to grow up."

To Mackert, the mindset of polygamy is one of control. Although the doctrine might say one thing, to her the subtext is clear. "Men: sexually abuse your children so you can control them forever. Keep them under your thumb; make them so beaten down so that they never find their spirit," she intones, adding, "I call it soul murder."

The Price of Incest

Beyond any moral issue, the taboos against incest are based in science. Simplistically, human beings are made up of genes, half of which come from the mother, half from the father. In turn, these genes are either dominant or recessive. When people too closely related procreate, their "gene pools" lack the necessary diversity that would be found if two unrelated people had children. That's because the incestuous couple already shares many of the same genes. As a result, it is more likely that two negative, recessive genes will be paired up. That is why inbred children have far higher rates of birth defects, learning disabilities, mental retardation, physical impairment, impaired fertility, and congenital birth defects. Stillbirths and infant deaths also are much more likely when blood relatives mate. Those children who otherwise survive are also more prone to illness.

"I know of several girls that have had babies that are severely deformed," reveals Bill Adams, a former Kingston employee. "And those babies usually die."

Lynn Jorde, a professor of human genetics at the University of Utah School of Medicine who researches genetic causes of birth defects, told the *Salt Lake Tribune*:

> For, say, parent-offspring or brother-sister matings, they share half their genes so half their genes are identical. So if you have any recessive disease gene, you have a higher probability of getting two of them. There have only been a few studies done on the biological effects of incest; it's obviously hard to get subjects. But the studies that have been done generally show that a fourth to half of those children have problems.

Even more disturbing is that many polygamist clans don't believe in seeking medical treatment. Speaking on an *A&E Investigative Reports* special on polygamy, Roni Baker, whose husband walked out on her and her eleven children because she refused to be a plural wife, says that while abortion is considered the work of the Devil, polygamists she knows think nothing of letting children born with defects suffer. She cites the case of a couple who gave birth "to a daughter born with two club feet and without a knee cap. The doctors told them it was correctable but they wouldn't have her fixed because God made her that way for a purpose. So here's this little girl who will be deformed and unable to walk."

To Baker, it was God who gave humans the ability to heal, so how could it be against his will to help the little girl? She concludes that polygamy is "not a religion where you go to church and worship and pray. This is so mind-bending that there's no room for reality."

Other defects seen among incest progeny include microcephaly, in which the baby's skull is malformed and small blindness spina bifida; Downs syndrome; kidney disease; and abnormal leg and arm joints. "You don't want to jump to the conclusion and say all of these are the result of inbreeding," Lynn Jorde warns. "But just on general principles, the offspring of uncle–niece, or half-siblings have an elevated level of genetic disease. There is no doubt about that at all. So when you see all of these diseases occurring in the children, it's possible some are the result of inbreeding."

And that possibility of children being born with horrible deformities and maladies, say doctors and scientists, is the prime reason for enforcing incest laws. "We do know there are biological hazards," Jorde states. "A fourth to half of father-daughter and brother-sister offspring have mental or physical deficiencies. It gets pretty bleak when it gets that close."

Rowenna Erickson says she has personal knowledge of the far-reaching effects of inbreeding within the Kingstons. "There's at least eight microcephalics, there have been two births that I'm aware of where they had fused limbs and the children died at birth or shortly after; there have been liver dysfunctions and schizophrenia is quite dominant."

The condition that killed Andrea Johnson, preeclampsia, is also considered a genetic condition and, according to former members, is a common ailment among pregnant Kingston women. Several Kingston offspring of incestuous couplings also have been born without fingernails, a disease that could also possibly be linked to a number of genetically caused abnormalities. Because of the secretive nature of the clan, direct medical diagnoses is difficult, admit authorities. However, occasionally there are leaks, such as when a Kingston wife in 1996 tried to find out why her two children's growth was stunted. Typically, she was vague about the children's parentage but eventually admitted to doctors that she was married to her half-brother. The diagnosis: dwarfism. After receiving the results, the woman divorced her husband and left the clan, too late to help her children.

Beyond the tragedy visited upon the children born with deformities is the more practical matter of who ends up paying the costs for these children as well as the consequences for the public. "If these couples are...mating in a way that increases genetic diseases, that the public ends up supporting, it becomes a matter of public interest," Jorde notes.

Linda Walker, who started the Child Protection Project website and who works as a legal consultant on civil cases involving child abuse and the church, says in an essay called "Fatal Inheritance; Mormon Eugenics" that it was the death of a childhood friend from an uncommon form of nephritis called Alport's Syndrome that first piqued her curiosity about the possible ramifications of incest and polygamy. People born with the disease frequently die in young adulthood and may also suffer from hearing loss and eye problems. Although uncommon, there appears to be a concentration of Alport's in Utah.

Walker also poses the theory that in addition to concern over authorities, another reason some children may not receive all the medical attention they need is that by seeking help, it's an admission that the child's bloodline is not perfect, which would fly in the face of John Ortell's original vision. But as each year passes, more tales of deformities and even new syndromes are reported, such as ulnar mammary syndrome. Other maladies become more common; in early 1990, the incidence of nephritis in the general population was revised up from one in ten thousand to one in five thousand. Beyond the incalculable human suffering involved, the amount of health care dollars needed to deal with the number of birth defects poses a substantial fiscal burden on the state's taxpayers.

The Order

While eugenics made a splash when the concept was first introduced half a century ago, in the intervening years, selective breeding has been shown to have disastrous consequences, particularly among humans. Whatever else they might be, the Kingston clan birth defect history is most surely a pointed and vivid cautionary genetic tale. However, there is no sign that the incestuous tradition has lost any internal momentum among the clan's leaders. As they have been since the time of John Ortell, the church leader, currently Paul Kingston, must sanction marriages among the clan members. However, former members say that Paul's brothers—Daniel, David, and Jesse—also have influence over who marries whom. Paul and the other high-ranking Kingstons who run the clan are simply called, "The Order." They inherited their status and place from John Ortell, who was a God-like figure to his followers. He regaled them with his visions and proclaimed himself to be the one true Mormon prophet then living.

According to former members, teenage girls in the clan tend to be married between the ages of fourteen to sixteen. Not all marriages are ordained; if an attraction happens naturally, it is possible for the young couple to have their marriage approved. Otherwise, marriages are arranged. However, leaders of the clan seem to have their pick. According to Bill Adams, a former employee of the Kingstons:

> Paul and Daniel spot the young cute girls, and they go to them and say, We've received direction from God to marry you. And then they shower them with gifts. The girls are told to go pray and see if you receive direction. It's sad in a way, because it's always the young cute girls. It's never the over-weight plump ones. It seems to me that somebody in the

group would get a clue as to what is going on here. But they don't. They don't question it. They're taught to be obedient.

Once married, these young women are expected to give birth once a year. And, says Adams, "None of those women goes to the hospital for births. Paul delivers most of the babies."

A curious side note is that male members of the Kingston clan who don't have the "good blood" running through their veins may find it difficult to find any wife. "You've got to realize that there's a shortage of females," explains Scott Stoddard, another former clan member. "And those Kingston boys take most of them."

After John Ortell Kingston died in 1987, the clan lost its one clear-cut leader. Control of the family passed to his seven sons from his first wife, as well as to another faction descended from Charles Elden Kingston's sister, Ardous. Formally, the president of the Latter-Day Church of Christ is John's septuagenarian brother Merlin, who is believed to have five or six wives. (Merlin's most dramatic moment in clan history may have come in 1977, when Ervil LeBaron made an unsuccessful attempt on his life.) But while Merlin may be the figurehead, it is Paul Kingston, a CPA and attorney, who is the Church's spiritual and economic leader. Members elected Paul to replace John Ortell over his three older brothers. As far as the clan is concerned, Paul is the only one in communication with God. Paul is said to currently have more than thirty wives and more than two hundred children.

As a youth, Paul attended the now defunct South High School in Salt Lake City where he was student body president. He was also active in sports, lettering in swimming and cross-country. He earned his law degree from the University of Utah. While most saw Paul Kingston as a popular, outgoing student, others caught glimpses of a less public side. Salt Lake attorney Ed Flint, a former classmate, told a reporter about attending Kingston's first marriage. "The weirdest thing is that he dated this one girl for a year and a half during high school and then about a month after school he came around with wedding invitations and he was marrying a different girl," Flint said. "We all went to the wedding. I don't remember it well, but there were a lot of women and a lot of children, you didn't see too many men and the ones you did see were pretty old."

Few outsiders knew the extent of the family business Paul would one day oversee. The Kingstons' Davis County Cooperative is headquartered in Salt Lake City and is believed to have holdings in Nevada and Idaho as well as Arizona and Mexico. The cooperative owns twenty-four private corporations, although the holdings are not always easy to trace. What is traceable shows a veritable empire. A glance through public records show the same P.O. box numbers and same family officers listed for each company. The operations include the Merlin Kingston–run Holtz, Inc., an enormous cattle enterprise located on Wine Cup Ranch that uses 677,000 acres of Bureau of Land Management property—an area twice the size of the greater Los Angeles metropolitan area. With approximately eighty-six hundred head of cattle, Holtz is the fourth-largest user of BLM land in the United States. The Kingston family attorney, Carl E. Kingston, is listed as the president of Holtz Inc. What strikes many who learn of the Kingston connection to Holtz is that a staggeringly wealthy family is enjoying below-market subsidies that cost taxpayers more than $100 million a year while overgrazing wrecks streams and drives wildlife to the endangered list; this in an age when individual ranchers are struggling to just survive.

"I think people should care about this," a spokeswoman named Liz Taylor for the Southern Utah Wilderness Alliance in Cedar City, Utah, says. "Not because they are polygamists, but because they are a major corporation. And they are getting quite a ride from the federal government."

Other businesses include an ice distribution company, A-1 Disposal, a trash-hauling company, a bituminous coal and lignite mine, a health spa, accounting firms, grocery and clothing stores, a preschool, and vending machine companies. Department of Commerce records indicate there are over forty businesses affiliated with the Kingston family and property tax records show they have twenty-three commercial and residential properties in Salt Lake County listed to the Kingston's Las Vegas–based World Enterprises, valued at over $3 million.

"This is a well-organized corporation," said former clan member Rowenna Erickson in a newspaper interview. "They are so secretive because polygamy is illegal and so is incest. They really detest publicity."

But some of their business activities seem predisposed to attract attention, in particular the Kingston-run Mountain Coin Machine Distributors, primarily controlled by Elden Kingston, John Ortell's nephew. According to a story in the *Denver Rocky Mountain News* by Lou Kitzer, "The amusement machine businesses the Kingstons run in Colorado, Arizona, New Mexico, Nevada, Utah, Idaho, and California are the type of prized cash-rich businesses that have frequently attracted organized crime interest. A report by the New Mexico Governor's Organized Crime Prevention Commission said that companies in illegal video gaming businesses are generally owned by organized crime, local racketeers, or legitimate vendors who are tied to organized crime."

Kitzer goes on to quote Merlin Symes, Mountain Coin's former Utah manager, as saying "the Kingstons bought illegal slot machines from Mafia-controlled companies in New Jersey. And they financed a $510,000, no-down-payment loan to a company that federal investigators said was also receiving funds from Denver's Smaldone La Cosa Nostra syndicate."

Elden Kingston, however, called Symes' allegations a "fantasy. I, myself and/or Mountain Coin is not now, or never has been, associated, involved or has any connection with organized crime, any crime family or any other illegal activity," Kingston said. "Our growth has been the result of hard work and careful planning, and most of all, making sure that all of our dealings were handled with honesty, integrity and a high level of customer service."

A former Kingston clan member who spoke to *A&E Investigative Reports* on condition of anonymity says she was involved in some underhanded dealings. "There was a time when the Kingstons were being audited by the IRS and worked late for a couple of weeks putting together a second set of books with false information so it would look like the businesses had paid the correct amount of taxes when in reality they hadn't."

If there is another hallmark of the Kingstons it is that today's leaders have inherited Charles Elden's frugality. Despite their vast wealth and cash reserves, many of the wives and offspring of the Kingston leaders live in squalid homes sparsely filled with tattered furnishings. "They live in poverty, sheer poverty," says Vicky Prunty, a founder of Tapestry Against Polygamy, a Utah organization that assists women who have left polygamous relationships.

Even though the men own the housing, women married to the Kingston brothers are forced to pay rent out of their minimum wage earnings. "The whole idea is they think they need to be self-sufficient," Stoddard explained. "You would be amazed at the lengths they go to save money. They even tell you you're only supposed to use three squares of toilet paper. And they used to go get garbage out of the back of large grocery stores and take it home and eat it."

Bill Adams, who has relatives in the Kingston clan, tries to understand why the women stay. He knows one woman who is thirty years old and has nine children:

> If you were raised in the whole group from when you were a kid, and the whole family, your cousins, brothers, sisters, everyone in your family is part of it, where are you going to go? And say if you have nine kids—what are you going to do? I used to have to inspect their cars. I've had a lot of the girls driving around in cars that were totally unsafe. I had one girl break down on me when I told her this car's not worth fixing. She was one of the leader's wives. He's a multimillionaire.

A former clan member, Laura Chapman, observes that finances are controlled to make it harder for women to leave. "They've set up their own currency, so these women don't have bank accounts or anything like that," she said. "It makes it even more frightening for them because they have to learn the basics. Leaving polygamy is like a slave in the south leaving their master. They have no way to exist without that master."

In an article published by the *Observer* newspaper, a source was quoted as saying that the Kingstons' frugality forces women and children to live in near-poverty conditions. While the men "have access to millions of dollars," they "don't feel responsibility for supporting their families emotionally or financially."

In the Spotlight

For a family that craves isolation and privacy, the Kingstons spend an awful lot of time in the news, much of it self-inflicted. Such as in July 1999, when officials with the Division of Child and Family Services took seven children between the ages of two and eleven into state custody after they were found home alone with no adult supervision. Authorities originally went to the house, owned by Ellery Kingston, a cousin of Mary Ann's father, John Daniel, after receiving a tip that a fifteen-year-old girl was being prevented from going to school against her will.

"The house was quite dirty and there was some construction going on," said Sandy police Sgt. Kevin Thacker. "They felt it wasn't safe to leave them there."

Then, in late November, a truck owned by the Kingstons' garbage company, A-1 Disposal, was involved in an accident that left the driver of the truck in a coma and injured four others. Six safety violation charges were filed against the company's operator, Ralph L. Anderson, the son of John Ortell Kingston and the brother of John Daniel, who is also listed as a partner in the company. Officials determined the accident was caused by faulty brakes, and the charges included a braking system violation, operation of an unsafe vehicle, headlight violation, no safety inspection, and expired registration.

An official for the Utah Department of Transportation said that A-1 was "one of the companies with the highest number of violations in the last ten years." In 1993, they were fined $10,000 for 215 violations, including operating a vehicle with unsafe tires, leaking wheel seals, having four of six brakes unadjusted or inoperative, and permitting a driver to drive after having been on duty more than seventy hours in seven consecutive days. Three years later, the company was fined $5,000 for thirty more violations.

A month following the accident, in December 1998, the Kingstons were in the news again when city officials severed business relations with A-1 because of its poor safety records and irregular service. A-1 Disposal had held the municipal garbage collection contract with the Davis County city since 1986, but city officials claimed they hadn't been aware of the company's spotty safety violations history. "We didn't know we could get that kind of information," said City Manager Collin Wood. "We were as surprised as anyone."

In February 1999, another truck with bad brakes overturned in a city intersection, although nobody was injured in that accident. But following yet another investigation, the state finally ordered A-1 to stop operating altogether in April 1999, an extremely surprising if not unprecedented action by the Utah Department of Transportation, which is generally more interested in compliance than extreme punitive measures.

"We've tried to work with them. We've fined them and cited them only to later find similar and repeated violations," UDOT spokeswoman Andrea M. Packer said. "They haven't addressed the safety and maintenance violations we've identified."

In 1987, John Daniel had a run-in with police after he allegedly pulled a gun on two youths he claimed were trying to break into his car, then took them to the Great Salt Lake, apparently to frighten them. He was charged with aggravated assault, aggravated kidnapping, and carrying a loaded weapon in a car.

One of the more compelling lawsuits involves Elaine Jenkins who filed a lawsuit seeking $1 million in workers' compensation in connection with the death of her former husband, Samuel Jenkins. He died in August 1997 after being run over by a shuttle car while working at the Kingstons' mine. Jenkins, who left the clan after divorcing her husband in 1996, wanted benefits for six of their nine children. She went into the legal battle prepared for the worst.

"They're really aggressive," she said in an interview. "You can't negotiate with them. That's part of their strategy—to wear the other person down. They have people in the group who lie for them on the witness stand." She claims that whatever Paul Kingston says, "is what they listen to. If he says this is Satan's attack on the group, most of the people will listen to that. People are still just as brainwashed as they ever were."

The mine where her ex-husband worked had been cited for safety violations and for running an illegal weekend shift. However, operation of the mine went on unhindered. "They still carry a weekend crew. They're still working illegally," she said soon after filing her suit. "But nobody's trying to stop them. They're going to keep doing it until somebody stops them."

The most interesting aspect of Jenkins suit is her efforts to seek the deed to her home, which was held by a Kingston-run company. She claims she has a right to the home because she and her husband paid for the house with their own money; however, as members of the Church, they turned over all their assets. But once given, it was going to prove extremely difficult to get it back. "If I lose this house, it's going to scare people more," she said.

Megan Chase became embroiled in a custody dispute after becoming pregnant. The father was the son of one of the high-ranking clan members. Chase refused to marry the young man after she found out the family were polygamists. She also accused him of being physically and verbally abusive, and threatening her and her parents. Although the court granted Chase a protective order, they also allowed the father visitation rights from noon to 8 P.M. on Sundays. Chase was trying to stop even that. "I do not want my baby down there," she said. "When they found out the baby was a girl they wanted her on Sundays. I know why. She's going to church with them."

Then in February 1999, Jason Kingston, who had allegedly been married to Andrea Johnson, the fifteen year-old who died in 1992, abruptly resigned from the state auditor's office—where he worked as a mid-level auditor—during an investigation into medical benefits he claimed for a niece, Rosalind. That niece also happened to be his wife, who he had married in 1993 in Nevada by a justice of the peace unaware of their blood ties—Jason Kingston's full sister is Rosalind's mother.

A review of court records shows that these are but a handful from the mountain of legal skirmishes the Kingstons have been involved in over the past two decades. From civil suits to welfare fraud charges to domestic disturbances to allegations of child abuse, the Kingstons have made a cottage industry of defending themselves. However, through most of the legal wrangling, few outside Utah knew of the Kingstons. But in the wake of Mary Ann's sensational allegations against her uncle and father, suddenly, the national media was zooming in on the family. The unwanted attention suddenly being focused on the family caused Elden Kingston to issue a rare public statement defending his family, who he said was being persecuted in the media and portrayed in an unfair light:

> There has been a lot of news media coverage that has tried to portray "the Kingstons" as some kind of secret religious group. They have been called names, ridiculed, discriminated against and persecuted, all because some of their religious beliefs were different than the majority of the people.
>
> The people that really know "the Kingstons" know these stories simply are not true and realize they are just normal people trying to make an honest living....
>
> I pay hundreds of thousands of dollars in state, local and federal taxes, and I try to comply with all the laws....I try to treat everyone as well as I possibly can. I believe in respecting all religious beliefs, in living and let live.
>
> All I would like is for others to do the same. I'm not sure what your religious beliefs are, but whatever they are, I respect them and wish you well.

Not only did the Kingstons' well-publicized legal woes keep their spin-control machine humming, it has also kept the family's lawyers busy. The main legal eagle is Carl E. Kingston, who also happens to be a Latter-Day Church of Christ leader. As an attorney, Carl is a member of the Utah State Bar and as such, was required to sign an oath to uphold the Utah Constitution—of which Article III specifically outlaws polygamy.

Even so, Carl is believed to currently have two wives; a reported third wife has since left the family. However, the odds of the state bar or any other legal entity taking action against Kingston for violating his oath, much less polygamy, is practically non-existent. Again, since the plural marriages are undocumented, it would take a former wife to go on the record for any reprimand to take place.

But the wall of silence that had enveloped and protected the Kingston clan for so many years was beginning to crack, ever so subtly. Mary Ann Kingston had put a face on the dark side of polygamy and the resulting court cases threatened to change the Kingston way of life forever.

Chapter Seven
GATHERING CLOUDS

Mary Ann Kingston's accusations presented both unprecedented opportunity and obstacles for the Box Elder sheriff's office. Seldom did anyone from within the Kingston family break ranks, much less offer themselves as a potentially damning witness in a criminal matter. For perhaps the first time, authorities were being presented with first hand information about polygamy-related child and sexual abuses within the emphatically insular clan, but the question was, would they actually be able to prosecute the offenders? And if they could, what would the ramifications be on the thousands of other active polygamists in the state?

From the outset, both opponents and proponents of polygamy recognized that the Kingston case could be an important conduit for voicing their beliefs and having them heard by a large, national audience. The media attention devoted to the Kingston allegations was modest in the beginning. However, as the case progressed, as charges flew, and as prosecutors pushed to make polygamy an unnamed codefendant in the case, Utah suddenly found itself a regular contributor to the nightly news throughout the nation.

When investigators presented police officials' affidavits alleging incest and unlawful sexual contact between Mary Ann and David, it was met by skepticism within the prosecutors' office, with one deputy county prosecutor telling reporters that the incest case was weak if it was only based on the teen's testimony. Others in law enforcement disagreed. "We believe there is enough to go on—the sexual crimes did not happen here, but in other jurisdictions," Lynn Yeates, chief deputy of the Box Elder County sheriff's department said. "And we are going to send those jurisdictions a copy of the reports and they can decide from those how to proceed."

What everyone could agree on was that in the end, it would come down to Mary Ann's word against her uncle's. As is usually the case with sex offenses, there aren't typically many witnesses.

On June 18, 1998, a month after Mary Ann gave her statement to the police, a July 22 hearing was set for John Daniel Kingston, who stood accused of one count of second-degree felony child abuse for beating his daughter. At the time, he was free on $10,000 bail. Mary Ann, on the other hand, was in protective custody, preparing for an ordeal that no one could prepare her for. "She is still scared her family will find her," Detective Scott Cosgrove said. "She just wants to go to high school and have a normal life. She is a brave girl. She's willing to testify and go through the whole mess."

The preliminary hearing was poignant and emotional for Mary Ann, dressed conservatively in a gray suit and white blouse, as she detailed in open court before First District Judge Ben Hadfield the harrowing incidents of the night her father whipped her. It was her first public appearance since calling authorities and the strain showed. Although fighting to maintain composure, Mary Ann's voice repeated cracked and she dabbed at her eyes with tissue during her testimony, which included statements regarding her polygamous marriage to her uncle, David Ortell.

When Box Elder County prosecutor Jon Bunderson asked her to identify the man who hit her, Mary Ann broke down weeping as she pointed toward her father, who was seated directly across from her seat in the witness box. John Daniel's attorney was his cousin Carl E. Kingston, who had asked that all spectators be removed from the courtroom. Judge Ben Hadfield denied the request.

Some questioned the appropriateness of Carl defending John Daniel. Investigators knew Mary Ann had worked as a receptionist in his Salt Lake law office. Others claimed Carl had presided over a secret ceremony in which his own daughter became the third wife of David Kingston—Mary Ann's uncle and husband. However, Carl refused to discuss the issues and most observers expected him to remain John Daniel's counsel throughout the legal proceedings.

When it was his turn to question Mary Ann, Carl Kingston tried to portray her as an overall wayward wild-child—a depiction she denied. Mary Ann was asked about relationships with other men and admitted on the stand she had once spent the night with a man in a hotel, where they drank and did drugs. But she maintained that the only person who had ever hit her was her father. The hearing was more of a formality than fact-finding mission and at its conclusion, Judge Hadfield ordered Kingston, then forty-three, to stand trial for second-degree felony child abuse. If convicted, he faced up to fifteen years in prison. He was to be arraigned the following Monday.

The Judge also rejected Carl E. Kingston's claim that the offense did not qualify as a felony but as the lesser Class A misdemeanor. The attorney argued, "If a parent slaps a child and the next week slaps him again, the child might have two bruises, but is the parent guilty of a second-degree felony? I would submit no."

Judge Hadfield saw it differently and told Kingston the extensive beating was more akin to torture than mere parental corporal punishment. "It would seem to the court that this was a methodical inflicting of continuous pain and suffering," he said.

Some of the spectators in the courtroom had more than just a passing interest in the proceedings; to them it was personal. A dozen members of the group Tapestry Against Polygamy, a support group of former plural wives, attended the hearings as both a show of support for Mary Ann and to draw a pointed legal line. "We wanted to show this young girl that we are here to support her," said one of the organization's founders, Rowenna Erickson, who herself was a former wife in the Kingston clan. "She has displayed profound courage in coming out like this."

At the arraignment, John Daniel pleaded not guilty to the charge, making no other comment before the court. Although receiving less press, a custody hearing had also been set for August 24, 1999, to determine whether or not John Daniel would retain any legal parental rights over his daughter, who was in foster care. Hoping to help Mary Ann reclaim her life and some sense of normalcy, the Utah Division of Child and Family Services announced it had set up a trust fund to help pay for Mary Ann's schooling, which she desperately wanted to resume.

By August 1998, the trust fund had received $3,000 in contributions, a third of it coming from a concerned Episcopalian minister in Florida, who said he learned of the trust fund via the Tapestry Against Polygamy website. In addition, the state Office of Crime Victim Reparations also agreed to provide $5,400 for remedial education for Mary Ann, who had been taken out of school by her family after only completing the ninth grade. The extra money would pay for a program that would enable her to catch up on two years of schooling in a single year. The unusual state effort was being made out of concern for her unique situation; when she ran away from her father, she effectively left her entire family. She was an orphan in the broadest context possible. "If you think about it, she's not going to have any support in the future," said Laurie Johnson, state Division of Child and Family Services caseworker.

While John Daniel was the first to face criminal proceedings, his brother's day in court would follow shortly. In late August 1998, David Ortell was ordered to appear in court September 1 before Third District Judge Ronald Nehring. Authorities had charged Kingston with two counts of incest and one count of unlawful sexual conduct with a sixteen- or seventeen-year-old, all third-degree felonies punishable by five years in jail. Like his brother, he was free on $10,000 bail—posted by Bail Bond Specialists, a company owned by a Kingston clan member.

Also like his brother, David made no statement during his brief appearance, as advised by his lawyer, Stephen McCaughey, a well-regarded Salt Lake City defense attorney. Instead, McCaughey denied the allegations on behalf of his client. When questioned by the media, the attorney also sidestepped the issue of polygamy, saying he didn't know whether David Ortell was a polygamist or not, but in any event, he couldn't comment further on the case until he had reviewed the police reports. "I just met him and he seems like a decent sort of guy," McCaughey said outside the courtroom.

In a related development, it was revealed that Mary Ann had reminded investigators about the 1991 investigation into her alleged rape at the hands of another uncle. However, because the statute of limitations had expired, prosecutors were prevented from pursuing that case or filing any criminal charges.

A day after David was in court, John Daniel's scheduled August 1998 trial was delayed until March 1999 following a surprising development. John had replaced Carl with another prominent defense attorney, Ron Yengich, who had a scheduling conflict. Now that the severity of the charges—and the state's determination to pursue them—had been fully revealed, both Kingstons had opened up the family's ample pocketbook and hired two of the best lawyers money could buy.

After David Ortell's preliminary hearing was scheduled for December 1998 before Third District Judge Robin Reese, his attorney, Stephen McCaughey, went on the record to publicly deny his client ever had sex with Mary Ann or that they were ever married, although he was quick to point out that the polygamous marriage was not "part of the charge anyway. The charge is whether he had sexual intercourse with her as an underage girl and as a niece. Our defense is that he never had sexual intercourse with her," McCaughey said. Another member of the David's defense team, Susanne Gustin-Furgis hinted at what the defense strategy was going to be when she said, "Everything will come out at the preliminary hearing," and, added that Mary Ann "has a very interesting background."

At a court hearing in the fall of 1998, McCaughey asked Judge Sandra Peuler to lift the court-ordered requirement that Kingston call in on a daily basis to Salt Lake County Pretrial Services because it was creating a hardship for David when he went out of town on business trips. Judge Peuler agreed to change the provision—but only if officials at Pretrial Services thought that Kingston's supervision was adequate. The issue indicated that there had been at least a modicum of concern among officials that Kingston might be a flight risk.

Harkening back to the early days of the Church, third President John Taylor had overseen the Latter-Day Saints from hidden exile. With the Kingston money and network of fundamentalist Mormon communities, it wasn't too far-fetched a concern. Plus, Box Elder Sheriff's detective Scott Cosgrove revealed that Mary Ann indicated there was a possibility the family might buy some property in Montana and flee before John Daniel got to trial. "They just can't see John Daniel going to court," Detective Cosgrove noted at the time. "Most of them are just watching what will happen. I think people are thinking he won't go to prison. They don't think we can convict him."

As expected, members of Tapestry Against Polygamy sat quietly watching the Kingston proceedings, their lapels adorned with purple ribbons, which symbolized the abuse they feel women and children suffer within the context of plural marriages. Afterwards, Carmen Thompson, director of public relations for Tapestry, noted, "This is just the kind of abuse a polygamist family is prone to. With such a strong patriarchal head, the wives are subjected to emotional, spiritual and physical abuse." She likened the women who suffered such subjugation to "Stepford wives," saying they became "like children— totally dependent."

She also revealed an interesting side note that the longstanding Mormon polygamist clans—many of whom were famous for seeking converts—were now facing pressure to convert from what she referred to as "Christian polygamist" groups. "Their major purpose is to convert Mormon polygamists to Christian polygamy," Thompson said, adding that she herself had once been a member of such a group. However, she described their style of plural marriage as being less rigid, as it were, insofar as families retained independence as opposed to being enveloped by a clan. Plus, incest was not favored. These groups preferred to add new blood whenever possible. "They seek women with children and single males," explained Laura Chapman, another member of Tapestry Against Polygamy. She added, "They are breeding at the nation's highest birth rate," Chapman said. "And every time polygamists are in the media, it attracts more sick people to join them."

The December 10, 1998, preliminary hearing for David Ortell was much more contentious than the hearing with John had been and revealed more about Mary Ann's life while in the clan—and her streak of rebelliousness. Of special note was the testimony indicating that the girl had fallen in love with another young man and had wanted to marry him. When questioned by defense attorneys about the young man, Mary Ann would become noticeably emotional. "Obviously, she had some feelings for him," noted Salt Lake Deputy District Attorney Dane Nolan. Mary Ann admitted she continued to see the boyfriend even after being married to David.

Looking more like a meek accountant than child molester, David Ortell was accompanied to the hearing by his first wife, Sharli Rae Jenkins Kingston. Once again, defense attorney Steve McCaughey vehemently denied that his client ever had sex with his niece, and categorized Mary Ann's story as having serious discrepancies. He claimed she was making it up just to be rebellious. "That's why she's saying this. It's her testimony versus whatever credibility issues develop," McCaughey said, adding, "We have to wait until the trial to hear Mr. Kingston's side of the story." But for Laura Chapman and other members of Tapestry Against Polygamy, the girl's story rang with a chilling familiarity, particular her testimony about being afraid to refuse her uncle's sexual advances. "All of us women who have exited polygamy, we feel her pain," Chapman said. "You do feel trapped. You have no options. You have your sister-wives, but you don't talk about the painful stuff."

Again, there was little doubt that the preliminary hearing would find just cause for trial. When the hearing was over, Judge Leon A. Dever ordered David Kingston to stand trial. His three-day trial was scheduled in Third District Court for April 20, 1999, before Judge David Young. He was charged with three counts of incest and one count of unlawful sexual conduct, all third-degree felonies. In a new development, prosecutors announced that after discovering in another interview with Mary Ann that their last sexual encounter took place between May 7 and May 15, 1998, a fourth count of incest would be prosecuted under a new, more specific law that had gone into effect on May 4, 1998. If convicted, Kingston faced up to twenty years in prison.

If nothing else, the pending Kingston trials opened a dialogue about a long-ignored practice that had been evolving out of sight for decades. Away from the oversight of authorities and hidden away from the general populace, had the fundamentalist polygamy groups devolved into dysfunctional clans rife with spousal and child abuse? Were women entering into plural marriages of free will, or were underage girls being forced into illegal and incestuous relationships? Authorities were now being asked these questions and were feeling the pressure to answer.

The last time anyone in Utah had been prosecuted for bigamy, the crime of having more than one wife, had been in the early 1960s. (Interestingly, although specifically outlawed in the state constitution, there was no statute against polygamy specifically.) The problems with these prosecutions had been repeated like a jurisprudence mantra—reluctant witnesses, witnesses disappearing, no record of the marriages because they're performed in secret, a concern regarding freedom of religion issues, public apathy, or disapproval of such prosecutions.

"Let me ask you this; would you want this office to prosecute every philanderer, every man who leaves his wife and shacks up with a girlfriend?" Salt Lake District Attorney Neal Gunnarson said in a 1998 *Desert News* interview. "In my personal opinion, they are feel-good statutes that are completely ineffective and shouldn't be there. Our society just patted itself on the back and said, We've got to make a stand against this evil."

Salt Lake County Sheriff Aaron Kennard added, "We don't go after it and my deputies are not going to go after it. Number one, because we have more important crimes. There is bank robbery, drive-by shootings, gangs, home-invasion robbery, homicide, rape. These are the issues of highest priority."

But suddenly, it wasn't just about consenting adults living an alternative lifestyle. Now there were women coming forward who had left the clans telling shocking stories of physical, emotional, and sexual abuse, child molestation, and women and their children living in forced poverty while systematically committing what many believe is essentially welfare fraud. But again, because of the way the Utah welfare statutes were written, it made prosecution tricky.

Since polygamous marriages were undocumented, and because the state wouldn't recognize a second wife because of the bigamy law, a plural wife applying for welfare assistance would officially be viewed as a single mother. And single mothers are eligible for such assistance. However, the spirit of the law is surely being sidestepped, especially in the case of the Kingstons, whose wealth is undisputed.

Because of the size of most plural families, the cost to taxpayers can be staggering when looking at food stamps, Medicaid, and other assistance. According to official records, in 1996, families in the polygamous community of Hildale, Utah, received more than double the amount of food stamps of other towns of similar size in the entire state because the federal program is based on the number of people in a family. According to the *Desert News*, one Hildale family had thirty-seven members and received $2,867 in January 1996. In Parowan, a town of roughly the same size, the largest household had only seven members. Similarly, Hildale's thirty-six households received $21,420 compared with Parowan's forty-four households, which received $9,532.

There was also the issue of girls being pulled out of school prematurely, depriving them of the education that might give them the tools to make it on their own, thereby making it that more difficult to leave the clans. Beyond that, many officials believe that children born into polygamous families are less apt to attend public school overall, in part because their fundamentalist parents don't want their offspring exposed to outside influences.

Even so, unwilling to begin what might be perceived as an assault on fundamentalist groups per se, Utah state officials in 1998 promised to aggressively pursue cases involving child and spousal abuse and incest while taking a hands-off approach to bigamy. Part of the new focus was the result of opinion polls that indicated more than 90 percent of their constituents wanted to see more attention paid to these kinds of crimes. State and local officials knew there were significant obstacles to this public mandate, but they also knew that with the world watching, excuses wouldn't be readily accepted.

Governor Mike Leavitt promised that his state would "not turn a blind eye" on victims of these crimes, but then deftly passed the buck, saying the ultimate responsibility lies with the attorney general and local county attorneys. The Attorney General's office, in turn, pointed out that they depended on local authorities to investigate and enforce the laws. But local police and sheriffs complained that their lack of resources, financial and otherwise, made it difficult to devote the necessary time and effort to ferreting out these crimes.

It was this kind of bureaucratic volleyball that frustrated people like Laura Chapman, who saw the flurry of activity as all bustle with little substance and suggested officials just hoped it would all go away. "When we asked for a task force on polygamy, we were kind of laughed off," Chapman said. "Our system is letting down these children."

Not everyone agreed with her dire assessment. For example, University of Utah professor Irwin Altman believes there is no more abuse in polygamous families than in monogamous ones. And fellow professor of constitutional law Ed Firmage, who also happens to be the great-grandson of Brigham Young, commented, "Religion is as much conduct as it is belief," so therefore some practices are protected under the Constitution. Beyond that, he doesn't see any advantage to prosecuting polygamy per se. "One thing is true—people will live with the people they love. It doesn't matter if you're talking about gays and lesbians, polygamists, or others." In fact, he sees some distinct societal disadvantages for purging polygamists, believing it simply causes the fundamentalists to become more insular and extreme. "When you're talking so much to yourself," he added, "you come to hear your own echo and it becomes the voice of God."

Chapman, however, says she speaks from experience, not academic theory; relating how her brothers started molesting her in her teens and how her father sexually abused her and her sisters. She also maintains that the reason these abuses occur is because of the inherent secrecy that permeates the clans. But even women who have nothing but happy childhood memories can grow up to see a different side. Jayne Voight, who grew up in a plural family, admits her change of heart came after she got married herself and her husband began marrying more wives. The emotional wear and tear convinced her it was simply an unhealthy way of life.

The Mormon Double Standard

In the first weeks and months following John Daniel's arrest, authorities experienced a noticeable jump in anonymous tips relating to possible polygamous families and activity. But after time, the flurry of activity vanished and people seemed to turn their attention elsewhere again. The same appeared to be true within the fundamentalist communities, where the news of the charges against John

Daniel and David Ortell seemed to spur a few women to try to leave. However, the increased attention of the group also resulted in a tightening of internal security, observed Elaine Jenkins, another former Kingston-clan wife, and created an "us against them" feeling within the group. But even if the clan didn't try to actively dissuade women from leaving the fold—either through family ties, verbal threats, or actual physical coercion—simply being a Mormon woman makes the struggle for independence that much more difficult.

While civil divorces in Utah are easily gotten, it is very difficult for Mormon women in general to obtain divorces in the Church because of the doctrine of celestial marriage. Women are told that "divorce is usually the result of one or both not living the gospel," and that a woman who wants a divorce is "untrue to the covenants she has made in the house of the Lord."

After a civil divorce, a woman's "temple recommend" is revoked; in other words, she is then considered unworthy to enter the Temple until she can prove to the heads of the Church that the divorce was not caused by adultery. To do this, the woman has to describe her sexual activities in a series of letters to the male church authorities. Once she is deemed worthy again, she needs to obtain a "cancellation of sealing" so she doesn't have to spend eternity with her ex-husband and so she can remarry in the church. In addition to the cancellation of sealing, Mormon women have always been required to obtain permission from their estranged partners and the Mormon church First Presidency before being allowed to remarry in a temple ceremony.

However, the cancellation of a sealing is not encouraged even after obtaining a civil divorce, even though a woman can be celestially married to only one man at a time. And after the death of a male partner, a female cannot be sealed to a second male; children born within a subsequent civil marriage are sealed to the first husband rather than their biological father.

It's a different story for men, although there have been some recent changes. Since February 1994, Mormon men must have permission from the First Presidency to remarry in the temple, but do not need permission from their ex-wives. Nor are they required to obtain cancellations of prior sealings in order to remarry "for eternity," which by extension allows men to accumulate numerous wives for the afterlife. If divorce is made difficult for the mainstream Mormon woman, it is magnified in the fundamentalist groups.

It's not often that outsiders get a glimpse into the inner sanctum of Mormon temple life, fundamentalist or otherwise, which is why Deborah Laake's book *Secret Ceremonies: A Mormon Woman's Intimate Diary of Marriage and Beyond*, created such a stir when it was published in 1993. And why, after its publication, church leaders excommunicated Laake for apostasy. Particularly upsetting to Mormon elders was her detailed description of the secret Mormon temple ceremonies, such as her wedding, which includes a ceremony in which her fiancé pulled her through "the veil" with a secret hand grip during a pre-wedding ceremony and told her, "Well done, thou good and faithful servant, enter you into the joy of the Lord."

While many took the book to be a simple exposé masquerading as personal memoir, Laake attempted to explain why some of the Mormon traditions were so detrimental and potentially damaging to many women's overall view of self and worth—such as her feelings about the "garments," or holy underwear, she was told she would have to wear all her life as protection from the Devil.

"The ones I wore on my wedding day in the temple were just like long johns—the fabric was thick and white, reaching to the wrists and ankles," she described. "I was told I must wear them night and day, that they represented the garment that God gave to Eve in the Garden of Eden, and would be a shield against the power of Satan until we finished our work on Earth. But I felt I was leaving behind me forever the worlds of desirability and youth. I was a freak."

She also spoke of how the male hierarchy makes it difficult for women to exert themselves. "Because of the patriarchal order in the Mormon church, the pronouncements of older men carry enormous weight," Deborah once explained in an interview. "When, for example, my father said we should use reusable condoms, it did not occur to me to question his wisdom."

Laake says she went into her marriage determined to make it work. Deborah had grown up believing that her only way to the higher levels of Mormon heaven was through her predestined marriage partner. "My success in this life and the next was dependent upon it," Deborah said. But she soon realized, "in trying to scale the heights of Mormon womanhood and become a model helpmate, I had to will myself into meekness. And because, like the vast majority of young Mormon women I knew, I believed that God wanted me at home, I set out to perfect my calling as a homemaker, even though I had no talent for it."

She divorced after just nine months and while still trying to cope with the emotional fallout of a failed marriage, suddenly found herself under outside scrutiny from her church elders:

> I soon found myself engaged in a battle against a hierarchy of gentlemen who were determined to hold my failed marriage against me. I was in no doubt that my sex life would be my church leaders' sole interest until I either remarried or died. Was I dating again, they wanted to know? Was I dating anyone other than Mormon men? Where did I allow my beaux to touch me? I realized they thought that a woman, once awakened, would always need to be watched extremely closely.

She also pointed out that while the Church may have officially banned polygamy, it is still an integral part of mainstream doctrine, which is what the cancellation of sealing is all about. "Men can marry 'for Eternity' in the temple again and again," without the cancellation of sealing, she explained. "When they lose a wife through death or divorce, she is still married to him in the next life. So in effect there's a policy of polygamy for men in the afterlife." She also argued that the inequality of all this was a source of spiritual dismay for many women who "know that in the next life they will be forced into a polygamous relationship with their divorced husband."

And therein perhaps lies the greatest issue for the modern Church of Latter-Day Saints. For as much as they say they officially denounce secular polygamy, the reality is, the Church sanctions—and performs—ecclesiastical polygamy within the temples every day. Their church leaders' decision to not address the issue directly is what critics find evasive. And the discrepancy has been the cause of friction between elders and members—with the Church frequently taking a hardline stance. In 1993, six of its more outspoken intellectuals and feminists were excommunicated, which was followed by an announcement that declared the church's three most dangerous enemies to be intellectuals, feminists, and gays.

In 1999, current Latter-Day Saints President Gordon B. Hinckley appeared on *Larry King Live*, and when asked about polygamy said, "I condemn it, yes, as a practice, it is not doctrinal." Considering the marriage ceremonies still being practiced in temples today, the statement seems dishonest at the worst or disingenuous at the least. While the Church excommunicates members found living in plural marriages, the very doctrines upon which the Church was built is irrevocably tied to the doctrine of polygamy. In fact, some would say it's a main foundation. Mormon women are taught that if they remain faithful to church doctrine, they will share their husband with other wives in the afterlife. If they question the implications of this, they are told to simply, "Have faith in a loving God's wisdom and judgment."

As in any group or society, there are more liberal and more conservative members in general, the Mormon religion is not particularly women's rights–friendly, which again fosters an environment in which abuses can spring. As children, girls and boys are taught the importance of the "patriarchal order." In fact, a handbook written for fourteen-year-old boys, states that, "The patriarchal order is of divine origin and will continue throughout time and eternity." Husbands conduct family prayers, bless their wives and children, and generally control the household. Girls are told that God wants them at home, while few boys are taught to clean up after themselves because they will either have mothers or wives to do it for them.

Chastity is stressed for girls. Without it, they might not be suitable for marriage. "If you sully your body by allowing boys to touch it in forbidden ways…no good man will ever want to marry you." In that great double standard, if a girl "lets" a boy touch her, it's her fault he won't respect her, even though he's the one doing the touching. According to Mormon Doctrine, "Loss of virtue is too great a price to pay even for the preservation of one's life—better dead clean, than alive unclean."

The irony is that at the same time a girl is being drilled about being chaste, she's being taught that it is her role to do a man's bidding; it is God's will that she please the men in their lives. Perhaps a telling statistic is that in a state that prides itself on family values and forbids the general sale of alcohol, in 1978, 70 percent of the teenage brides were pregnant at their weddings. And a young woman is more apt to be raped in Utah than she is in California.

What particularly galls some women is that the entire structure makes them feel like so much property. A former church-goer named DeeVie told Andrea Moore Emmitts of the *Salt Lake City Weekly* that even though she no longer believes in the doctrine, she didn't want her name in the books as being sealed to her ex-husband. "I'm essentially his property on some record somewhere. I don't believe in polygamy and I don't want it on any records that I have any part of it, because he doesn't own me and neither does the church."

In an effort to correlate current official teachings with doctrine, the effort is made to downplay the importance of plural marriage, saying it is temple marriage, not plural marriage that is the "new and everlasting covenant"—even if it directly contradicts the Doctrine and Covenants. The impasse is made clear in a comment by the sixth President of the Mormon Church, Joseph F. Smith, when he noted:

> Some people have supposed that the doctrine of plural marriage was a sort of superfluity, or non-essential to the salvation of mankind. Some of the saints have said, and believe, that a man with one wife will receive an exaltation as great and glorious if he is faithful, as he possibly could with more than one. I want here to enter my protest against this idea, for I know it is false.

Valeen Tippetts Avery, Women's History Professor at Northern Arizona University in Flagstaff and former president of the Mormon History Association, says such waffling results in confusion. "What you have is people trying to get divorced going to church leaders and they're told what is believed by that leader," she says. "People have to be careful when the church is doing theology and history. The Mormon church has a hard time doing both."

It is precisely this conflict between the Church's public stance and what is still fundamental in the faith's doctrine that creates a don't-ask-don't-tell atmosphere when it comes to clans such as the Kingstons. And when looking at what revelations upon which the Latter-Day Church was founded, it's easier to understand why groups like the Kingston's believe that they are the true keepers of the faith and following God's will.

A footnote about author Deborah Laake: plagued by depression for much of her life, she developed breast cancer, which she beat. However, after her mother died and Mormon leaders would not allow Laake to eulogize her during an upcoming church funeral or even sit in the front of the church with the family, she seemed to emotionally melt. On February 4, 1999, she committed suicide at forty-seven years old.

Whether or not her issues with the Church in any way contributed to her depression, Laake offered a unique look into one woman's perspective and brings into clearer focus just how much courage Mary Ann Kingston showed by breaking away. Because even within the mainstream Church, once you are outcast, the isolation is complete. Laake spoke of the circumstances around her excommunication:

> It began with a phone call from a local church official I'd never even heard of. They held a trial, I was invited but didn't attend—I knew I would be talking to deaf ears. Then the news of my excommunication arrived, in a letter, in which I was informed that they had appointed one of the church's officials to defend me. Defend? He said that as I had broken my vows, none of my family could ever trust me again. As I stood there reading all this, I felt incredibly frustrated and powerless. This was the exact feeling I'd had as a Mormon woman. These men believed they had done the most terrible thing to me by excommunicating me, they thought they had ruined my eternal life...and they had done it viciously and without any insight into their own motivations.

When asked how she remembers the Mormon girl and woman she once was, Laake answered, "With affection. It's a bittersweet feeling. Yeah, I feel protective, but also very separated from her. I've moved on."

It should be noted that while Mormon Temples are the most secret facet of Mormonism and are completely different from neighborhood Mormon chapels, it's a world apart from the daily life of most practicing Mormons. Not only are no non-Mormons are ever allowed inside a temple once it's dedicated, most Mormons are not permitted in either. Only those who have passed the stringent requirements of worthiness earn a "temple recommend," which permits them to enter the Temple. According to church leaders, less than 20 percent of adult Mormons have valid Temple Recommends and less than 10 percent of adult Mormons regularly attend the Temple.

But the real issue of the polygamy question isn't temple passes or interpretations of doctrine, or even if the Mormon Church is being duplicitous in trying to oppose plural marriage despite the fact that polygamy remains a basic tenet of the religion. At the very heart of polygamy is the emotional, physical, and spiritual impact of the institution on women and, most importantly, young girls. Are minors having their civil rights trashed by being forced into unwanted plural marriages; is it child abuse to impregnate a teenage girl and then have her live in poverty with little hope of a different life; as a society, can we stand by and turn a blind eye to incest that results in horrible birth defects? Even if it were determined that polygamy is protected by the Constitution, child abuse and sexual molestation is not. Does the practice of polygamy provide an environment in which abuse thrives or is it being unfairly attacked?

In the end, perhaps only women who have lived both sides of these questions can provide the answers.

Chapter Eight
WOMEN AT ODDS

As the firestorm of controversy swelled in the wake of the Kingston arrests, it polarized opponents and proponents of the polygamy issue, with each side seeing an opportunity to present its case to an interested national audience. On one side were plural wives who defended their family life as being both righteous and loving. On the other were women who had, in their words, escaped from polygamous marriages and who told a far darker tale.

But it's not only modern women speaking out. Looking through historical documents, it becomes clear than the emotional effects were the same 150 years ago. Anne Eliza Webb, one of Brigham Young's wives, in writing about her own mother said, "Polygamy...was the most hateful thing in the world to her, and she dreaded and abhorred it, but she was afraid to oppose it, lest she be found fighting against the Lord." And again, women felt they had no choice but to accept it because they were told to fight it would deny them heaven. But who would want to be part of a system that prompted the likes of Heber C. Kimball to note, "I think no more of taking another wife than I do of buying a cow."

Many women, however, were duped. Male missionaries would convert women who would then be encouraged to come to Utah to be with other Mormons. Only after leaving their family and friends, and whatever money they had, moving, did they learn about polygamy. By then, they were stuck. Worse, because of the competition that was frequently found between wives who yearned for attention from their husband, the women found themselves isolated from the other sister-wives. For women living at the turn of the millennium, the situation was starkly similar.

In a report on the television newsmagazine *20/20*, Barbara Walters prefaced the segment by commenting, "Shocking. That is absolutely the only word, when you see this, I think...after you watch this report, you may ask yourself how can this still be going on in America?"

The women interviewed on that show spoke of the emotional torment of being a plural wife; of the psychological brainwashing that is used to keep women fearful of the outside world and therefore in their place within the polygamous marriage; of young girls forced to marry virtual strangers or, even worse, close relatives. Laura Chapman went on the air to call polygamy, "the systematic abuse of women and children. The deprivation and poverty of the human soul is just horrible."

Carmen Thompson of Tapestry Against Polygamy, who was married to a Christian polygamist before leaving the lifestyle, says, "I truly believe that the act of sharing your spouse is emotional abuse. I've seen it in women's faces, and my shoulder's been there when they've cried on it. It's very difficult to lay in bed at night, trying to believe you're doing what God wants, listening to your husband in the next room having sex with another partner. It's so dehumanizing," she says. Along with the emotional abuse of sharing your spouse, she says there was a lot of isolation and deprivation. "Suppressing your emotions in polygamy is the only way you can survive as a woman. If you try to deal with your emotions, they'll destroy you."

The issue of polygamy has become the purpose in the lives of Chapman, Thompson, Vicky Prunty, Rowenna Erickson, and Lillian Bowles, the founders of Tapestry Against Polygamy, an outreach and support group that offers counseling, therapy, legal advice, health care, and other assistance to women and children leaving polygamy. The women who founded Tapestry became acquainted through mutual friends who saw they shared the same commitment to helping women trying to escape the polygamous lifestyle. Erickson says, "We had a meeting and from that began our organization. We found that we had mutual goals, mutual desires—all we had to do was find each other."

Prunty adds, "We are unraveling the threads of the tapestry of polygamy." Each woman speaks with the voice of experience, for all of them were once plural wives and all of them speak of the reality of polygamy as hellish. Prunty, who was married to two polygamous husbands, says, "We know the high costs of leaving are worth it. We are showing other wives that we have done it, too. They can find happiness outside of polygamy."

She also sounds a warning, saying that women and children are little more than slaves and some wanting to leave have been threatened with blood atonement. "Women who leave polygamy can be in real danger," Prunty says. "Men have been known to threaten harsh punishment and even death. Some women have died trying to leave. The need for our organization may be far greater than any of us knows."

Consider that even Social Security numbers are unknown to many of the women because such governmental documents are considered "the mark of the beast" by fundamentalists. Many children born in clans never have a birth certificate because they are born at home. Likewise, some children are never sent to school. "When you're coming out, you pretty much have to step into an entirely different world," Prunty observes.

Learning how to set up a bank account for the first time or go shopping at a regular grocery store can be intimidating. "One lady from the Kingston group said that even going to a restaurant and trying to figure out what she wanted on the menu was something that was very difficult to do," Prunty said. Plus, many women don't have modern clothes to wear.

Not only is a plural wife usually lacking in practical and social skills or education, because these marriages are not sanctioned by the state, it is more difficult for these women to collect child support or alimony from their husbands once they do leave. And although it is difficult to leave the family system, Prunty says she wants other women to know it is possible that they are not alone.

Laura Chapman knows those feelings of isolation. Chapman, who grew up in a polygamous family, says her father sexually assaulted her at least a dozen times as a child, as he did her sisters. However, because sex was a forbidden topic, she didn't feel she could turn to anyone in her family for help. "It's like the big denial, even that they're all sharing the same husband." But, she also says, "There is nobody questioning his authority. Probably the safest place for a pedophile is in a polygamous community."

"These are men that live above the law," Prunty comments. "It's unofficial lawlessness. They're getting away with, basically, anything that they want in the name of religion." To which Rowenna Erickson pointedly adds, "Polygamy is abuse. It is not of God."

Erickson, who was a member of the Kingston clan, adds, "There are no boundaries with these men. They're married, and they're God. Whatever they say, that's what they want." By way of backing up that claim, Thompson claims she knows of a case where two eight-year-old girls had been married off to forty year-old men. The accusation sounds unbelievable, but even a cursory jaunt around the Internet will reveal personal ad sites for polygamists looking for women of all ages.

Lillian Bowles, who was raped when she was five years old and married off at seventeen, says, "You are completely brain-washed when you are there. And to leave, I know for myself I had to hit the point where I was ready to go to hell. I acknowledged to myself, to God, to my family, that if going to hell was the price I had to pay—okay. I'm in a different place now. I don't feel like I'm going to hell in my life now. But it's a very lonely spot to hit to be willing to trade that."

However, along with one of her sisters, Lillian Bowles took the rare step of confronting the leaders of their polygamous community with the charges that their father had forced his wives and children to live in extreme poverty and that he allowed family members and other men to sexually molest his daughters. "To me, by not talking about it is keeping it secret, is supporting it." After an investigating by church leaders, her father was removed from his powerful position on the Priesthood Council and later issued an apology to his family—but such an outcome is extraordinary and rare.

More typical is Chapman's experience. The mother of four daughters and a son, she left her marriage after her husband announced he was going to marry his eighteen-year-old first cousin. But once she decided to leave, she realized she didn't have anywhere to go. She was afraid that if she left the state, she would lose her children because she was broke. "So I turned around and went back to the YWCA, and they almost didn't let us in because nobody was beating me. There were years where I didn't know if I could get through it. And I would wake up and go out and stand outside on my porch and look up at the sky and go, Is there a God? I hope there's a God, and I hope I get through this. I hope there's a happy ending." Although she has managed to build a new world for herself, Laura still says, "Polygamy ruined my life."

Unlike Chapman, who was born into polygamy, Vicky Prunty chose it—at least for a while. A native Californian, Vicky converted to Mormonism when she was ten years old. While attending Brigham Young University, she met her first husband who was seven years older than she was. It wasn't until after they'd been married a while and she'd had two children that she and her husband decided polygamy was the right way to serve God. "Once we had married, my husband and I started investigating early teachings of the Mormon Church. We really wanted to please God and not man, to live the gospel as it first originated under Brigham Young and other early leaders. We believed that polygamy was a way of living by the commandments and preparing ourselves for Zion, when Christ would come back."

They moved from their home in Arizona back to Utah and joined a small fundamentalist group. Seven years after their marriage, and now with three children, her husband found the next women he wanted to marry. Vicky had to give her husband to this new wife in a ceremony, which she says is typical. "I put her hand in his. I felt uncomfortable with it, but I wasn't convinced that it was wrong." But she soon discovered the pitfalls.

"When my husband went to business dinner parties, we accompanied him alternately," Vicky recalls. "I lived upstairs and she lived downstairs and we pretty much shared the middle floor. She had a nice big wedding and reception. I had to hide in the background—I was told to act like a friend of the family—because he wanted the image of marrying monogamously for his career. I'd just had a baby a few days earlier. It was so difficult. It was not natural, for me at least. Yet the whole time I was trying to convince myself that polygamy was right and I was wrong because of the religion behind it."

But Vicky's idea of what polygamy would be had been very different from the reality. "I had always thought that plural marriage would be more charitable, something you do to help women without husbands, the single women." Instead, she realized her husband had chosen her sister-wife "because of her body proportions. He had told me he wanted someone who was shapely. That hurt me, and I realized that he was more in it for himself than anything else. I felt as if I was the martyr of the whole thing. It was just a charade."

She says eventually she had an epiphany, although, "It took me a while; that the dynamics and the institution did not emancipate a woman. I only realized this when all of a sudden our partnership turned into a dictatorship. In monogamy, our relationship wasn't perfect but it was pretty balanced in terms of power. But when he became the husband of two wives, the only way to keep order in the home was to become more powerful."

When Vicky decided to leave, the full weight of her situation came to light. "What was I supposed to do without money and all these kids? I also have a copy of a scripture he wrote in which he said, 'If the wife is subject to her husband's law, then she truly has no right to refuse his taking other wives beside her in her lifetime. She is, after all, under his dominion.'"

Hoping to bring Vicky back under control, her husband told her she must be possessed by demons "because I was rebellious and unhappy. Some of the other men in our group would try and exorcise me." After eleven years of marriage, she finally left when she realized she'd put herself "in a position to be used for his glory, his ego."

Not only does polygamy affect the wives, but the children of the household as well. On one hand, Prunty believes, "It's great to have a large family, to think of humankind as all being brothers and sisters and taking care of each other." However, in practical terms, children get caught in the middle, especially when one of the wives leaves. When Vicky's children visit their father, they are told his other wife is their mother because Vicky is a sinner and she no longer belongs to the family. "That's the sort of indoctrination we go up against." It frustrates her because although just as damaging as physical abuse, this kind of "emotional and mental abuse is much harder to prove. It's their word against mine."

In some cases, the children don't even know who their father is; because it's illegal and authorities are more prone to pursue incest or welfare fraud charges, men with plural families usually don't want their blood ties revealed. Although official statistics aren't available, a newspaper investigation indicated that 33 percent of residents in two polygamous towns on the Arizona border receive state assistance compared with 4.7 percent for the rest of the state.

Prunty turned around and went into another plural marriage with a family she knew that seemed, "very happy in polygamy." She didn't want to be a full-fledged wife but wanted to be part of the family as a third wife so her kids could have a father figure. Her disillusionment was complete when the husband admitted to her, "He never believed in polygamy; that he had just taken wives because he wanted to have sex with more than one woman. Of course it shocked me and I had to run into the bathroom crying and wondering what was going on. I felt sick because I had actually started to fall in love with this man."

In retrospect, Prunty says, "Any woman who shares her husband and believes she can get through these emotions and become a stronger woman and be happy sharing with her sister-wife, I don't believe it. I think this a drug for men. The power and the control is a drug. It's stimulant. It makes them feel good. It makes them feel good to have a harem of wives."

Vicky went through some hard times before reclaiming her life and turning her pain and energies toward trying to help others. With the perspective of time and experience, she now says, "If a woman wants to be treated as an equal and she wants a partnership in rearing her children, monogamy is probably the way. If she wants to have a husband who has sex with other woman and she wants to be submissive and have lots of children, then she perhaps should go into plural marriage." She equated it with being a single mother, "except you still have a leader. But you're usually lonely and don't have much money."

Carmen Thompson, who had been one of eight wives of a husband who couldn't hold steady job, empathizes. "The bottom line here is we are single mothers, we just don't have the freedom of single mothers. I remember thinking, I'm playing mother. I'm playing father. I'm playing provider. I'm taking care of the house. I'm doing everything and what is he doing? He floats in here once a week and [sleeps with] me and leaves." But for many years, during which she had five children, Carmen felt "what I was doing was God's higher law and that He wanted me to do this."

Like Thompson, looking back Prunty says she also simply saw things differently than she does now. "Now I think that polygamy is designed to oppress women and to keep them in bondage to men. Choosing polygamy because of religion, because you fear that if you don't chose it you'll be damned for eternity, is very different from choosing polygamy because you really want to take in a lonely widow—to be kind to family, friends, and neighbors."

When looked at dispassionately, it's understandable why women are prevented from continuing their education and pushed into marriage at some young ages, because it's less likely they will rebel. "They prey upon women who aren't strong, with low self-esteem," Prunty notes, adding, "I didn't grow up in it so it was easier to get out. We're finding thousands of children are being brought up in it and their lives are ruined. It's not like some women in Denver or California or New York getting involved in this, because they just wouldn't. These are Utah women that have been taught that they are inferior to the male sex. Getting out of it is very difficult." To her, the basis for a polygamous marriage is nothing more than "power and control." And through Tapestry Against Polygamy she hopes to bring light to the issues. "It's been so hush-hush. It's like Utah's dirty little secret."

Rowenna Erickson says that in the Kingston clan, most of the girls get married between fourteen to sixteen years old and immediately start having children because they are expected to bear one child a year. But, she says, "They cannot keep up financially, and the children live in poverty, and the mothers are overwhelmed." Beyond that, "there's arguing amongst the women, and there's a lot of eating disorders because they try to keep slim for the husband because they want to catch his attention because they don't see him very much."

Of all the Tapestry women, none has been more visible than Erickson, who is also the most outspoken member of the organization. As far as Erickson is concerned, "Polygamy is the biggest con in the world," she says bluntly. "Men are in it for sex, not religion. It is power and control in the name of religion."

Interestingly, Rowenna's parents were not polygamists—but only because her father, a Lutheran, didn't believe in it. However, Erickson says, her Mormon mother "idealized it. She felt that, since she hadn't done it, at least one of her children should. Also, she thought she'd get religious 'credit' and that she'd be more likely to get what we called 'celestial glory' in the hereafter."

A devout follower of Charles Elden Kingston, Rowenna's mother thought nobody in the family would reach that highest level "unless a daughter is married to a leader of the Kingston church. So my mother groomed me for a life in polygamy. She conditioned me to think polygamy was a sacred thing." So Rowenna prayed and believed God directed her to the man she was to marry.

In 1960, when she was twenty years old, Rowenna became the second wife of Leon Kingston, the firstborn son of Charles Elden, the Church of Christ founder. Leon's first wife was Rowenna's older sister. Now, Erickson admits that looking at it objectively, marrying one's sister's husband is not normal. "But when you're in that sort of group it seems completely normal; your thinking, doing and being are all controlled by the church. If the church said something, we jumped."

Erickson acknowledges that even though they believed they were following God's will, the situation was difficult, especially for her sister:

> It was very, very hard for her. She didn't know how the first wife typically feels, as no one had talked to her about it. She became depressed. She was angry, hurt, and jealous. We talked about it at the time, but it was still hard. In polygamy, the first wife thinks she's going to live "God's law" by having a "sister-wife," and it turns out to be hard. So my sister blamed herself for not being able to please God.

The discomfort was present from the start. Leon and Rowenna consummated their marriage while her sister was in another part of the house they all now shared. After eleven years and five children, Rowenna and her kids moved into a tiny rental house and eventually gave birth to three more children. Her sister, a midwife, delivered them all. The poverty she experienced was emotionally and spiritually depleting. She lived on food stamps and collected recyclable cans and babysat—for thirty-two cents an hour—for extra money. Although Leon worked as a warehouse manager, he gave a lot of his earnings to the Church. Between his two wives, there were fourteen children and simply not enough money to go around. Worse than the poverty was the debilitating loneliness she felt.

"I had no affection, no attention from this man. Intimacy was never talked about. I remember I'd shower at night and I'd just cry in the shower so no one could hear me then. It was horrible. I never loved him. When I was pregnant he wouldn't even ask when the baby was due." Even though her husband visited her on alternate nights, "I was just a vessel to him to bring souls down from heaven," Erickson says but adds, "I was dutiful and never refused him. It was very formal and sterile because my marriage to him had to be secret because it was illegal. It wasn't even known at first within the Kingston group because they had been investigated by a grand jury in 1959 so it was all relationships were secret. I was pretty miserable."

And out of typical concern over possible action by authorities, her children thought he was their uncle—she told them their real father was away in the Army. "It was cruel because they kept expecting he would come home sometime and be their father," she says now. "They imagined all these wonderful things about him. They certainly didn't like the man they thought was their uncle—who in fact was their real father. He reprimanded them so much and never showed any love or affection."

In 1985, a twist of fate would change Erickson's life. While watching television, she happened upon a hypnosis demonstration on the *Phil Donahue Show*. Inspired, she saved enough money to start taking classes in hypnotherapy at an institute in Salt Lake City and eventually earned her certification. Suddenly, Rowenna had an avenue to the outside world, and the exposure to people and ideas outside her fundamentalist clan opened her eyes and mind. Erickson says she realized "what a lie I had been living. I went on this big spiritual quest and realized I'd never loved my husband and that I was unhappy. I thought, OK God, all these women here are complaining about you and thinking you're not very nice to them and how could a God love women and tell them they had to live polygamy?"

With her newly raised consciousness, Erickson felt compelled to speak out against the child abuse she saw around her, the neglect she knew of firsthand, the rampant incest within the clan, and the young teenage girls being forced to marry. So, in 1992, she wrote a letter to a Church of Christ elder, "telling him off for never preaching love and for ruling by fear." For her efforts, she was excommunicated. Fortunately, all her children were grown so custody wasn't an issue. However, her marriage was as good as over, although it took her until 1994 to make it official. "I realized that I couldn't still be a polygamist and help people get out of polygamy," Rowenna says.

Once free, she could look back on her life and view it with clear eyes; she didn't always like what she saw. "I began to become aware of a real discrepancy between the spirituality of polygamy—that it's the ideal marriage—and the poverty and abuse that polygamous families actually live with," Rowenna says. "Polygamy was one big lie. I'd been duped. It's demented. Polygamists are not as spiritual as you're led to believe. These guys are really sick—there's wife-swapping, ménage à trois, use of pornography. The sexual acts and the incest and the actions against women and children are so sick. There's no end to it."

Erickson recalls when one of her relatives was married as the second wife, "the first wife went on the honeymoon with them. And they had two beds in the hotel room and she and her husband had sex in front of the other wife. Supposedly it was supposed to help her not feel jealous. So she would know it's just like what goes on with her and him.

"Women's feelings and emotions have been abandoned. Horrendously."

And because of that kind of manipulation Rowenna says, "You have to be rehabilitated from this. It has taken me years." As she explains, "Women who leave polygamous marriages are frightened. You're taught that you're nothing without your husband. It seems so stupid now. I'm ashamed and embarrassed. We were so obedient to the organization, so loyal, and we kept all the secrets. We weren't supposed to complain or question the church authority or God would disapprove. It's a big scam."

And yet, in some ways, leaving was the easy part. Now Erickson had to figure out what to do with the rest of her life. "I had been dying inside. I became sick with asthma, I was depressed and stressed out and I had so much tendonitis and bursitis in my hip, I was bedridden. I was broke. Although I'd been given a house by my former husband, I had no skills that would help me get a job."

What she did have, though, was the support of her children. "My children really encouraged me to get out, otherwise I might not have been able to." In fact, she says, "My children were way ahead of me. They thought polygamy was stupid all along and were waiting for me to catch on."

Then in a most unlikely turn of events, Rowenna became an activist. She found the best way to move on with her life was to confront her past. She talked to whomever would listen about the abuses and alleged illegal activity of the Kingston clan. From the media to the IRS; from accusations the Kingstons paid less than minimum wage to actually stealing property, she rabble-roused— but not without more than a little angst. "I still feel a little guilty talking about some of their inner workings because I was so conditioned," she admits. "Like in Satanic ritualistic abuse and cults, they're taught never to reveal information. Some people have been programmed to kill themselves before they would reveal any information. But in the group, they teach the child that if they ever leave, they'll go to hell."

But more than anything, she wanted to send a message to anyone caught in a plural marriage that there was a way out. And she found a way to do that through Tapestry Against Polygamy. Tapestry has helped over three hundred women who came to them with by now familiar tales of incest and abuse.

Elaine Jenkins, who left the Kingston clan, is grateful for a group like Tapestry, in part because of their efforts to made the public aware. "The public in the past has been so hostile—especially after the welfare fraud cases," Jenkins notes. "It was scary. That's why I didn't leave then. People didn't realize people were victimized in the group, and now it's starting to come out. It makes it easier to leave with the public support on the outside."

Especially in light of the Kingston arrests, other polygamists clans sought to distance themselves from the more shocking aspects being revealed, such as the Kingston incest. But for most women coming out of polygamy, and even those who stayed in it, it was the emotional devastation of such a system that wreaked the most enduring havoc. After Ruthann Stephens, who grew up in the Owen Allred–led Apostolic United Brethren, left the group, she suffered the loss of her children, who now believe she is condemned to hell. "I don't believe polygamy inherently is a full, balanced, harmonious way of life," she says with pointed understatement.

Then repeating the refrain heard by so many other women, Stephens talks about the numbing mind control the principal fosters. "This whole concept of living life as other people dictate to you through their lectures, through their looks, through their admonitions is a deprivation of spirit and soul. And I just felt myself drowning more and more as I just gave up and give to what I thought other people wanted from me. It asks you to make a lot of sacrifices and people believe sacrifice is the way to God. I don't believe God asks you to make sacrifices. I believe people do."

Rowenna Erickson believes the only way polygamy exists is through such mind control. "I've seen so many women say, It's so wonderful, we're so happy, he's such a good father to my children. Polygamy is a subculture. You can never get beyond a particular level of intellect or state of mind, state of being, you're always at this ceiling you can never go beyond that. You ever see the movie Stepford Wives? That's what we all were," she notes, referring to the movie where flesh-and-blood wives were replaced with subservient automatons.

Carmen Thompson contends polygamy isn't good for the man, either. "A man in a polygamous situation has very little time for anything other than running around putting out fires of jealousy. He has no time for his children, he has no time for himself. I would be surprised if he had time for God."

A Question of Support

When asked if polygamists should be jailed, Erickson admits there's a difference of opinion within the group, with some believing polygamists should be prosecuted to the full extent of the law, while others worry such a legal assault would force the fundamentalists further underground, making escape that much more difficult. "I just want the abuses prosecuted," she said, along with increased sensitivity and awareness by authorities. "There was a case in Colorado City, Arizona, about fifteen years ago where a woman tried to run away and she was returned to her husband by the police."

Carmen Thompson said dryly, "State officials have said it's probably easier to prosecute the mafia than it is polygamy—interesting choice of words, because this really is organized crime on many levels. The reality is, if a man was marrying his niece and lived in mainstream society, you can bet the state would get him and he would serve jail time. But because they hide behind this cloak of religion, the state's afraid to do anything about it....I don't believe there are any successful polygamist relationships. But the bottom line here is, good, bad, or indifferent—it's a third-degree felony in the state of Utah. It's against the law. And it doesn't matter if it's good; it's a crime."

At least one lawmaker braved an opinion against prosecuting polygamists. GOP Utah State Representative David L. Zolman commented, "If laws against adultery aren't enforced, why enforce laws against polygamy?"

But as the furor over the Kingston case and other abuses within the fundamentalist polygamy clans grew louder, Utah officials were spurred to action—whether out of genuine concern or the awareness that with the upcoming 2002 Winter Olympics, Utah could be in for some unwanted negative and embarrassing publicity over the issue, especially if it appeared the politicians running the state were burying their heads in the sand. "They practice all kinds of things we try to clean up in Third World countries," Democratic State Senator Ronald Allen was quoted as saying. "Early polygamy attracted feverishly religious people. Now, it's pedophiles and abusers."

So in January 1999, the Utah Legislature's House Health and Human Services Committee unanimously approved a bill aimed at cracking down on child marriages by raising the state's marriage age from fourteen to sixteen years in most cases. However, the bill would still allow marriages among fifteen-year-olds when a judge deemed a marriage is in the best interests of the children, the marriage is voluntary and both parties have completed premarital education. It also required pregnant teens to be given counseling, including the option of adoption.

"There may be some fifteen-year-olds who are more mature than sixteen- or seventeen-year-olds, and I feel like a judge is in a lot better position to make that determination," said the bill's sponsor, Rep. Carl Saunders, who a year earlier had proposed a bill that would have imposed an outright ban on marriages for those younger than sixteen. That bill passed the House committee and the full House but failed in the Senate by a single vote. While members of Tapestry were pleased, they also felt it would have little effect on plural marriages because they were already illegal anyway.

People like Erickson are frustrated because some influential organizations have weighed in on the side of plural marriage. The American Civil Liberties Union, for example, believes that criminal and civil laws prohibiting or penalizing polygamy violate constitutional protections of freedom of expression and association, freedom of religion, and privacy for personal relationships among consenting adults.

Political columnist Katha Pollitt debated that view in *The Nation*, writing:

> What's wrong with legalizing polygyny? Consider the phrase consenting adult. After much Sturm und Drang, Utah raised the age of consent last year from fourteen to sixteen—fifteen with the permission of a judge, who is barred by law from asking questions that might uncover coercion. Girls cannot refuse to be "home schooled," and school authorities don't insist that such schooling means math and history and English and science, with progress measured by tests. Instead, they look the other way when girls are pulled from

school to work for free in clan businesses, as was the Kingston girl, while awaiting the summons to marry....

Nobody would argue that cultural diversity is an absolute value overriding every other consideration. No one I spoke with at the ACLU had a problem with rejecting religious or cultural defenses of child abuse, domestic violence or female genital mutilation. "Violence is different," ACLU director Ira Glasser told me. But if the ACLU is going to draw a line at all, why only there? Why not see polygyny as a human rights violation, a contract so radically inegalitarian—he has fifteen wives, each wife has one-fifteenth of a husband; she can have no more mates, he can have as many as he likes—that it ought to be illegal? That some women may find this arrangement acceptable doesn't mean the law should permit it, any more than the law should let people work for a dollar an hour, or sell their kidneys, or clean houses off the books and wind up with no Social Security.

But the fact is, there were women who found the arrangement not only acceptable but preferable. Somewhat amazingly, the Utah Chapter of the National Organization of Women went on the record saying polygamy could be a solution for the problems of working mothers. "It seems like a pretty good idea for professional women, who can proceed with their careers and have someone at home they can trust to watch their children. It solves the day care problem," said Luci Malin, vice chairman of Utah NOW in an interview with Joyce Price of the *Washington Times*.

Ellen George, state secretary for Utah NOW, added, "This isn't blatant support for polygamy....But maybe it can work for some people, and maybe it can make raising children easier for those trying to juggle careers and motherhood." The organization added that their support was provisional that "those involved in such arrangements are consenting adults."

Journalist Elizabeth Joseph created a stir when in 1998 she announced she not only fully supported polygamy but was part of a plural marriage herself: "I've often said that if polygamy didn't exist, the modern American career woman would have invented it. Because, despite its reputation, polygamy is the one lifestyle that offers an independent woman a real chance to have it all."

Joseph painted a picture of domestic tranquility. "I know that when I get home from work, if I'm dog-tired and stressed-out, I can be alone and guilt-free. It's a rare day when all eight of my husband's wives are tired and stressed at the same time. I married the best man I ever met. The fact that he already had five wives did not prevent me from doing that." To her, polygamy wasn't subjugating women; it empowered them. "Polygamy is an empowering lifestyle for women. It provides me the environment and opportunity to maximize my female potential without all the tradeoffs and compromises that attend monogamy."

To those who had escaped from fundamentalist clans, Joseph's situation was clearly the exception that proved the rule. The majority of women in plural marriages have no education, much less a good-paying job. Joseph had money to pay for food and clothing and a life outside the home. Joseph entered into her situation as an adult of her own volition. The environment Joseph presents as empowering for her simply doesn't exist within the structure of fundamentalist clan families. In addition, Joseph obviously isn't required to be a baby machine, as are the girls in the Kingston clan and other fundamentalist groups. Life as a polygamous independent was worlds apart from life inside a clan.

In a personal essay posted on www.polygamy.com, a pro-polygamy website, Mrs. Mary Ben David, offers a less feminist-based endorsement of plural marriage:

> There are many myths and untruths about the polygamous lifestyle, and there are many different forms and practical applications of the theory. The only guide we have is the Bible, the Holy Word of God, which should guide and enlighten each Christian as we strive to be obedient to God's will for our lives.
>
> Speaking as a woman and a polygamous wife, I have not found that women are exploited or subjugated. Rather the

opposite is true. Women achieve more freedom and expanded horizons than in monogamy. Why? There are two or more to share the housework, the cooking, the childcare, freeing each one to have more time to herself to pursue independent goals and objectives. Exploitation and subjugation may occur in some situations, but that also occurs in monogamous marriages. The form of marriage is not the problem—the individuals involved in the marriage and their attitudes are the problem. A polygamous marriage based on Biblical truths and precepts, as all marriages should be, should meet the same standards as any monogamous marriage. Husbands should love their wives, and wives should be submissive to their husbands, based on Biblical principles.

Mrs. David does acknowledge that, "abuse and exploitation should not be tolerated, as they should not be tolerated anywhere in our society. Polygamy is not abuse. It is a lifestyle ordained by God for some people. Polygamy is not for everyone. But for some it is God's calling and God's special blessing. It must be based on Biblical principles and lived in obedience to God's will. To those whom God has called, it is a special treasure."

Elsie Allred, one of Owen Allred's eleven wives, agreed that polygamy was a special calling from God. "You find you faults, your jealousies, your feelings but it helps you learn how to control them, how to understand them. And it's beautiful when you learn to overcome it."

In direct response to Tapestry Against Polygamy, plural wife Mary Potter formed a new pro-polygamy group. Called the Women's Religious Liberties Union, the group generated considerable media attention by threatening to sue the state—in order to have the law banning bigamy repealed. As with Rowenna Erickson, the polygamy issue is personal to Potter. Years earlier, her husband Royston had been fired from the police force after it was learned he was a polygamist. He sued the city of Murray in federal court in 1983, challenging the ban on polygamy. A U.S. District Court judge rejected his claim that polygamy was a practice protected by the U.S.

Constitution. Two years later, the Tenth Circuit Court of Appeals agreed, saying that monogamy is the "bedrock upon which our culture is built."

Making the interaction between the two groups even more complicated is that most of the women on both sides know each other, so the rhetoric can become very personal. The WRLU officially denounces abuse, but says that Tapestry greatly exaggerates its prevalence, claiming it is no more common in polygamous families than in monogamous marriages. "There are a lot of women in polygamy who are happy," Potter said during a press conference to introduce the group. "I feel that the government shouldn't interfere with people's lives and religion."

Many women in plural marriages are afraid of being identified as such and would not speak publicly on the issue. Via the anonymity of email and letter, Tapestry's Laura Chapman admits she has received angry missives from women in the Kingston clan. "Even though we're here to help, we're a threat to them," Chapman says.

Although secrecy and discretion seems the reasonable course to take for polygamists, there are some who are willing to broadcast their beliefs to a national audience, regardless of the possible retribution. On the ABC network newsmagazine *20/20*, several plural wives discussed their lives and lifestyle. Wendy Malstrom maintained, "None of us were forced into this. We chose to live this type of family situation," although she does admit, "the rest of our extended family thinks I'm nuts. My friends think I'm nuts."

Her sister-wife, Pam, also acknowledges there can be jealousies but, "you learn to overcome those feelings. I've gotten to the point where I love these women just like I do my own blood sisters....Even though I struggled with my feelings, I knew this was something that I needed to do and to live."

When asked if they thought their husband loved them equally, sister-wife Laura said she didn't think so, but Monique disagreed. "He loves us equally, but that doesn't mean that we all get the same thing. It's what each of us need." Pam added, "It's just like a mother with each one of her children. You love all of your children, but yet each one of them have a different personality and have different needs." She spoke for all the sister-wives when she said, "We would rather share one good righteous man than have a rotten husband all to ourselves."

And therein was the rub; the women Tapestry was helping had failed to find good, righteous men. Did any number of success stories negate the horror stories of the women starting to come forward? The trial and John and David Kingston would polarize the state as well as the nation, forcing citizens to reevaluate their views on whether or not polygamy was truly God's will or a smokescreen for criminal behavior society would otherwise refuse to condone.

Chapter Nine
THE TRIALS

As dawn broke on the new year, officials in Utah braced themselves for the unknown. 1998 had ended on a dour note amidst charges of vote buying by the Salt Lake City Olympic bid committee. Although the 2002 Games were secure, Utah's image was posing for a black eye. According to reports, the International Olympic Committee was investigating $400,000 spent by the Salt Lake bid committee on U.S. college tuition for thirteen foreign students between 1991 and 1995—six of whom just happened to be relatives of IOC members who voted in the 1995 balloting that awarded the Games to Salt Lake City. In addition, Utah's largest health-care provider, Intermountain Health Care, admitted that through the bid group, it had supplied free surgical services in 1994 to at least two IOC members or their relatives. One member of the Salt Lake Olympic Committee told *Sports Illustrated*, "Despite what the IOC says, putting on the Games isn't about the athletes. It's about money."

And perhaps not so coincidentally, there were many who would say that polygamy wasn't about religion; it was about control and power. Ironically, however, even though polygamy was at the heart and soul of the two Kingston trials, it was not considered an official factor in either case. Although the Olympic scandal was embarrassing to state residents, the upcoming Kingston trial stood to do far more damage to its national image.

The first round occurred February 8, 1999, during a routine pretrial conference in the 1st District Court. John Daniel Kingston, charged with child abuse, did not attend. The hearing was meant to simply confirm his March 3 trial start date on the second-degree felony child abuse charge. However, in a surprise move, Judge Ben Hadfield ordered the trial moved from Brigham City to Logan, Utah, because of pretrial publicity. Defense attorney Ron Yengich explained that he and the prosecutor, along with Judge Hadfield, had polled over fifty potential jury pools from Cache, Weber, and Salt Lake counties about their familiarity with the case, and the Cache group was the least aware. It was then Yengich filed his motion to move the trial to First District Court in Logan, in the court of Judge Gordon Lowe, but with Hadfield still presiding.

"I guess people in Cache County don't read the same newspapers or watch as much TV," he commented after the judge granted his change of venue motion. "Nothing against the good people of Box Elder. I just believe it will be easier to get a better jury in Logan. Questionnaires indicated there was a lot of intractable opinion about this case," much of which was unfavorable to his client according to Yengich. "Under those conditions, Logan is a better choice for this trial."

Although the judge granted his motion, he also let it be known he wasn't pleased that Yengich's client wasn't in attendance. "It's the policy of this court that the defendant be present for a pretrial conference."

Yengich took the reprimand in stride and also took the opportunity of the hearing to talk about the case, claiming his client was innocent of the charges. Although he admitted he had no alibi witness for John Daniel Kingston in the alleged beating of his daughter, the attorney said he was planning to summon "other individuals she had been associated with" who are responsible for "some if not all of the injuries." He added that, "the prosecution's theory of the case is wrong." But when pressed for names of the witnesses, Yengich said he still hadn't been allowed to interview Mary Ann to learn their names. It was obvious he was picking up on Carl E. Kingston's earlier insinuations that her injuries were actually caused by some teenage boys she had met.

Jon Bunderson, the Box Elder County Attorney prosecuting the case, said about the change of venue, "It was the judge's call." But he objected to the delayed trial dates—April 21–23—that accompanied the new location, because it overlapped with David Ortell's scheduled April 20–22 trial in Salt Lake City. Bunderson's primary concern was the emotional toll on Mary Ann, the pivotal witness in both cases. "She is still just seventeen years old," the prosecutor said to the judge in open court. "Having her testify in one trial then turn around in another trial may be too much to ask." Diane Balmain, the girl's guardian ad litem, an advocate appointed by juvenile court for the girl, joined in the objection, asking for more time to talk to the girl about her wishes.

However, Yengich said the simultaneous trials were necessary to reduce the risk of publicity in one case influencing the other. "It seems to me with the kind of publicity these cases will generate, even though both juries will be advised not to look at the news or listen to the news, we will be much safer if one trial is not following on the heels of another."

In the end, Judge Hadfield agreed to keep the matter open. The judge also ruled on another defense concern—the anti-polygamy demonstrations and protests, from signs to pins. Although he didn't name them, it was clear he was referring to the Tapestry contingent who came to every hearing wearing their purple support pins. "Whomever they are, I'm certainly for an open trial, but leave these demonstrations away from the jury," Yengich said. "This case should be decided on the merits of the evidence, not fear or intimidation from anyone's presence in the courtroom. I'm sure these are nice enough people but, frankly, I'm just as concerned with the signs in the hallways where the jury may see them as with the ribbons.

"You have places sometimes in a trial like this where the rights under the Fifth and Sixth Amendment to a fair trial conflict with the rights of free speech. Judge Hadfield will have to rule how he will weigh those two fundamental rights in this trial."

The judge advised those in attendance at the hearing that he would instruct bailiffs to remove overt pins, signs, or badges expressing an anti-polygamy view during the John Daniel's upcoming trial. His order extended to anyone parking in the court parking lot or using the sidewalks or any other part of the courthouse grounds. The ruling came after Yengich complained to the judge that at two hearings for his client, a few protesters held signs critical of Kingston and polygamy.

Laura Chapman, for one, was defiant. "We'll wear them and see what the judge's bailiffs do," she said.

Normally, Logan, Utah, is more suited as a winter vacation spot than as a media hot spot. Located an hour and a half outside Salt Lake City, the city of fifty thousand is nestled in the heart of beautiful Cache Valley and is home to Utah State University. But in the spring of 1999, Logan's typical tranquility was jarred by the focus being trained on the Kingston trial. Because of the expected onslaught of media and the ongoing public attention, Judge Hadfield issued an order laying out guidelines for the trial.

Media outlets received faxes stating anyone wishing to attend the trial had to be in their courtroom seats five minutes prior to the start of each day's sessions. "Once the court session begins, the doors will be secured and no one, except court personnel or counsel or their support staff, will be allowed to enter or leave the courtroom," the fax read. According to a court clerk, the reason for the strict time guidelines was more for jury selection than the actual trial. Already worried about pre-trial publicity, the judge didn't want prospective jurors being tainted by any gossip they might hear about the case. Also, Hadfield limited the number of people in his courtroom to make room for potential jurors and media representatives. Any spectator who did get in would be allowed to leave, but would not be granted entrance again until a recess.

State court communications director Jan Thompson said, "When a judge is aware of a high-profile case with widespread interest by the media, local, state, and national news, he'll issue an order like this. It's obviously an unusual case when you have to decide where you're going to put all the satellite trucks."

Other trial regulations stated reporters could not conduct interviews in the hallway adjacent to the courtroom, and loitering in the hallway was also prohibited. There would only be one pool photographer, who would represent all of the media, allowed in the courtroom during the trial, but the photographer was banned from taking pictures during the jury selection and witness-examination phases. Video cameras were not allowed.

"I commend Judge Hadfield his understanding media interest," Thompson said. "It's a privilege to have a still camera in Utah courts, and he made a concession to have a camera in the court during certain parts of the trial." The judge's primary concern about cameras was that they would compromise Mary Ann's anonymity.

In commenting on the order that no posters or placards would be allowed on the court premises, including the parking lot, during the trial or that nobody was allowed to wear any type of badge or photograph that "could be construed as communicating a message to the jury," Thompson noted, "We want to keep the political debate out of the courtroom. Child abuse trials are not uncommon, but the interest in polygamy is."

Prior to the beginning of jury selection, fourteen news organizations had secured press credentials, including the *Daily Telegraph London*, the *Guardian London*, and the BBC, plus the court retained four unreserved press passes to be passed out on a first-come, first-served basis. The presence of the BBC heightened the awareness that the case had taken on international significance, whether because of the subject matter, the fact it was happening in the next home for the Winter Olympics, or a combination of both. But even though anyone looking at the case knew polygamy was an integral part of what had happened, it seemed amazing to some that it was the one issue prosecutors had chosen to ignore completely. Their official party line: the case is about child abuse, pure and simple. However, the reality was that everyone familiar with the case or the Kingstons knew better and it would be impossible to screen out eight jurors and three alternates who had no knowledge of the Kingston lifestyle.

Carmen Thompson, executive director of Tapestry Against Polygamy, said there was no doubt what the case is about. "I can tell you that the prosecutor doesn't see it as a polygamy case, but the public does see it as a polygamy case." And, she added, "When you see crimes stemming directly from the polygamy issue, the polygamy should be prosecuted."

But the judge would do everything in his power to minimize the impact of such attitudes and awareness. On the first day of jury selection, seventy-five prospective panelists filled out questionnaires and were screened by the judge and attorneys for both sides. After the weeding out process, those left would return in the afternoon session to be interviewed individually. "This case is receiving considerable news media coverage," the judge told one group of prospective jurors. "For that reason I am telling you—you must not discuss this case with anyone."

Interestingly, some rival polygamist clans took the opportunity of John Daniel Kingston's pending trial for a little self-serving publicity. Owen Allred, leader of the five thousand–member Apostolic United Brethren, clucked, "They think all of us are guilty of child marriages. That's so far from the truth." He blamed practices like that for sullying the public perception of all polygamists and in essence, putting their lifestyle as a whole on trial. "It's the very reason this whole thing is coming down," Allred said. "Generally speaking, our people are very peaceful, mind-your-own-business people."

Actually, there is no Utah law against polygamy specifically, and prosecutors contended in the pretrial frenzy that prosecuting bigamy, the only related law on the books, is extremely difficult, making it fiscally inefficient at the very least. They preferred to focus on the related charges they felt they could prosecute, in this instance, the vicious beating of Mary Ann by her father. "I think the jury will understand this case has very little to do with polygamy and everything to do with child abuse," said Scott Wyatt, attorney for Cache County.

But not every official agreed with that stance. "To me, the underlying problem is the polygamous relationship that exists and they ought to be prosecuting that relationship, not just the child abuse," Dexter Anderson, a Millard County prosecutor, told the Associated Press. And Anderson was doing more than just giving a sound bite. The previous month he had filed bigamy charges against a man allegedly married to five women—the sixth such case he had pursued since 1986. "I don't think (polygamy cases) should be any more difficult than any other kind of case," he said. "To me, it's a law just like any other law and it's our sworn duty to prosecute violations."

As the start of the trial hovered, Logan officials braced for a potential avalanche of media, with more than three hundred press credentials having been issued. The courthouse parking lot was manned with Logan police officers prepared to avert a gridlock and to check each driver as he or she entered. "We're not expecting trouble," Sheriff's Lt. Dave Bennett said. "We're just expecting a lot of people."

However, as the court session opened, there was an unexpected lack of activity, almost as if people had forgotten the hoopla that was supposed to happen. "We didn't know what to expect," Officer Eric Collins said to a local newspaper. "I'm glad things are calm." Tapestry Against Polygamy was represented by two members. Carmen Thompson explained that their primary job was to help women wanting to extricate themselves from plural marriage, not just to be court watchers. "We're just here to offer support," she said. "We will not use a victim's situation to further our cause." And despite Laura Chapman's words challenging Judge Hadfield's order, the Tapestry women refrained from wearing their signature purple ribbons.

In the end, it was much ado about nothing. In a surprise move, with the jury selection process only halfway complete, John Daniel Kingston pleaded no contest to child abuse, preventing a trial that would have brought his family and himself under intense scrutiny. Under the plea agreement, the state agreed to reduce the charge from second-degree to third-degree child abuse, which carries a penalty of up to five years in prison. The original charge carried a possible penalty of one to fifteen years in prison. Judge Hadfield set the sentencing date for June 29.

In open court, he refused to take a guilty plea and when speaking to the judge, John Daniel said he was agreeing to the plea because, "I feel like this has gone on too long. The court has offered me this no contest plea." And after seeing his daughter in the courtroom, "I feel like it would be in her best interest not to put her through more than what she has already gone through." Mary Ann stood crying as she watched.

However, it seems as if the plea left Mary Ann Kingston without the one thing she wanted most: to hear her father apologize for his actions. "She still had some fight in her," Detective Scott Cosgrove said. "She wanted her father to admit to the charges and say he was sorry." Apparently, although he didn't admit it in open court or to reporters later, according to Cosgrove, who had remained in touch with Mary Ann, that's what John Daniel did via a note he passed to his daughter while they were still in the judge's chambers working out the plea agreement. "She wanted him to say, 'Yes, I'm guilty,'" in court.

But he admitted to it in the note," Cosgrove said. "He said he was sorry and that he still loved her. It kind of broke her down a little." Spectators in the courtroom say it was obvious the girl had obviously been crying when she entered prior to the plea. Cosgrove added that for all her spunk, she also wanted "to get this taken care of and get on with her life."

Cosgrove didn't discount that the girl might have succumbed to the pressure as well. "There is possibly pressure from the family now, saying, 'Take care of this', which should have been done months ago, and we shouldn't be here today," he mused, then added, "But that's my personal feeling."

According to Prosecutor Bunderson, the plea agreement that was struck was similar to an offer that had been made to Kingston several weeks prior. But it was only after John Daniel slipped his daughter the note that she agreed to accept the lesser charge. Bunderson acknowledged that Mary Ann, "became emotional toward the end of this process, which included her reading that note from him. Our position in making this particular offer was that in the long run we don't think it's going to make that much difference in the punishment that he ultimately receives."

A no contest plea is essentially the same as a guilty plea, except it cannot be used against the defendant in any future civil cases that might arise. In other words, had Mary Ann wanted to sue for civil damages arising from the beating, the no contest plea could not be used as evidence against her father. But from his standpoint, Bunderson thought it was a win-win situation: they got a conviction and spared the teenager the ordeal of a trial. "I'm hoping it sends a message that people who mistreat children are going to suffer the consequences," he said.

As part of the process, Prosecutor Jon Bunderson detailed the case against John Daniel—that he had beat his daughter thirty times with a belt, that "she counted twenty-eight before she fainted....She woke up the next day on a couch and he told her he was going to strike her ten times for each thing he believed she had done wrong." Judge Hadfield then addressed Kingston. "You're not contesting what Mr. Bunderson is saying?"

Coolly, John Daniel answered, "I'm not contesting that that would be the evidence presented."

The judge responded, "I will treat your no contest plea as if it were a guilty plea in all respects."

Outside, Kingston gave a curt statement to the assembled press as he was hustled into his attorney's car, noting "The state offered a chance for a no contest plea, which does not admit guilt and that's what I'm saying."

Perhaps the most surprised person at the turn of events was Kingston's defense attorney, Ron Yengich. "That's what he wanted to do; it's not my choice," Yengich said. "The people that are most important in this case, which are the defendant and the alleged victim, basically decided they were going to settle it."

Outside the courtroom, both sides of the polygamy issue added their opinions. "This is the first time that we've actually seen a polygamist accused and prosecuted and the outcome was good," Tapestry's Carmen Thompson told reporters. "I think the message that is sent is that women and children in polygamy can trust the outside world and the justice system does work. Now, girls and women can realize that they can use the justice system, that they have power. They don't have to be victims." However, prosecutor Bunderson still refused to focus on polygamy, reiterating, "This isn't anything other than a child abuse case."

Defense counsel Yengich commented, "I think that is the sexy aspect of it," referring to the polygamy angle, "using that in the broadest term. Obviously there are overtones with other issues because of statements that were made in the police reports and the feeling that have been engendered by people who have been participating on the periphery," another not-too-subtle jab at the Tapestry group.

But for Tapestry cofounder Rowenna Erickson, it was a case of sticks and stones. "I feel absolutely wonderful because it's an admission, at least, of what he actually did," Erickson said. "I know this girl really did something for a lot of people, she's opened the way for other girls. I bless her for what she's done."

But the teenager's ordeal was only half over, as the prosecutors turned their attention toward the June start date of David Ortell's incest trial. While waiting, Mary Ann filled her life with school and adjusting to post-clan life in her foster home. Despite her obvious inner strength and fortitude, it was still a difficult time. Mary Ann held no desire to see her father. She also stopped seeing her mother after feeling pressured by her to drop the charges against her father and uncle.

But she wasn't alone. In addition to her foster family, Mary Ann also found support in her court-appointed guardian ad litem, as well as her Division of Child and Family Services caseworker and a counselor. But it was obvious that Mary Ann was a unique young lady. Despite not having any money, she repeatedly turned down offers to sell the exclusive rights to her story to producers. Not that she rejected the idea, but she didn't think it was the right to do until the entire matter was behind her. She would have a ways to go before that time came.

However, a slight, almost imperceptible change seemed to be taking place regarding polygamy. Quietly, without fanfare, some authorities were carefully testing judicial waters that hadn't been disturbed in almost half a century. Prosecutors in the central Utah cities of Richfield and Fillmore filed bigamy charges after receiving complaints from ex-wives, who were being assisted by Tapestry. The first to be prosecuted was Steve Bronson, who agreed to a "plea in abeyance," meaning his crime would be expunged if he lived only with his lawful wife for the following year.

The second man charged, Mark Joseph Easterday, initially planned to fight the charge. Easterday, a disabled vet and open polygamist, complained, "I'm caught between a rock and a hard place. Who am I going to go with, the law or my religion?" While he agreed that offending polygamists should be prosecuted for incest or abuse, he also said, "I served honorably in the service for eight years and defended the freedom and rights of fellow Americans, and now I'm being persecuted for living my freedom. I just hope the time comes where America wakes up." In the end, Easterday, pleaded no contest to adultery, a misdemeanor, avoiding jail time.

In both cases, the prosecutors said they were simply enforcing the law. "Do we get to pick and choose?" asked Paul Lyman, who prosecuted Easterday. It was an attitude that the Tapestry women were hoping would spread to prosecutors in Salt Lake City.

In May 1999, David Ortell's lawyer tried to have prosecutor Dane Nolan removed from the case on the grounds Nolan may be a material witness. In his motions, defense attorney Steve McCaughey said he intended to call prosecutor Dane Nolan as a witness because he obtained information about the case during an interview with Mary Ann that had not been disclosed in prior interviews with police or social workers. The interview in question resulted in the state adding the fourth charge against Kingston when Mary Ann revealed a fourth sexual encounter that had occurred in April. "This is an unusual situation where you have a prosecutor interview the complainant witness and she makes a new allegation," McCaughey said. "Usually, we have a police officer who does the interview and there is a tape or a transcript."

He went on to say, "This is the first time this allegation had been mentioned. The prosecution has never produced any type of recording of this fourth allegation, which has the obvious potential to impeach the alleged victim, and thus exculpate the defendant." The attorney went on to say he intended to "call Nolan as a witness for the defense, to impeach the alleged victim, undermine the state's case and support the defendant's contention that he is not guilty of the charges."

In addition, McCaughey asked Judge David Young to order Nolan to make himself available to be deposed by the defense, after which he should be thrown off the case. In highly creative legalese, the attorney also charged that, "A lawyer from the Salt Lake County District Attorney's office should not be representing the state of Utah in this prosecution because his performance in cross-examining Mr. Nolan as a defense witness would be hindered by his responsibilities to his coprosecutor, Mr. Nolan, and by his own interests in office politics and morale."

Judge Young, however, ruled that the defense could not depose Nolan. In answering McCaughey's claim that, "Our defense in this case is that she has made inconsistent statements on numerous occasions," prosecutor Nolan pointed out to the court that the defense had police transcripts and a preliminary hearing transcript to use in their preparation. A caseworker who had also been present during the interview could be subpoenaed by the defense. But the most compelling argument occurred when Nolan reminded the court that McCaughey had the opportunity to question Mary Ann about the \incident when she was on the witness stand in December during the preliminary hearing.

Young agreed. "It seems to me there is no basis for getting a deposition from the prosecutor," the judge determined. "He learned of that in an appropriate investigative interview." However, Young also ordered Nolan to submit any pertinent information obtained during the interview to the defense. The judge also denied a prosecution motion asking that the jury hear the details of Mary Ann's beating at the hands of her father.

David Ortell on Trial

Unlike his brother, David Ortell refused to take a plea bargain, and his criminal trial on three felony counts of incest and one count of unlawful sexual contact was on track to start. His defense was simple: he didn't do it. He didn't marry his niece nor did he ever have sexual intercourse with her. When the case first unfolded, Kingston, through McCaughey, denied even knowing the girl, but later admitted he did. Their overall strategy was to paint Mary Ann as a troubled teen who was making it all up. Although he wouldn't identify them, McCaughey said he would call five or six witnesses but declined to say whether his client would take the stand in his own defense. Unlike some other high profile cases, this one was expected to go the jury after just a couple of days.

As in John Daniel's trial, jury selection was of critical concern to the defense and it took the better part of the first day of trial in June 1999 to seat the panel of eight jurors from the prospective pool of fifty. During jury selection, prospective panelists were asked if they had any associations currently with polygamy, but were not asked if any of their ancestors were from polygamous families. Again, spectators were barred from exhibiting any form of anti-polygamy protest, be it visual or verbal, in an effort to prevent tainting the jury in any way. Although nearly half of the pool was female, an all–white male jury was seated. "This is unheard of," Carmen Thompson said in disbelief.

Defense attorney McCaughey was also incredulous when the pool of fifty potential jurors was asked how many had followed the case, even marginally. Nobody raised their hand. "I've never seen anything like it," McCaughey said. Everybody who has ever watched a court drama on TV knows you can be disqualified for knowing too much about a case. And the media interest in this case was intense.

Many national news programs were referring to David Ortell's case as "Utah's trial of the century." As expected, several regional and national news organizations, such as the *Los Angeles Times*, NBC News, and the ABC newsmagazine *20/20*, were all following the story, as was the BBC and Geraldo Rivera. In one of the more surreal moments, just prior to the start of the trial, a news bureau in New York called Judge Young to ask if the trial could be delayed until one of its reporters arrived on the scene. The judge was not accommodating.

Although Judge Young himself made it clear that the trial was not about polygamy but about incest, he felt compelled to address the issue, telling jurors, "The fact that he is alleged to be a polyga-mist...should really have no bearing in this case." But it did, although the prosecution would be hard pressed to explain how.

In his opening statement, McCaughey was brief and direct. The defense would show, he said, through the victim's inconsistent state-ments, that his client never had sex with his niece. He also urged to look for the "conflicting and contradictory" statements in the Mary Ann's testimony. He said, "Listen to the discrepancies in how many times the alleged intercourse occurred, where the alleged intercourse supposedly occurred, and when, the dates, the alleged intercourse occurred."

The prosecution's entire case would live or die on whether the jury believed Mary Ann's story. To help do that, the prosecution tried to paint a virtual picture of what life inside the Kingston clan was like; how free will was systematically and intentionally destroyed, how husbands were chosen through close blood ties, and how young girls were programmed from birth to be babymakers and plural wives.

Nolan wanted the jury to understand why Mary Ann, obviously a bright young woman, would have agreed to marry and then have sex with her uncle in the first place without putting up a fight. He tried to describe in detail the circumstances surrounding their wedding, which included David Ortell's fourteen other wives and the family pressure she was under to go through with the marriage. The defense objected, saying the other wives were irrelevant and calling for Nolan to establish some kind of foundation as to how she learned they were Kingston's plural wives. The Judge asked the prosecutor why the testimony was relevant to an incest case. "The fact that the other wives were there welcoming her goes to her beliefs in regards to her expectations of her role in the marriage," Nolan argued. "Detail in this case is important. She should be allowed to tell us everything she remembers about the wedding." Despite Nolan's argument, Judge Young sustained the objections.

During a break in the proceedings, Douglas White, a lawyer for Tapestry Against Polygamy, criticized the judge's rulings. "It's a disservice to the jury," White said. "They pull eight guys off the street and ask them to hear a case like this and only give them part of the puzzle. It's like trying to prove there's a tenth floor to a building without any evidence of the first nine." White went on to say, "There was no reason to thread the needle like that. Do they think they're going to offend us by talking about polygamy? Like we don't know about it?"

Back in the courtroom, when asked why she gave conflicting statements to authorities, including police officers investigating her charges and social workers assigned to help her, Mary Ann testified she had been terrified to reveal her family secrets. "I still was not sure if I was going to get out of the group," she said. "I was so scared, I didn't dare tell inside secrets."

While women like Rowenna Erickson could deeply identify with Mary Ann's fear, could anyone who hadn't been so indoctrinated believe an individual could be so frightened and confused?

Slowly and methodically, Nolan had Mary Ann describe her life. She recalled her father, John Daniel, told her when she was about thirteen to "start preparing for marriage and who I should marry," with that union having to be approved by Paul Kingston. She also explained that she knew her school days were numbered because girls in "The Order" don't get the luxury of education. "It wasn't part of the plan, I guess," she said.

When David called her on October 13, 1997, to tell her they would be wed in two days, Mary Ann says she panicked. "I was kind of in shock because it was in two days and I needed more time," she said. But the decision was out of her hands. As previously described, her uncle had chosen the date October 15, because she would be his fifteenth wife, which is also why he later gave her a ring with fifteen diamonds, which she later turned over to authorities. Her mother and father had approved the date and so had Paul. She was trapped with no way out.

The night of the ceremony, Mary Ann and David left the church around 7:30 P.M. when he drove her to the Olympus Park Hotel in Park City, where they spent the night. Although she was able to stave off sex that night claiming she was menstruating, David consummated their marriage in January 1998. He had sex with her three more times, until she ran away in May.

The courtroom sat in riveted silence throughout her testimony, which spanned two days: four hours of direct examination on Tuesday and several more of brutal cross-examination on Wednesday. Throughout the questioning, Mary Ann remained calm, responding so softly at times that the judge asked her to speak louder. Although empathy could be read on the faces of the spectators, the jury seemed unmoved. Outside the courtroom, the members of Tapestry cheered her bravery and fortitude. "Good heavens, the girl is just a hero," Laura Chapman said. "She's incredible."

Although the judge did his best to minimize discussion of the Kingston's Church of Christ polygamy clan, some inclusion was inevitable, when Christine Gustafson, a member of the group, testified.

"Are you aware of the Kingston group?" prosecutor Dane Nolan asked Gustafson.

"Yeah," Gustafson answered.

"Are you a member of the Kingston group?"

"Yeah."

"Is the defendant a member of the Kingston group?"

"Yeah."

Judge Young allowed this particular line of questioning was to let Nolan show whether or not Gustafson, a defense witness, had a bias toward David Ortell Kingston. According to Mary Ann, Gustafson also happened to be David Kingston's fourteenth wife—a categorization Christine denied on the stand. Gustafson said she was a single woman with no children who worked part time as a bookkeeper. As to how she knew David Ortell, she admitted they were blood related but said nothing about being married. Gustafson did acknowledge, however, that girls in the group generally do not have a high school education and are married off to whomever clan leader Paul Kingston—David Ortell's brother—approves of.

Gustafson also admitted that Kingston had asked her to live in the run-down apartment located at a Kingston-owned coal yard one day after he moved his niece there. She testified that she believed she was sent to live with Mary Ann to keep her under control. The defense hoped to use Gustafson to help portray Mary Ann as a wild, incorrigible teenager, with testimony about the girl sneaking out in the middle of the night and not returning until the next day. And Christine admitted she is the one who called Mary Ann's mother, Susan Nelson, when she failed to come home the night of May 21, 1997. When Gustafson finished her testimony, she sat on a bench directly behind David Ortell.

Whatever points Gustafson may have scored for the defense were erased by Sharli Kingston, David Ortell's legal wife. They had been married since June 8, 1984, and together had six children. Like Gustafson, she denied Mary Ann had ever been married to her husband, nor had there ever been a secret ceremony. She also claimed she was the one who accompanied David Ortell to the Olympic Park Hotel on the night of October 15, 1997.

Sharli testified that because it was a tax deadline day, her husband, a CPA, had been in the office working all day. When he finished, they drove to Park City and checked into the hotel. According to Sharli, they spent the night, did some sightseeing the next day, had dinner, and then drove home. She speculated to the jury that Mary Ann fabricated her version of the day's events after hearing Sharli talking about her and David's trip to Park City at a birthday party a few days later.

Upon cross-examination, Dane Nolan asked Sharli to draw a picture of the hotel room where she said she had stayed with David. He then compared it to a drawing Mary Ann had been asked to draw. Both sketches were then compared to a diagram presented by the assistant hotel manager, Kevin McDougal. The differences were quickly apparent. Sharli's drawing neglected to include that the room had two sinks, two nightstands, a large closet, a TV that was positioned on top of a dresser, or that the hotel pool could be seen out the window—descriptions Mary Ann had accurately made. It was clear that Sharli had never been inside the hotel room in question.

During his closing argument, Nolan would tell the jury that her inability to recall the room meant all her testimony should be "completely disregarded." However, later, he showed more compassion. "She is in a tough situation," Nolan said. "Her husband is charged with four serious crimes. She's at home with six children, so you can understand her desperation."

In trying to explain Mary Ann's differing accounts, Nolan told the jury to put themselves in her position, talking to strangers about a terrible time in her life. She was afraid to tell the truth at first out of fear what would happen if she did—and then had to go back. "Her future at that moment, in her mind, is very uncertain. When you're young, you don't know what's going to happen, you don't know how adults are going to react," Nolan said. He urged them to concentrate instead on the hard evidence that proved a wedding had taken place—the wedding photos and a wedding ring. He also rebutted the defense contention that she had made up the entire story because of a bad relationship with her parents. If that were the case, why involve the uncle? And finally, he stressed the importance of the hotel room diagram. How could she be so accurate unless she had been in that room on the night of her wedding?

Of course, the defense wanted the jury to consider little else but the fact Mary Ann had not told the same story from the beginning of her ordeal. McCaughey singled out at least eight different versions of events the girl had given to authorities. He sought to undermine the prosecution's case by dismissing the importance of the wedding. Whether or not there had ever been a ceremony or a ring or a night spent in Park City was irrelevant, he argued, because none of it had any bearing on whether or not David Ortell had sexual intercourse with his niece. "Marriage doesn't mean sex," McCaughey said. Ironically, it was McCaughey who most directly addressed polygamy, saying it had been the "motivation to get away from her situation by accusing her uncle of incest."

The two-day trial ended without David Ortell Kingston taking the stand. And as the all–white male jury of eight headed in to deliberate, both sides held their collective breaths. Four hours later, they told the clerk they had reached a verdict. As the men filed back into the courtroom, they avoided eye contact with everyone but the judge. There were four counts of incest and unlawful sexual conduct, each to be decided independently. Judge Young looked at the paper in his hands and read the findings of the jury to the courtroom.

On the first count, the jury found the defendant, "Not guilty." An audible gasp came from the Kingston side.

On the second count, the jury found the defendant, "Not guilty." Smiles were beginning to appear on the Kingston clan members present while a cool emotional mist of disbelief began to chill those who had fervently believed the girl's story. Had the judge's decision not to let the full scope of Kingston clan life be explained been the edge David Ortell needed to convince the jury of his innocence?

On the third count, the jury found the defendant, "Guilty." Suddenly, smiles turned to shocked tears for those seated behind Kingston, with women grabbing for each other's hands and clinging to one another for support.

On the fourth count, the jury found the defendant, "Guilty."

David Ortell Kingston had been convicted of two counts of incest and unlawful sexual conduct, both third-degree felonies. Throughout the reading of the verdict, Kingston showed no emotion, not even when Judge Young ordered him to be taken into custody. He was immediately handcuffed and stood while the judge set a July 9 sentencing date. At the discretion of the judge, each count carried a prison term of up to five years. After David was led away, Sharli and other family members hurried from the courtroom, refusing to make any statements to the media. Co–defense attorney Susanne Gustin-Furgis said, "I'm kind of shocked by the verdict. I think they just split the baby."

It was an unusual verdict. In the end, the jury convicted Kingston on the March and May incest and unlawful sexual charges, but acquitted him on the January and April charges, the latter two incidents being where Mary Ann's story had been deemed inconsistent. The only thing that prevented David Ortell from walking away a free man was the power of Mary Ann's testimony. And perhaps some of the jury members had to know this kind of lifestyle existed in Utah. On the other hand, the two not guilty verdicts indicated not how close the defense had come to picking the perfect jury for an acquittal. None of the jurors interviewed wanted to be identified for the public record, but of those who spoke to reporters, one commented that the split verdict spoke of the difference in opinion among jury members more so than the evidence presented. "Whenever you have eight individuals, certainly you will have the potential for eight points of view," he said.

The jurors revealed they chose not to take a poll when they first started deliberations, opting instead to begin a methodical review of the evidence. After refreshing their minds, they began the internal debate when differences in opinion emerged. "We kept coming back to the jury instructions, to give us direction on the things we needed to say," a juror said. "The final verdict was very much my decision."

Although polygamy was the tacit codefendant in the case, jurors maintained it didn't play a factor in either the convictions or acquittals. "None of the four charges against Mr. Kingston had to do with polygamy, and it was not part of our decision-making conscious," one juror told the *Desert News*. "I think it was obvious in the sense that the situation was obvious."

Another juror summed up the process by saying, "All I can say is that we went through all the evidence item by item very carefully and analyzed all the evidence for every one of the counts before we made our decision."

For seventeen-year-old Mary Ann Kingston, the news of the verdict came via a cell phone call. Bill Burnard, director of the Children's

Justice Center in Logan, says, "That lifted a big load off her shoulders. We heard it around Bountiful. She just lit up. It was the best I'd ever seen her. She was so happy. She was a totally different person."

Although they would have liked to see David Ortell convicted on all counts, opponents of polygamy saw the outcome as an inspiring victory that gave hope to others, both women and children, wanting to escape polygamous lifestyles. "This case makes a difference," said Tapestry attorney Douglas White. "It certainly sends a message that the state of Utah is willing to prosecute these cases." He also predicted there would be more cases to come. "It's clear, it's present— there is danger in the courts for polygamists in Utah."

For the prosecution, any conviction was a good conviction, so Nolan was reluctant to classify the verdict as a compromise, as the defense counsel had done. But he did take the opportunity to reiterate that the verdict, although about incest, was inseparable from polygamy. "Polygamy is part of the background in the case," Nolan told reporters after the verdict. "To understand the case, you have to understand the people." He also praised the grit of Mary Ann Kingston, calling her, "Extremely courageous. It takes a lot of guts, bravery, moxie, and backbone to go to court and say what she did. It's something I could not have done as a seventeen-year-old."

But while Mary Ann's ordeal in the court system was over, the end of the trials simply marked the beginning of new challenges—and controversies.

Chapter Ten
THE AFTERMATH

Apparently, David Ortell believed any mention of polygamy during the trial was too much. On June 14, 1999, Kingston's new defense team—Todd Utzinger and Hakeem Ishola—filed a motion before Judge David Young requesting a new trial on the grounds prosecutor Dane Nolan introduced "irrelevant and highly inflammatory evidence" regarding Kingston's "alleged" polygamist lifestyle; defense attorneys Steve McCaughey and Susanne Gustin-Furgis failed to keep such improper evidence out of the trial and should have moved for a mistrial; and new witnesses had come forth since to refute Mary Ann Kingston's testimony.

Todd Utzinger said, "Our concern is that Mr. Kingston be given a full and fair opportunity to clear his name. Despite the judge's best efforts to exclude evidence that was irrelevant, prejudicial evidence made its way before the jury, and we think he's entitled to a new trial that's untainted by irrelevant and inflammatory evidence." Speaking of the new witnesses suddenly ready to come forward, Utzinger said at least one "can shed light on the whereabouts of the alleged victim in some of the time periods that she claims to have been with the defendant. From what we've learned so far, we believe that on some of the dates in question she could not have been with Mr. Kingston because she was in fact with other individuals."

In a surreal situation, not uncommon in American jurisprudence, the defense attorneys were asking the judge, in essence, to admit his own wrongdoing, insofar as allowing in what little information Judge Young had about David Ortell's polygamist ties. While Utzinger seemed to go out of his way to give the judge credit for sustaining as many defense objections as he did during the trial, he still argued, "The problem we have is that once the drop of ink has been put into the jug of milk and the jug shaken, you can't get that ink back out, and our concern is that despite the best efforts of Judge Young to keep this issue out, it got in." However, even Utzinger acknowledged that the standard for granting a new trial was daunting, but felt it still should be done.

Prosecutor Dane Nolan was furious that Utzinger filed the motion for a new trial even before reading a transcript of the original trial. He accused the defense lawyer of "recklessness" for alleging prosecutorial misconduct and inadequate assistance of counsel. "He did that apparently without doing any research. I worked very hard to try to earn a good reputation as a prosecutor and in five minutes of typing a motion that reputation took a major hit," Nolan said.

Life outside the Kingston Clan

While David Ortell's attorney busied himself with judicial appeals, Mary Ann Kingston looked to her future, while taking care not to exploit her past. She still declined to sell her rights for a movie and turned down all requests for interviews. Bill Burnard, director of the Children's Justice Center in Logan, said at the time, "Those options are out there, but she doesn't want to come forward yet. She knows she'll be giving up her confidentiality. It has to be the right time for her."

Mary Ann's counselors and the court seemed intent on protecting the girl in whatever way was at their disposal. One way was to preserve her anonymity, which resulted in a court order banning the media from taking and publishing her photo. During David Ortell's trial, one photographer inadvertently broke the rule when he took a picture of a prosecutor, who was holding a portrait of Mary Ann in her wedding gown. When she found out, the teen panicked and her team of social workers and counselors immediately contacted the photographer and appealed to his sense of decency. The photographer turned over the negatives.

Although they tried to minimize the risk, some of the people advising and counseling Mary Ann privately worried that she still faced the potential of physical danger from members of the Kingston clan who might harbor ill-will towards the girl for having sent both Kingston brothers to jail. At the very least, it was clear she was a pariah. Karl Perry, a deputy attorney general who helped prosecute her father, said, "The Kingstons played some games early on. They wouldn't give her back her portable stereo. First they said she never had one. Then when they finally gave it back, it was trashed." He also confirmed there had been rumors that the Kingstons were looking to find where she was living.

Whether safety was a consideration or not, Mary Ann was planning to attend college out of state. "There's probably not a whole lot of places in the state where she can go where she wouldn't run into someone from the Kingston group," said Burnard. And perhaps not surprisingly, she was considering a career as a lawyer because, according to those in contact with her, she felt the law had literally saved her life.

While the physical wounds and bruises had long since healed, recovering emotionally was a much longer process, as was the effort to reconcile her own beliefs from what had been her clan indoctrination. But showing the remarkable resiliency of the human spirit, Mary Ann was by all accounts a typical teenaged girl in many regards. After having caught up on her studies via private instruction, she went back to public high school, where nobody knew of her situation. And from the outside, she indeed seemed like a typical teen— she enjoyed being with friends, liked going to the movies, and had a healthy interest in boys her own age. Unlike the beaten girl at the pay phone, this Mary Ann had flowered as a young woman.

"She's very headstrong," said Karl Perry. "Once you understand that system she got out of, no way she's average. A lot of the girls in the Kingston clan are watching her, thinking about trying to get out."

Interestingly, unlike the women of Tapestry Against Polygamy, Mary Ann didn't seem interested in using her experience to become an advocate against polygamy; at least not at the moment. One of her counselors told Tim Gurrister of the *Standard Examiner* that, "She didn't leave thinking I'm going to get these people. She did not intend to be the icon of polygamous runaways. She just took a walk. It was Sunday, everyone was in church, and she hoped she would have the courage to call someone when she got to a pay phone. She didn't know there was any kind of support group out there."

And even though she found a strong circle of people wanting to help her, there were a lot of issues only she could resolve within her own heart and head. "She's going through a lot of, 'What do I believe compared to what my parents taught me'," the counselor added. "She still struggles with that, wondering how much to believe out of everything her parents told her."

On June 29, 1999, John Daniel Kingston returned to court for his sentencing—fifteen minutes late and accompanied by over a dozen family members. Although Mary Ann didn't speak herself, her presence was still keenly felt when her guidem ad litem read a letter from the girl to Judge Ben Hadfield. It was poignant and uplifting, heartbreaking but hopeful:

> I want the Court to know the many ways I have been hurt because of my father's actions on May 23, 1998. The bruises and wounds to my body healed many months ago. The damage to my spirit is taking longer to heal. His actions through these criminal proceedings have made me suffer more.
>
> When I was talking with the prosecutor and my guardian ad litem about what result I wanted from the criminal process, I told them what I most wanted was for Daniel to say that he had done wrong. He gave me a note, through his lawyers, saying that he was sorry for how I thought he had hurt me, that he loved me and wanted me to have a good life. I felt good that he had said he loved me, and that he wished me well. I felt bad that he could not admit that he had done wrong. If he loves me like he says he does, it seems that he should be able to tell me he is sorry for something we both know happened and that we both know was wrong.
>
> My lawyer and the prosecutor have explained to me that because of the way Daniel plead "no contest" rather than "guilty," he can't admit that he has done wrong. I cannot feel safe until I know he admits he has done wrong. And I am afraid for the other members of my family who will know what he did, and that he has not said that it was wrong. They

will know that he can do it again, because he doesn't believe that what he did was wrong.

I am worried for my family, and that no matter what happens today, they will not have safety. My family was and is very close to my heart. I had many good friends in the group that I have missed and will never forget. My heart is broken that I know I can never be with them again. I do wish all of them good and happy lives.

I know that in my family's eyes, I have done wrong. I hope that I can be forgiven by them for the things they feel that I have done to hurt them. My family's opinion of me was and is important to me and I live every day with the pain of knowing that they are disappointed in me. Even now, every day I feel a lot of guilt because I know that they feel that I have let them down. I didn't want to live the lifestyle they did, but I didn't know how to do that and not lose my family and all of my friends.

When I started having outside friends, my father and uncle arranged it so that I was never alone. I didn't have a phone, and wasn't even allowed to go to the store for myself. And then when I stayed out with those friends, I was taken to the Ranch and beaten.

I have lost every person and every thing I knew to be my family. I have lost the life and every thing I knew growing up.I was never taught that there is a way to live happily with people that you don't agree with. I am learning that, and many other things now. I will never forget my family and the group and the life that I had before, but I will move on and become a better person for all of my experiences. I will make it.

I don't want to go back on the agreement we made that Daniel not have to go to prison. I only want for him to tell me that he knows that what he did was wrong. I want to believe that he is sorry for what he has done. I don't believe that he is sorry. I am his daughter, and I love him as my father. He was the person I looked up to the most. I had always counted on him as my father to be my protector. He was my idol. Mostly, I wanted him to approve of me and love me for who I was. I still want that, more than anything.

I still love Daniel very much, and I will never forget the good things he taught me, like hard work and family ties. I wish I could call him "dad," but I never did and now I never will be able to call anyone "dad," and I will never really know what that relationship should be like.

I love my family and friends from the group and will never forget them.

The wounds and bruises to my body have healed and can be forgotten. The hurt to my soul has been much harder to heal.

To the end, John Daniel refused to admit culpability. He told the judge he loved his daughter very much, which is why he agreed to a plea. "I didn't want her to go through the embarrassment of a trial. This has been a difficult but growing experience for me." He said, "I'm sorry for the pain and suffering that I have caused her and anyone else." He also wished his daughter well in "becoming the good person I know she can be."

Just prior to the sentencing, John Daniel's attorney, Ron Yengich, encouraged the court to treat his client as he would a more anonymous person. "He is a good provider," Yengich said. The lawyer also assured the court and Mary Ann—who was present—that she was in no physical danger from anyone in the Kingston clan. "It is his concern, it is his desire that nothing happen to her," Yengich said. "And he wants to assure the court that no one, at his direction, concurrence, or desire, would harm her in any way." However, one former Kingston clan member observed, "She betrayed him completely. And he'll never forgive her because she has committed the unforgivable sin by running away and speaking publicly about who her father is."

Sentencing

Although John Daniel could have faced up to five years in prison, Judge Hadfield sentenced John Daniel in June 1999 to seven months in jail, fined him $2,700, ordered him to pay any restitution for medical or psychological costs Mary Ann may endure from her beating, ordered him to avoid any contact with his daughter unless supervised by his probation officer, and required him to complete an anger-management program. However, the judge also said he would consider reducing the jail time if John Daniel apologized to his daughter in writing and took responsibility for beating her. "Obviously in telling you that, I'm not satisfied at this point," Hadfield told Kingston. However, the odds of John Daniel putting an apology in writing seemed remote at best. Kingston would also be granted release time to work after serving the first two full weeks in jail.

Afterward, former Kingston wife and Tapestry Against Polygamy founder Rowenna Erickson told the *Standard-Examiner* newspaper on June 30, 1999, she seriously doubts John Daniel Kingston will ever be truly sorry, and even if he did apologize, "it won't come from the heart; it will just be for the court." Erickson added that while the girl "got some type of vindication, but the fact that he wouldn't admit what he did was wrong is just the type of mind-set that they have because polygamous men never say they're wrong." That said, in the eyes of the Tapestry group, justice had been served. "We thought it was a victory for the victim, and it's a beginning for the future of similar cases."

Around the same time in a different courtroom, Third District Court Judge David Young denied defense motions to delay David Ortell's sentencing. He also denied Todd Utzinger's motion to grant Kingston a new trial on the basis of misconduct by prosecutors and incompetence by the defense. But neither ruling prevented the attorney from filing a motion to arrest sentencing, which could still result in a new trial for Kingston. Although David Ortell had hired Utzinger to handle all his appeals, Kingston would still be represented by his original defense team during the sentencing. However, Susanne Gustin-Furgis expressed her frustration with Utzinger to the judge, saying she believed the motion libeled not only her but her co–defense attorney Steve McCaughey as well as the prosecutors. She was also unhappy that Utzinger advised Kingston not to speak with the Adult Probation and Parole officers who were preparing a pre-sentencing report.

Judge Young gave both the prosecution and the defense attorneys who had represented David Ortell in his criminal case a personal vote of confidence, saying he saw no evidence of misconduct by the prosecution or incompetence by defense attorneys. "They succeeded in getting acquittals on two of the incest charges," Young noted. "As far as I'm concerned they did an excellent job in representing the interests of Mr. Kingston."

But now David Ortell's fate was in the hands of the judge and on July 9, 1999, Kingston appeared in court to be sentenced. Kingston's attorneys pleaded for the court to keep the jail time to a minimum, suggesting six months behind bars. However, Deputy District Attorney Dane Nolan urged Kingston get the maximum, pointing out that in addition to everything else, David Ortell had put Mary Ann potentially at risk for a sexually transmitted disease. "It has been reported to me that he has fifteen wives, therefore, you can assume he is having sex with them. And someone having that many sexual contacts, you can assume he's a risk for disease."

Defense attorney Susanne Gustin-Fergis painted a far different picture for Judge Young, calling her client kind and caring, "He's not a bully. He's not aggressive, he's not the evil, domineering patriarch he's been described as in the media." She also criticized the Adult Probation and Parole division's recommendation for the maximum sentence, characterizing it as being politically motivated. "There is a lot of political pressure to exact the maximum penalty of Mr. Kingston because of the nature of this case." But, she pointed out David Ortell had already been severely punished. "His life has been shattered and his heart has been broken."

Part of the defense problem in the sentencing was that Kingston continued to deny his guilt. Expressing remorse often improves the chance for a lighter sentence, but Gustin-Fergis, didn't have that to fall back on. Instead, while acknowledging that Kingston continued to deny his guilt, she also told the court he could still benefit from a lighter sentence combined with probation and therapy. "All sex offenders have a degree of denial," she argued. "That's the role of therapy, to lessen the denial and establish a degree of empathy with the victim." And since, in David Ortell's case, the basis for the offense was "a religious practice, not a compulsion, so he can be treated more easily. The offenses are accompanied by a marriage ceremony in Mr. Kingston's case, not by entrenched fantasies, compulsions and drives...He is not going to be out molesting the community at large. He understands that he will only be able to have sex with his wife, Sharli, and he is willing to follow societal norms regarding that."

She also argued that Kingston was a victim of "some misguided family instruction and teaching." Summing up, the defense asked the court to consider six months in jail, two years' confinement in a halfway house, and enrollment in a counseling program.

Dressed in a red prison jump suit, David Ortell spoke briefly, asking for mercy from the court and expressing concern for his niece. "I have no hatred or resentment toward her at all. I feel sorry for her," Kingston told Young. "I hope she has a real good life and gets out of life the things that she wants." David Ortell also told the court of his concern for his family. "I do have a large family with young children who need their father," Kingston said. "I don't know what my family and children will do without me to help them."

Young, however, proved to be unmoved by the calls for mercy. He believed the case merited much stiffer penalties. He ordered David Ortell Kingston to serve the maximum sentence—five years for each count to be served consecutively, meaning a ten-year prison sentence. He also fined Kingston $5,000 on each count and ordered him to pay counseling costs for his niece. In issuing his sentence, Judge Young noted that while David Ortell might be a victim himself of his family's "mistaken dogma," it was the judge's duty to consider the fact that Kingston was still a polygamist. "In this sentencing, polygamy is an issue. Thus, I can't protect other relatives of yours without imposing this sentence." Young also commented that to ignore the polygamy issue would be "like ignoring a five thousand–pound elephant in the living room."

Young also told Kingston that "your family is wrong" in its beliefs about incestuous relationships. "You have been taught in such a way that relationships with nieces as plural wives is okay and that is flat out not true," Young said bluntly. "In the relationships of family, in the relationships of marriage, in the relationships of conception of children, you are willing not to abide by the law." Young also said the fact he saw no indication Kingston believed having sexual intercourse with his niece was wrong factored into his decision, as did his doubts Kingston had or would denounce the family's incestuous, polygamous practices any time in the future. "You have lacked the judgment to recognize that mistaken illegal doctrine that you have followed."

Despite his harsh words on polygamy, Judge Young stressed his primary concern was for other female Kingston family members, not necessarily society at large. "It's a very closed society that he lives in, and if he is out in the community…he is going to continue to engage in that lifestyle and continue to commit illegal acts." As David Ortell was led out of the courtroom in handcuffs, he mouthed the words "I love you" to Sharli and their five children.

While the defense expressed dismay at the verdict, Prosecutor Nolan felt the punishment fit the crime. "He chose to engage in this lifestyle, and he chose to engage in this conduct," Nolan said, who added that it was particularly just because, in light of the incest among the Kingstons, "if a child is conceived in that relationship, it faces a greater risk of being born with birth defects, mental retardation, et cetera."

Although Kingston would most likely get out of prison on parole before serving a full ten years, the sentence shocked the defense lawyers—as well as members of Tapestry Against Polygamy. "We're surprised. We didn't expect it to be so strong, and we're happy about it," Carmen Thompson said. Rowenna Erickson added, "This is the first judge we have seen that has a real understanding of what polygamy is. I know they're shaking now," she said, referring to the Kingston clan. "Their whole structure is beginning to shake. It's like a low-level earthquake. I want an end to it and I see an end in sight. I do."

On Appeal

However, it seemed as if there would never be an end to the appeals filed on behalf of David Ortell. In late July, Todd Utzinger and Hakeem Ishola filed another motion for a new trial, again based on the polygamy inclusion. According to the papers filed, Kingston "was denied due process because his trial was tainted by numerous references to the irrelevant and prejudicial issue of defendant's alleged but unproven polygamous lifestyle. The issue of polygamy is so potentially inflammatory and so inherently prejudicial...that the jury should have been insulated from that issue entirely." The motion went on to say "despite the court's efforts to keep the jury untainted during the trial, the polygamy issue crept into defendant's trial in a most insidious manner." The new motion also argued that even if the court decides the references to polygamy during the trial didn't constitute a due process violation, "it should grant a new trial based on prosecutorial misconduct," and the defense counsel's failure to keep Kingston's "alleged polygamous lifestyle," out of the trial. "Almost from the very start of its opening argument, the state raised the specter of polygamy," the motion states. Moreover, "once it became clear that the issue of polygamy had made its way before the jury, trial counsel should have sought a mistrial instead of allowing the case to go to a tainted jury."

On a cold January 7, 2000, David Ortell was back in front of Judge Young hoping to be granted a new trial. During the hearing, against the advice of his lawyers, Kingston took the stand to testify, hoping to convince the judge his original defense attorneys had been incompetent. "I felt like the only hope I had for a fair trial was that we focus on the charges and focus on the discrepancies of those charges," Kingston recalled, saying he had asked McCaughey, "What if polygamy came up in the course of the trial? He told me that he would object strenuously."

At one point, Young asked Kingston point blank if he was a polygamist. Kingston insisted, "I am not." Then he added, "If the question is do I have children from other ladies, the answer is yes."

Steven McCaughey and Susanne Gustin-Furgis both took the stand and testified they felt it was necessary to bring some aspects of polygamy into the case in order to show the girl's motives for trying to leave the Kingston clan. "You have to explain the background," Gustin-Furgis said. "The normal person would be saying, Why would this person be having sex with his niece? and polygamy explains that.

I think we were in agreement that polygamy was going to come into this trial. The question was how much."

Kingston told the judge that when the "alleged wedding" between he and Mary Ann was brought up during the trial, David Ortell says he thought his attorneys should ask for a mistrial but McCaughey didn't want to do that. He believed the all-male jury gave them their best chance for an acquittal. "In my judgment, there was no reason for a mistrial," he said. "We couldn't ask for a better jury."

McCaughey told the court he was happy with how the trial went and admitted he was so confident with their case that he considered not calling any witnesses once the state rested its case. But David Ortell insisted on presenting more evidence. However, he also said it was McCaughey's idea for his wife Sharli to testify. "I felt like she shouldn't come," Kingston recalled. "But he felt like she needed to come—so she did come." McCaughey admitted it had been a mistake because Sharli had come across as untruthful. "The only thing I'd do different was I wouldn't put Mr. Kingston's wife on the stand," the lawyer said.

In the end, Young said he still believed Kingston had received an adequate defense, despite the numerous polygamy references. "Be realistic about this; it seems to me there had to be some reference. There had to be, in this case, some facing of that fact by the defendant." He also said McCaughey and Gustin-Furgis had "carefully, adequately, and thoroughly represented" their client.

Although he again denied the motion, he did allow Kingston and his attorneys to file a written version of the discrepancies they say McCaughey and Gustin-Furgis did not bring out at trial, meaning the issue was far from over. "Technically, we're still before Judge Young," Utzinger said. Dane Nolan was prepared for more hearings. "Certainly there's going to be an appeal so it's not the end of the story today."

Beyond the Kingstons

The Kingston trials also gave impetus for charges of polygamy to appear in Utah courts. Tapestry Against Polygamy had their sights set on another notorious polygamist, Thomas Green, who had declared publicly he and his wives believed in plural marriage. Green had become a frequent guest on talk shows and news magazines promoting his lifestyle, declaring it was his religious right and presenting his family as being persecuted by narrow-minded individuals. His family includes wives Linda, LeeAnn, Hanna, Cari, and Shirley. Green's first wife divorced him after Thomas received his personal revelation that he should have more than one wife.

"I'm a different husband with each of them," says Tom. "Each one of them has different demands. I'm like oxygen, okay? I mean, for example, if Cari is hydrogen and we get together, then we become water." In musing about giving his bevy of young wives, all at least half Green's age, equal physical attention, he once commented in a *Men's Health* interview, "Never in all my adolescent fantasies did I dream of this."

For their part, the wives present a united front. "If I didn't have Tom, I'd be married to some yes-man," says LeeAnn. "I'd rather have a little of a real man than all of a jerk." Her sister-wife Shirley agrees. "None of us would want a man who is [pussy-whipped]."

However, the state of Utah was initially more concerned with finances than passion. In the summer of 1999, the Utah Office of Recovery Service filed five lawsuits in 4th District Court in Nephi to collect back child support Green owes his five wives. Since the women are legally single parents, the state has been providing assistance for them and their twenty-five children. Green retorted by saying the assistance wouldn't be necessary if he didn't have to spend so much time fighting anti-polygamy efforts and could devote more attention to his family business, which consisted of selling magazine subscriptions over the phone.

In some ways, the Green case had the potential for being more pivotal than the Kingston convictions had been, primarily because neither Kingston was charged with bigamy. Of course, the odds are Green would never had been charged had it not been for the Kingston case. It was as if the court of public opinion had slowly begun to tilt and the days of Utah's version of don't ask, don't tell were gone. But some believed that the Green case might be the one that could ultimately force the Supreme Court to weight in on the issue and decide if polygamy was a protected religious practice. In 1879, it ruled it was not, but Green and other polygamists thought the current court might be more sympathetic to their cause.

"It's a question that begs to be answered," says defense attorney Ken Brown of Salt Lake. "If it's not hurting anybody, it's not otherwise a crime, then aren't you being prosecuted for exercising your religious belief? That's a good test case and a good case to defend."

Even Prosecutor David O. Leavitt noted, "A court in 1999 or the year 2000 or whenever it gets there may look at it differently," Leavitt said. "There are potential First Amendment arguments and those should be raised."

But Green seems less inclined to believe the Supreme Court would reverse its former ruling, which is why he hedged against waging an all-out assault against Utah's bigamy law. "I don't mind going to jail for my beliefs," he said. "But why start out on a journey if there's no hope of arriving at the destination? If I thought we could do it, I'd say, all right, let's do it."

Despite all the talk about First Amendment and freedom of religion issues, Carmen Thompson of Tapestry was resolute. "It is not a religious issue. The bottom line is it's against the law," she said. And that's the mantra Tapestry has been repeating to law enforcement agencies and prosecutors all over the state. While some authorities were starting to hum the same tune, others were more resistant. Prosecutors in Utah's urban counties say the bigamy statute is awash with constitutional problems. For one, it forbids cohabitation without defining it. Kay Bryson, Utah County attorney, says the law may be too vague, adding, "It just leaves too much discretion to the prosecutor or to law enforcement or to the judge and that brings to my mind whether or not it's constitutional."

It was those doubts Tom Green played on when he went on the talk shows. "We're not criminals. But we're guilty of obeying a commandment that's part of our religion. We're practicing civil disobedience concerning one specific law," he said, adding, "If some are guilty of other crimes, fine, prosecute them." Which is exactly what prosecutors did. And in June 2000, Tom Green was ordered to stand trial on charges of child rape and criminal non-support—based on Green's own television appearances on *Judge Judy, The Jerry Springer Show,* and *Dateline,* which were played in open court during the hearing.

Prosecutor Leavitt noted, "All I can say is that whenever someone confesses to commission of a felony on national television in my jurisdiction, I'm going to prosecute him." As it happens, Leavitt is the brother of Utah Governor Mike Leavitt.

Green, then fifty-one, was also charged with four counts of bigamy. However, the judge said he would render a written ruling on the bigamy charges at a later date because Green's attorney had filed a previous motion in May to separate the bigamy charges from the child support and rape charges. In the court papers, John Bucher argued that the various charges stem from different alleged criminal episodes which Utah law forbids combining because it could prejudice a jury if prosecuted together. The reasoning is that a jury hearing evidence of the rape may be more inclined to convict on the bigamy charges.

Leavitt disagreed. "It is my belief that child sex abuse, criminal non-support and bigamy are the triple crown of the practice of polygamy. Those who argue they are not, are wrong. In most cases, you don't discover the child sex abuse until you go after the bigamy."

In addition, attorney Bucher also asked Fourth District Court Judge Lynn W. Davis to compel Leavitt to provide details of his allegations, including the child rape victim's name and the date and place where Leavitt believes the crime took place.

Despite the ambitious scope of the prosecution, the Green case clearly demonstrated the difficulty in prosecuting bigamy as the law is currently written—especially without any current or former wives willing to testify. Winning a conviction under Utah's bigamy law—which, specifically, is the act of marrying one person while still being married to another—requires evidence of at least one legal marriage.

In Green's case, he had carefully staggered his court-sanctioned marriages so that he officially has been married and divorced from three of his current wives, and unofficially wed the other two, meaning there was no marriage license obtained from the state. "Legally, I'm single and available," Green has noted. Leavitt had to convince the court that at least one of Green's unions as an ongoing legal marriage, despite the fact he is either divorced from or has never been legally married to each of his partners.

It was an uphill battle. In March 2000, Leavitt had tried to establish that Green had married Linda Kunz in 1986 when Kunz was just fourteen years old. Although they divorced in 1989, Leavitt maintained in court papers that the two continued to live as husband and wife and "each has cohabitated with the other...in the sharing of a common abode that each party considers his or her principal domicile...that they have participated in a relatively permanent sexual relationship akin to that generally existing between husband and wife." However, the court declined to address the issue then, citing the lack of pending charges. But now that Green had been ordered to stand trial on the other charges, the judge could no longer duck the issue.

At the preliminary hearing in June, Green was accompanied by his four wives. One of them, Linda, told the media, "We want our family to stay together." Green went on to tell reporters, "I don't think I'm going to be convicted of anything. The only thing I'm guilty of is building a family." It was obvious Green was starting to feel the pressure, much of it supplied directly or indirectly by Tapestry. But the group's advocacy was beginning to rankle many polygamists, particularly Green. So in early June 2000, the Greens sued the group for defamation for contending he used the guise of Jesus Christ and God to seduce young women. He said they labeled his wives as junior high dropouts and claimed Carmen Thompson, Tapestry, and its attorney lied when they suggested on television news programs the Green family is incestuous and abusive. In return, Green and his wives are seeking about $60,000 in damages, which, if victorious, will be used to start up a polygamists' legal defense fund.

"They have crossed the line of being a help group to being a hate group," Green said. He also called the members of Tapestry bitter, revengeful "loose cannons" that exaggerate facts and know nothing about his family. "Anyone who takes time to get to know my family will disagree with their stance," he said.

Green particularly took umbrage to the notion women in plural marriages and their children are trapped and need to be rescued.

"Where are these people who are clamoring to get out of plural marriage? I don't see them," he said. Two of his wives, Linda Kunz Green and LeeAnn Beagley Green, claim that they live with Green by choice. Both also were married to him when they were fourteen. "This is who we are. This is what we want," LeeAnn said. But, Green says, just because plural marriage is his lifestyle doesn't mean he's foisting it on his children, the way the Kingstons do. He gave examples of how several of his children have chosen to live traditional lifestyles. "It's not like we're brainwashing our children to follow in our footsteps or else," he said.

While Green remained free on a $150,000 property bond for his Juab County homestead, called Greenhaven, the lines of public opinion were being drawn. In an article published in the *Salt Lake Tribune*, John R. Llewellyn observed:

> Right or wrong, fact or myth, whether we like it or not, the Mormon fundamentalist religious movement has evolved into a bonafide subculture with its own literature, heroes, symbols and communities. Why? Because the practice of plural marriage has been allowed to grow and flourish in Utah for nearly fifty years with impunity. Since the fiasco of 1953, when Colorado City was raided, politicians, lawmakers, law enforcement and religious leaders have turned a blind eye, tantamount to sweeping polygamy under the rug...
>
> Polygamy in Utah is a mess and disgrace with no realistic solutions. The Utah Legislature turned down two bills asking for money to combat polygamy. Practicing polygamists are safe in one county but not in another.
>
> Rep. David Zolman, whom some polygamists see as a modern Moses who will eventually deliver them from political bondage, made it out of the Republican Convention unopposed, in spite of his public defense of the polygamist lifestyle. What kind of messages are these events sending to the nation?

It seemed that as more people looked into the issue of plural marriage, the polygamy subculture was made up of two distinct groups—

the independents and what some have called "the cults." In Utah, the majority of polygamists belong to one of three clans—the Kingstons, Rulon Jeffs's Colorado City–based Fundamentalist Church of Jesus Christ of Latter-Day Saints, and the Apostolic United Brethren group led by Owen Allred. As Llewellyn points out, "Ethos, unification and momentum in these three groups, as oppressive as they may be, are so strong that it is doubtful that they will ever be eliminated short of 'ethnic cleansing.'" The tacit inference is that because of the political clout, wealth, and sheer numbers of people in these organized polygamist clans, authorities will remain essentially helpless to make a dent into their practices. Both Allred and Jeffs literally run incorporated polygamist cities, by which they oversee the school systems in those cities, control all the land the people live on, and are able to indoctrinate their children, particularly girls, to be subservient from young ages with no outside influences to the contrary.

In July 2000, Warren Jeffs told "the Priesthood people" to separate themselves from "the apostates" around them. The most obvious result of this order was seen in the classroom when attendance at local schools dropped by 75 percent, as the clan began educating nearly one thousand children at home. Church elder Daniel Barlow, who is also the mayor of Colorado City, says the reason for the pullout was simple. "The public schools won't let us teach about our heritage."

Others have different opinions. "If they send their kids to school, then people ask questions" about their lifestyle, says Carol Lear, a lawyer for the Utah Office of Education. Roz McGee, head of the policy group Utah Children, adds, "Some of these clans are so patriarchal, so closed, that it's difficult to get state agencies to respond." One case that authorities were looking into involved a mother named Lenore Holm who claims that Jeffs's church officials ordered her to leave her home—located on church property—after she complained about a celestial marriage they had arranged for her sixteen-year-old daughter. Rod Parker, an attorney for Jeffs's church, denied the story.

However, the independents, like Green, tend to just live by their own creed and do not claim to have priesthood authority over anyone. In fact, polygamists like Green are actually scorned by the clans, precisely because they won't acknowledge the authority of these other self-appointed prophets. Although it is the clans that represent a much greater danger to their adherents, it will be the independents like Green who will be much easier targets for prosecution.

It is this dichotomy and inequity that makes some people hesitant to affect a concentrated effort against polygamy. It was to those people Green appealed when he put together a twenty-page memo to County Attorney David Leavitt, in which he explained why prosecuting him would be a legal and political mistake. "I am not afraid to go to jail or prison for my religious beliefs. To do so would be to follow in the footsteps of some noble men. It would be an inconvenience for my family, though," Green wrote in the memo. He urged for authorities to legalize plural marriage and encouraged them to prosecute physical and sexual abusers in any group, including polygamists. However, he said that labeling all polygamists as participating in incest or being abusers and molesters was comparable to cultural genocide. "I don't know of any polygamist who thinks crime and victim crime should be covered up," Green said.

Soon, it seemed everyone would be weighing in with an opinion. But the issue of polygamy had grown far beyond the revelation first presented by Joseph Smith. As John Llewelyn of the *Salt Lake Tribune* noted, "You can't combat the practice of Mormon fundamentalism unless you understand its purposes, motives, economics and political agendas in context to the frustrations and needs of adherents.

"Maybe that's why polygamy has grown to be a giant, out-of-control tar baby."

Chapter Eleven
A NEW AWARENESS

Now that Utah's long-held little secret had been dragged into the national spotlight, proponents on both sides were left to wonder, What now? Was the conviction of David Kingston an expression of a new public mandate or simply the outcome of an extraordinary case brought by an extraordinary young woman? While everyone seemed to agree that incest and blatant sexual abuse should be prosecuted, there was no consensus of whether polygamy itself should be the object of unsolicited legal action. In fact, some anthropologists believed it should be studied, not prosecuted. But most people's view was colored not by academia but by ethics.

"If a proper case is put together and presented to me, we'll prosecute it," Salt Lake District Attorney David Yocom said shortly after the Kingston convictions. That said, Yocom also indicated he has no plans to seek out prosecutions because "we've got rape, robbery, and murder," to go after. Then he added, "However, if the Legislature said, 'Here's some money designated for the purpose, we could put together some damn good cases.' Then you've got to ask society, do you really want to spend the money?"

Although the resistance to prosecuting polygamists was still strong, Carmen Thompson believes the zeitgeist is changing and that politicians are slowly becoming more amenable to taking a stand.

"We've never done anything like this before," Thompson said. "We're breaking new ground by prosecuting crimes within polygamy, as well as polygamy itself." Thompson reminds people that the issue goes far beyond two adults involved in an alternative lifestyle. "When children are involved, it is no longer just about two adults having consensual sex. I've seen the effects of children growing up in polygamy. It's difficult for them to understand there are laws they have to obey; that you can't just pick and choose. That you have to obey man's laws, not just God's laws."

Tapestry Against Polygamy wants to create a task force to address crimes committed against women and children living in polygamous situations. And Thompson says, "Meanwhile, we have gone down into the trenches. We are handling things case by case, as they are brought to our attention. Whether by a victim or a public outcry, we contact prosecutors and push for prosecution."

Others, however, say that if you prosecute polygamy, then other alternative lifestyles might be put under equal legal scrutiny. Or, as the Women's Religious Liberties Union states, if polygamists are prosecuted, the state better prosecute "fornicators, adulterers, homosexuals, sodomizers, unwed mothers and those who perform acts of bestiality." Beyond that, how to prove the crime of bigamy remained the key issue.

But opponents of polygamy were frustrated that authorities were not pursuing at least incest charges against several members of the Kingstons. In his trial, it was revealed that John Daniel and his wife Susan—Mary Ann's parents—were half-brother and sister who had ten children together. It was also known that David Ortell was married to at least two other nieces besides Mary Ann. And the Church of Christ leader, Paul Kingston, was also married to a half-sister. The *Salt Lake Tribune* challenged prosecutors, printing an article in which it was pointed out that according to their marriage certificate, the former auditor for the Utah State Auditor, Jason Kingston, was married to his niece, Rosalind. In addition, the paper also listed Jesse Kingston, Paul Kingston's brother, as having married his half-sister, Janice Vesta Johnson, in a civil wedding in Elko, Nevada.

In addition to the existing documentation already on file, opponents of polygamy say that other evidence, such as DNA, should be enough to prosecute for incest. But Lake District Attorney David Yocom is hesitant, saying he would prefer "a real, live victim to take to court." Without that, he feels, "We'd be venturing into awfully new ground."

Legal waffling aside, the biggest obstacle to stopping the crimes associated with plural marriage are more emotional in nature than legal. Just as rape victims carry an innate shame at having been assaulted, it was hard for women in polygamy to publicly acknowledge that a close relative had sexually molested them or married them against their will because doing so reflected badly on the woman herself. People might ask, how could she let that happen?

Beyond that, it wasn't strangers doing the molesting or marrying; it was family, which added another layer of guilt. Then tack on the fact that families are left even worse off financially than they already are should a man with many wives and scores of children be sent to jail. And as anyone who worked with abused children knows, the biggest conflict comes because usually, no matter what horror has been committed against a child, that child still tends to love the parent. Cap all of the emotions involved with the belief that even if they did come forward, law enforcement would turn a blind eye, and it's easy to see why the practice had been able to flourish unabated for the last half century—until Mary Ann Kingston stepped out of the shadows.

In the end, even though neither John Daniel nor David Ortell was convicted of being polygamists, the mere fact that they were convicted of something would prove to be the most important legacy of the trial. Charles Castle of NOW says, "This decision will bring a flood of women out of these groups that have just been hedging because they thought these people would get a slap on the wrist and would be back to assault and beat them."

Even though a new dawn was breaking for women who wanted out of plural marriages and for their children, it was clear the political lines being drawn were still hazy. The reticence of most politicians to condemn polygamy was made clear by Utah Governor Mike Leavitt in a July 23, 1998, news conference, when he indicated he believed polygamy might qualify for freedom of religion protection under the U.S. Constitution. "These people have religious freedoms," the governor told reporters, adding that most of the polygamists he knew growing up were "for the most part hard-working, good people." He also noted, "This does not define our state. It is part of our history that endures." He also acknowledged the plural marriages in his own family tree.

The impromptu comment created a firestorm of controversy. The fact that Leavitt's own family once practiced polygamy, and that critics already referred to him as the "Governor from LDS" for his open embrace of Mormon values, set off a warning bell within the anti-polygamy camp.

Within days of the governor's remarks, Tapestry Against Polygamy sent the following letter to the governor and to news organizations. Dated, July 27, 1998, the letter read:

Dear Governor Leavitt,

We as refugees of polygamy, come to you with grieving hearts. We now realize that polygamy is a titanic in disguise, poorly crafted for the interest of greed and power. When we finally had the courage to leave our abusive relationships behind and jump overboard to safety, no one was there to catch us. And as we drifted afloat, in confusion and despair, no one was there to lend us a hand. Others who were safe saw us, but they closed their eyes pretending we did not exist. In our innocence we believed this journey to be right, we followed our patriarchs.

Governor Leavitt, we know you did not design this craft, but we know you have within your hands the power given to you by the people of this great state of Utah, to alter this course. When you took office you swore an oath to uphold the state's constitution and the laws of the land. While the laws say polygamy is illegal, you have been quoted as saying, "...we have a long history of dealing with it," We, along with many women and children, believe that the state has a long history of NOT dealing with it.

When you indicate that polygamy may infringe on freedom of religious expression we wonder at whose cost, the polygamist or the children?

Our Governor is elected by the people to represent society, keep order, and to ensure our best interests. How can we feel comfortable re-electing a Governor who does not have an opinion concerning actions which are against the law?

Polygamy is against the law, abuse is against the law, and incest is against the law. We don't believe our Founding Fathers would ever have wanted abuse to be protected behind religious freedom.

Governor Leavitt, we petition you to enforce the laws of polygamy until, if at such a time, they are repealed. If at such time, the people decide that this lifestyle legalized then laws should be established to prevent any abuses. Right now is not the time to consider future legislation or policies, but to enforce the laws that currently exist. You have publicly implied that you have no intentions of enforcing anti-polygamy and bigamy laws, which is contrary to the obligations of your office. In the eyes of the honest, law-abiding citizens of Utah this is deplorable. We demand action.

Governor Leavitt, we must be assured those women and children exiting polygamy have their temporal needs met. Their physical, mental, and emotional health is vital to their productive membership in today's society. These needs are not being met. We, as the membership of Tapestry Against Polygamy will not be satisfied until all these human rights are guaranteed. The state of Utah has consciously turned a blind eye to some of the most vulnerable victimized sector of our society. Which has resulted in physical, mental, and sexual abuse. Too often when these women and children leave, mere survival forces them to return to their abusers. They become powerless within the court system. We demand action.

You swore an oath when taking office as Governor to uphold the constitution of the State of Utah and laws of the land. The time to take action is now.

Board of Directors & Supporters of Tapestry of Polygamy

Hoping to avoid a major public relations nightmare, Vicki Varela, the governor's spokeswoman, made it clear her boss took polygamy seriously. However, she also defended his position pointing out that he was the wrong person to attack. "He can't answer why it isn't prosecuted. He's not a prosecutor," she said, adding, "Polygamy is against the law. Everyone knows that. Whether the question of religious freedom is part of the discussions with local law enforcement officers is something they have to address."

But Governor Leavitt was prompted into calling another press conference to clarify his stand in person when he learned the then-new pro-polygamy group had thanked him, as did Carol Gnade, executive director for Utah's American Civil Liberties Union, for what they perceived as support of the polygamy cause. The timing couldn't have been better for Mary Potter's Women's Religious Liberties Union, which held its first meeting a few days after the governor's remarks, especially since the group's goal was clearly political—repeal the state law banning polygamy. According to Potter, legalizing the principle would eliminate the need for clans to be secretive, saying it was the bigamy law that "causes people to go underground. And I believe if we bring people out, that would bring more opportunity for the young. And people have been oppressed and repressed in this state because of that law."

Carmen Thompson of Tapestry Against Polygamy again pointed out that the clans are isolated because that's what keeps the women subservient and pliable. "We're concerned that if it is legalized, or if it is decriminalized, it will make no difference on the polygamous communities. We believe that they pretty much are practicing outside of the law as it is, and if there was a law enforced, it would make no difference to them."

At his news conference, Governor Leavitt assured voters he wasn't going to support such an agenda. "Polygamy is prohibited by the Utah Constitution. It is against the law and it should be....I think this can be used as an opportunity to make it clear: Whenever there's any kind of abuse...we should aggressively respond." He also stressed that the attorney general had given the issue a new priority.

Now with the ball in her court, Utah Attorney General Jan Graham acknowledged her office would educate prosecutors and law enforcement on the unique problems of victims within the polygamy clans. "Crimes within the polygamist community can and must be prosecuted," Graham wrote in a statement released to the media.

"The claim of religious freedom is no defense to the crimes of statutory rape, incest, unlawful sexual conduct with a minor, child abuse or cohabitant abuse.

"We have shown with domestic violence that secrecy, denial and fear can be dealt with to enable victims of physical, sexual and emotional abuse to get to safety and to ensure that abusers are punished. The approach to women and children who are trapped within polygamy should be the same."

It seemed as if Governor Leavitt couldn't stress enough that his previous comments in no way indicated he supported individuals who broke the law. "I just want to assure that the position of the state is clear," he said, denying he was in any way aligned with any group that wanted the state to legalize polygamy. "I do not support that," Leavitt said. "Those who would advocate changing the law simply because they go forward and we don't enforce them....I don't think that's the right solution either. There is a teaching ethic to the law. There is a community standard establishment of the law. I think that's an important reason to keep those in place."

He also did a mea cupla when admitting, "I'd like to make an important point; I learned this week that the First Amendment guarantee of religious freedom is not among the reasons prosecutors do not prosecute. Although the recent furor over polygamy has been unpleasant, the recent discussion has a positive consequence if it focuses attention on a lifestyle where abuses too easily can be shrouded in silence and secrecy."

Now that the topic was being openly discussed, the Governor found himself answering even more questions:

> There are people who practice it for reasons they believe are religiously significant to them. This has been a long-standing legal debate, not just in Utah but in the United States. If there are abuses of human rights, if there are civil liberties that are being abused, and we need to follow up on this, that would be very important and I think that's done. I would call on local prosecutors if anyone is being abused, domestically or otherwise or if their human rights are being

violated or their civil rights, they need to act aggressively. Period.

However, Leavitt refused to directly comment on the lifestyle itself or officially urge prosecutors to directly crack down on the practice. "I've talked to federal prosecutors. It's clear to me they don't intend to change their practices. As I have talked to state prosecutors...and local prosecutors, they have told me the same thing. That is their priority for the reasons I have already enumerated. I do not expect that will change."

At the time of this press conference, the Kingston cases were fresh in everyone's mind, especially the irony of John Daniel being represented by his cousin, who is a member of the clan. So Leavitt was quizzed about the practice of appointing practicing polygamists to state positions in government and having lawyers practicing law who are known polygamists. The governor then passed the issue to the state bar. "I know the bar is going to undertake that discussion, and I'll leave that one to them. I suspect there are people that live lifestyles that I might not agree with that I've appointed to places and that have been appointed in other states. I have not seen that as the sole criteria for those appointments."

However, when pressed about whether polygamy should be considered a factor in appointing an individual to state office, Leavitt clarified his stance. "No, I'm not saying that. I'm not saying that. I recognize that there may have been one or two people who practice this. I have not made it a criteria for my appointment. I do not know whether they are or whether they aren't. If you ask them, they'll tell you they're not. And for the same reasons it's difficult to prosecute these cases, it's difficult for governors to know whether they are or they aren't either." In other words, "It's a policy that sometimes you just don't know."

In the end, the governor seemed philosophical about being both a product of familial polygamy and now being in a position of having to, at least officially, denounce it. Leavitt said, "I am among thousands of other Utahans who have somewhere in their heritage multiple families. That has nothing to do with my life today. There is no place for it in modern society, and therefore all I can do is delineate what I think is right today."

On the heels of Leavitt's scrutiny by the media, the *Salt Lake Tribune* published a series of articles on modern polygamy, in which it wrote that some of the more prominent communities of polygamists collect more welfare than anybody else in the inner-mountain west.

Howard Berkes of the NPR program *All Things Considered* noted that the issue of polygamy might have a long-term effect on Leavitt's professional life. "I'm not sure that this is necessarily a big political problem for the governor within the state," he said in a report. "It may be more of a perception problem for the governor outside the state as some consider whether he's suitable for, you know, national political office perhaps, and it only draws more attention to an uncomfortable part of Utah's past for the state and for the leaders of the Mormon Church."

Almost as an afterthought, Berkes added, "Utah will be host to the Winter Olympics in the year 2002 and you know, reporters will be paying more attention to Utah as the Winter Olympics of 2002 approach."

Politics and Public Opinion

Not only would the media be more attuned to what was happening in Utah, but there seemed to be a political ripple effect occurring as well. As anti-polygamy advocates grew more vocal, proponents of the practice raised their voices, too—much to the chagrin of the Mormon Church. During 1998, several Church leaders spoke out publicly on polygamy. LDS President Gordon B. Hinckley said, "I wish to state categorically that this Church has nothing whatever to do with those practicing polygamy. They are not members of the Church. Most of them have never been members. They are in violation of the civil law."

In a case of political déjà vu, legislators in Washington D.C. were again wrestling with religious issues that could have an impact of polygamy. The Religious Liberty Protection Act was receiving a lot of Beltway attention and similar legislation—often called Religious Freedom Protections acts—was being proposed in a number of state capitals as well. Because the practice of polygamy was being defended beneath the umbrella of religious freedom, there was a distinct possibility that the issue of plural marriage could become a point of contention if any of the measures became law.

The Religious Liberty Protection Act, RLPA, states that the government must show a "compelling interest" before placing any "burden" on religious groups or practice. What worried many about these measures is the potential for chaos and abuse. Under the guise of RLPA, practices from forced female circumcision to animal sacrifice could be protected under the "religious exercise" umbrella. In addition, certain groups could contend drug use was part of their religion and claim immunity from prosecution. Polygamists most certainly would argue that certain practices currently viewed as abusive are their protected right under the First Amendment. Other critics point out that if the measure passed, the courts would be inundated with litigation related to RLPA.

Ellen Johnson, President of American Atheists, notes, "It creates a double standard in the application of law and justice. RLPA is not about guaranteeing legitimate rights for everyone—it says that certain activities can be practiced by religious believers, churches and faith-based groups, while the rest of society cannot have these privileges." To Johnson, it was a dangerously slippery slope. "Where would it end? What if a Muslim sect wanted an exemption from the bigamy laws? All that any bigamist would have to do is declare him or herself a believer."

Of course, the real issue for women like Rowenna Erickson is that the whole culture of polygamy, the mind-set of religious-based patriarchies, is set up to oppress women and deprive them of basic civil rights. Another Tapestry activist, Vicki Prunty, says polygamy leaves women brainwashed and subservient. "I believe people should be allowed to believe whatever they want but not practice whatever they want," she says. "There's a difference between religious freedom and religious abuse."

Although for many years polygamy was viewed by outsiders as simply an odd and perhaps even old-fashioned way of life that injured no one, the point anti-polygamy advocates were trying to make is that the practice of plural marriage is rife with victims—even if the victims themselves couldn't or wouldn't acknowledge it. To some, polygamy clans had much more in common with mind-bending cults than mainstream religion. Most of the women involved in the polygamist lifestyle have never known anything different. They have been conditioned through isolation to be obedient and denied the education necessary to make an informed choice about how to live their lives. Some, like Mary Ann Kingston, have a stronger sense of self and unusual courage to break free, but most do not.

Public opinion was divided with a majority holding the view that "if they're not bothering anyone and no one is getting hurt, leave them alone," while others felt the polygamous environment inherently subjugated women. The *Herald-Journal* newspaper of Logan, Utah, interviewed six randomly picked residents and asked their opinion on the issue. Arlene Cooper of Wellsville was emphatic. "I don't think women and children feel like they can speak out for what they really want." Herself a practicing Mormon, Cooper was bothered with the way polygamists used the previous acceptance of the principle by the Latter-Day Saints as justification for their current lifestyle of promoting illegal marriages. "Maybe it was all right at that time, but it is different now and it should be treated different now," she said, her reasoning largely pragmatic. "If you were married to twelve women, how could you possible be a good father to that many children? Do you think they even know who their own children are?"

Despite his public atonement, not everyone was appeased by the governor's comments. Leavitt's perceived about-face infuriated those who supported the practice of plural marriage. Sale Lake attorney Scott Berry, who has represented polygamists' interests in Colorado City, Arizona and Hildale, Utah, noted, "The ceiling fell in and in no short order it was explained to him (Leavitt) that religious liberty doesn't apply to fundamentalist Mormons and he's more or less backing up as fast as he can ever since. Religious freedom extends to everybody from Native Americans to Hare Krishnas," Berry said. "But fundamentalist Mormons don't get it."

Berry went on to say that prior to the Kingston case, his advice to his clients was, "You've got nothing to be ashamed of with your religion. I think the world has changed. You can identify yourselves as organizing your family according to this principle without fear of legal retribution." However, as the rhetoric on both sides of the issue grew more heated, he now says, "I'm not sure that is the case anymore."

Then-Republican State Representative David Zolman, who had been vocal on numerous occasions in defense of polygamists, went on record saying, "They are a political reality. We need to make a place for them. They live in America, America guarantees liberties to all comers and it must apply to people who feel committed to have more than one marriage choice." Zolman, a professional genealogist, who was narrowly defeated in the November 2000 election, believes his efforts on behalf of polygamists cost him his House seat.

"Some of you warned me, 'Do this at your political peril.' You were right. Please forgive me if I have offended you in this impossible dream. I appreciate your patience and understanding. I feel less pain at being rejected at the polls than I do being silent against prejudice over a century old."

Even if others had been more politically prudent and not spoken up, apparently Zolman wasn't alone in his feelings. During the 1999 state legislative session, there was very little discussion among elected Utah officials about a topic that was generating national headlines, although there were two proposals that were indirectly related to polygamy. One was to raise the minimum marriage age to sixteen years old, although Rep. Carl Saunders went out of his way to make clear his bill was not at all directed at polygamists. "It had nothing to do with that. I don't want it associated with polygamy at all," he said. The other bill proposed allocating $750,000 to train prosecutors and fund investigations of incest, sexual abuse of minors, welfare and tax fraud, and failure to pay child support. The bill's sponsor, Democratic Sen. Ron Allen, said the bill would pay for itself if after just forty prosecutions because of the money saved from fraudulent claims. "The money's going to come back to us," Allen said. "And in terms of human rights violations, we can't put a dollar figure on this."

While many of the state's polygamists wondered when the other legal shoe would drop, some went on the offensive. Owen Allred, leader of the Apostolic United Brethren, told the *Salt Lake Tribune*,

"We believe in free agency. If my daughter doesn't want to stay in the group, she has free will. She has the right to do what she chooses." Allred would say on another occasion that because plural marriage was such a difficult undertaking, eighty percent of his congregation in fact chose monogamy. "It takes twice as good a man to have two wives as it does to have one. If you have three wives, it takes five times as good a man to do it, if you are going to have harmony in your family."

The church leader went on to say that the Apostolic United Brethren was considering making proof of financial and moral responsibility mandatory before entering into plural marriage. "Oh, they're not going to like it, not one bit," Allred admitted. "But what too many of them don't understand is this: There are more men damned for trying to live celestial marriage than there will ever be saved." Allred would later add, "Most of the world feels that plural marriage is just so man can have more sex. And I hate to admit it; too many men marry for that purpose. Then when they have a family, they don't take care of it."

Convicted polygamist Tom Green appeared on NPR's *Talk of the Nation* to state his side of the issue. "I was raised a mainstream monogamous Mormon," he told host Lynn Neary. "But in my study of history I discovered that the concept of plural marriage was a key element to my theology. My great-grandfathers went to Canada a hundred years ago to keep from going to prison in Utah, but my mother's mother taught her that it was a wicked practice, and so I had to rediscover my roots in studying Utah history and I had to make a determination for myself as to whether or not I was going to cling to my theology in its original form or be satisfied with the modern form or chuck it altogether, and my convictions brought me back to my original Mormon roots."

Green's wife Linda, who comes from a polygamist family, spoke of their relationship. "I married Tom when I was fourteen years old. He was a friend of the family and we met each other through friends, and I fell very much in love with him and I've been with him ever since. I'm twenty-eight now. We have six children together. And we've built a very successful relationship together."

Green, though, is careful to highlight that even though he considers the five women he lives with his wives, it's in the spiritual sense, not the legal sense. "It's polygamy, not bigamy. Bigamy is a crime, the criminal elements of which are fraud and deceit—fraud upon the state by claiming to get a marriage license when you're not eligible for one, and deceit by deceiving your partners into thinking they're the only spouse. Neither one of those things has happened in my situation."

Tom Green and the Legal Fight against Polygamy

In the end, Green's attempts to skirt the law through religious freedom by appealing to the public failed. In fact, it's quite likely his high-profile is what ultimately brought the legals powers that be to bear down on him. As Juab County's Prosecutor David Leavitt told Howard Berkes of NPR, "Why Tom Green? Because he confessed to a felony on national television, basically, that's why. If Tom Green would have laid low and kept to himself, I wouldn't have known that he existed. You do your crime in public you're more likely to get caught."

Green himself seemed to understand his plan had backfired. "I think there's been an unwritten understanding in Utah that if you want to be a polygamist and raise a plural family like our ancestors all did, like the founders of Utah did, we'll look the other way as long as you just hide in the closet and shut up and don't let anybody know you're here," he said. "But as soon as you talk to the media and start to defend your beliefs to the public, then we're going to nail you for embarrassing the rest of us."

Despite their common religious ancestry, the lines were clearly drawn between Green and David Leavitt when jury selection began for his trial, and the stakes for each side were clear.

"We'd like to defend the case on the idea of religious freedom and on the idea that the bigamy statute doesn't apply," stated Green's attorney, John Bewer, who added that his client was "really quite interested in establishing that now may be the time for the government, and for the people, to allow an exercise of religion such as this. Then if it's a legitimate exercise of religion and can be shown to be that, isn't there room in this country for this particular practice?"

On the prosecution side, it was a matter of a man breaking the law and flaunting it. A man with five wives, at least three of whom they believed he had married when they were legal minors between the ages of thirteen and fifteen, who together had produced twenty-five children, most of whom were on state assistance. Green was also charged with criminal non-support and child rape, although the rape charge would be prosecuted in a separate trial that had yet to be scheduled.

Held in Provo, Utah, the prosecution of Green became the first modern showdown between the State and polygamy—sort of. Again, Utah doesn't specifically have laws on the books again polygamy, only the harder to prove bigamy, which Green hoped would be his best defense.

"Polygamy is not bigamy," he pointed out during jury selection. "Bigamy includes fraud on the government when you go and try to get another marriage license when you already have one enforced, and deceit, where you deceive your spouse into believing they're the only one. Polygamy doesn't do that."

For years, Green had believed that because he had been careful to legally divorce each wife before marrying another, that he was in the clear of the bigamy charges. However, after almost a year of studying the case, prosecutor David Leavitt eventually figured out how to overcome that obstacle by applying a common-law marriage statute aimed at welfare cheats. He found a judge who agreed and declared Green legally married under the common law to one wife, even though they were legally divorced. Simply stated, the Utah law defines common-law marriage as two people living together, assuming marital rights and duties and holding themselves out as married. After that key victory, the trial was next, where the state would try to prove that Green was tacitly married to his other wives as well.

Once Leavitt had his legal foundation, it was simply a matter of presenting the evidence, much of which, ironically, had been supplied by Green himself during his frequent television appearances.

Even though Leavitt believed he was on solid legal ground, it still wasn't clear how a jury would decide the case. The prosecutor admitted to NPR's Berkes, "I have had concern for a great deal of time whether we will be able to find enough of a jury pool who either doesn't know about the Tom Green case or who don't have feelings about polygamy on one side of the fence or the other, which would render them impartial in their deliberation. Polygamy is not an issue which most people don't have an opinion on, and so that causes some concern."

Leavitt wasn't the only one worried about the jury pool. Green had his own concerns. In another irony, he worried about the jury being comprised of Mormons. Juab Country is home to one of the more orthodox Mormon communities in the state and Green felt the jurors might feel the need to publicly condemn him because they know polygamy is officially condemned by the Church.

However, when Green tried to suggest that polygamy has a proud Mormon history, Leavitt was ready with a tart response. "None of my ancestors took thirteen-year-olds to wife," he said. "None of my ancestors impregnated thirteen-year-old girls. The practice of polygamy in the nineteenth century is vastly different from the practice of polygamy engaged in by Tom Green." In any event, 4th District Judge Guy Burningham had decreed that religion could not be a defense in Green's criminal case, a ruling that the defendant objected to and felt hurt his case because freedom of religion was at the heart of the historical Mormon doctrine.

But during an evidentiary hearing in the chamber of Judge Burningham prior to the trial, it was clear this trial wasn't going to be forum on religion. Judge Burningham limited the testimony from two controversial authors, Ogden Kraut and D. Michael Quinn, that the defense wanted to call to the stand only to what advice they gave Green regarding plural marriage and nothing more than that. "I will not allow it to be a fundamentalist soap box," he said.

Judge Burningham also shot down the defense request to have Governor Leavitt called, which prompted Prosecutor Leavitt, his brother, to quip, "Cross-examining the governor does have some unique appeal to me."

Bucher's rationale for wanting to question not only the governor but former Salt Lake County Attorney David Yocom and former

Attorney General Paul Van Dam was to show that state leaders made statements assuring the public that polygamists would not be prosecuted. It was these statements, Bucher argued, that led Green to assume he would not be targeted by prosecutors. Again, Burningham was ruled against him. "Ignorance of what the law is, is still no defense."

In any event, Leavitt argued, although Green married and legally divorced each of his five wives, under Utah law, any marriage as the result of a "religious ceremony" could be considered a legal marriage, with or without a marriage license. In view of that, Green should have known that by "marrying" five women he was violating the law, Leavitt said.

Jury selection took place May 14, 2001. Because of concerns over pretrial publicity and the very controversial nature of the case, the number of prospective jurors, seventy, was double the usual amount. Each was asked about the news reports they might have seen and any opinions they may have formed. They were also asked whether they were members of any group that believes polygamy is wrong and, if yes, if that belief makes it difficult for them to be impartial.

Once the jury of five women and three men was seated, the prosecution began its case on a Tuesday. David Leavitt wasted no time using Green's own words against him, playing video clips of Green's various television appearances, including *The Jerry Springer Show, Dateline, Sally Jesse Raphael,* and *Queen Latifah,* during which he somewhat cheerfully admitted he participated in actions that state law deemed illegal, such as incest and bigamy.

In one such clip, Green responded by saying, "Unfortunately, the legal descriptions cover what is abhorrent in society and, at the same time, cover what I think is quite virtuous in our relationships."

The prosecutor spent significant time outlining the Green family tree, which included him marrying sisters, Hannah and Cari Bjorkman, one of his mothers-in-law, and a wife's cousin. Kunz Green, the self-described CEO of the wives, is the daughter of Beth Cook, Green's second wife. Two other current wives, Shirley and LeeAnn Beagley, are daughters of June Johnson, a former wife. Johnson is Cook's sister and lives next door to Green to be close to their four children. The marriages to girls aged thirteen, fifteen, and sixteen were also dissected.

"If you don't think that bigamy hurts people take a look at the marriage license of Linda Kunz," Leavitt said, showing the jury that Kunz was married to Green when she was thirteen, after a "courtship at a dinner table" while her mother Beth Cook, who also married Green, looked on and consented. While Utah law requires parental consent for such young marriages, the circumstances surrounding these unions shows its failings when seen in a polygamous context.

Likewise, Leavitt told the jury that in the case of Hannah Bjorkman, "Mom said 'yes' and Tom took her away and the rest is history," Leavitt said, reminding the jury that all of Green's wives were raised in polygamous families with the exception of Allison Ryan, who was "spiritually" married to Green for three weeks before leaving the family.

During a break in the proceedings, Green seemed agitated. "They presented excerpts from the tapes to try to put things in the worst possible light, to try to make me look like a predator of young women," he told a group of reporters. "What we're really about is about a family, not about some old guy preying upon young girls."

Linda Green was defiant. "We've never denied it. I mean, we've told it to the world. So the jury might as well hear it, too. We're proud of the fact that we consider ourselves a family and that we're married to our husband and that these are our children, and I'm not afraid to say that."

A major part of the prosecution's case was that Green's marry/divorce/cohabitate lifestyle was part of a scheme to fraudulently collect welfare. To that end, Leavitt called an investigator who specializes in crimes within closed societies to testify that Utah had paid $54,420 in child support to the Greens from August 1995 to June 1999. But as the prosecution's case continued, tempers began to flare. On Wednesday, May 17, Leavitt questioned two of Green's wives about the child welfare payments they received while living with him.

"What did you do with the food stamps?" Leavitt asked one of the wives, Shirley Beagley, who is the mother of six children.

She answered sharply, "To buy food. I wouldn't have applied for food stamps if I wouldn't have needed them to buy food."

Beagley was the focus of some unexpected courtroom drama when she tried to take the stand holding one of her children, who was severely handicapped. Leavitt reacted strongly, calling the maneuver a "cheap trick seeking sympathy," reminding the court that it had been predetermined that no children would be allowed in the courtroom.

But in the end, the case might have come down to her answer to Leavitt's question of whether or not she felt married to Green. "Yes," she said. "I entered into an eternal ceremony with Tom."

But a closer look into Green's idea of heavenly matrimony might give others pause. In 1988, LeeAnn Beagley, then thirteen, went to a juvenile court to complain that he had sexually molested her, a charge she withdrew when she married him two years later. In 1997, June Johnson alleged that he slapped her. Since his first wife died, four of Green's nine following wives have left him. Although Tom has repeatedly claimed sex is the least of his interests, during the 1990s, his wives would arrange conjugal visits when they were ovulating so that their children would be born around the same time. Those same-age groups are called teams A to F in the Green clan.

But to hear Green's current wives, and at least one ex-wife, speak, it was hearts and flowers. June Johnson claims that she had no qualms about her older daughter Shirley marrying Tom. She admits, "It was harder when LeeAnn married him. She was only fourteen and Tom and I tried really hard to get her *not* to marry him. But she was adamant. She was in love with him. How do you stop that?"

One way, prosecutors felt, was by putting Tom behind bars, and to do that they systematically presented his lifestyle to the jury. Among the witnesses they called included several of Green's children, associates, and current wives. After three days, it was the defense's turn, but their case really boiled down to one issue: would the jury believe Tom Green when he testified?

Speaking to the jury, Green explained that although he believed himself to be celestially married to his wives in the eyes of God, he did not believe himself legally married, and therefore not guilty of bigamy. "In the eyes of God I consider myself eternally married," he said, but added, "I consider myself legally single." In addition, while Green admitted he and his wives and their children lived together on the compound called Greenhaven, he added that because he lived in his own trailer, he therefore did not legally "cohabit" with the women.

Several times during his testimony, which began on Thursday, May 17, Tom Green broke down as he recounted the hardships his family had endured. He told the jury he had become a polygamist after studying "my history, the history of my family, the history of my faith, and the history of my state," then described how he and his family had been evicted from a mobile home park in Sandy in 1993 and lost a three-year-old in a trailer fire that destroyed their home in Utah's west desert.

After a second trailer was struck by a drunken driver, then destroyed in a wind storm, Green said he was forced to apply for approximately $54,420 in state dental, medical, food, heating, and living assistance. Throughout the hard times, Green testified he struggled to support his family by selling magazine subscriptions throughout the West and Midwest.

However, Green's testimony was contradicted by a surprise witness Leavitt called to the stand late Friday. Larry Beckwith, president of Allied Publishing in Fresno, California, was Green's boss. He told the jury Green had worked almost twelve years as a contract salesman. According to Green's 1999 tax statement, he earned $31,983, but according to Beckwith, Green did not earn that money. Out of the approximately 258 magazine subscriptions, Green was personally only responsible for nineteen—his wives sold many of the rest. Moreover, of those contracts, about 72 percent of them canceled within five months, meaning Green actually owed Allied Publishing over $27,000. When asked what it meant, Beckwith said dryly, "It means Allied Publishing really took a bath on that one."

The testimony severely tarnished the credibility of Green, who had testified that he was responsible for all of the money to support his family and that he worked as much as his conscience would allow. But according to the figures presented by the prosecution, for at least the year 1999, Tom Green was only responsible for 7.4 percent of the family income.

Earlier, Green had described his family as a "beehive" working together in his business to support the family, prompting Leavitt to remark, "I'm sure his family is like a beehive and that his wives are busy queen bees. The something he had to do is that he made them go out and get those contracts."

Deliberation in the case began Friday evening at 8:45 and it took the jury just three hours to reach a verdict. They found Tom Green guilty on all counts, which included four counts of bigamy and one count of criminal nonsupport.

Underscoring the emotional nature of the issues on trial was a report of threatened violence that had been made, which prompted court officials to delay identifying the eight jurors. Shortly after verdict was read, Jan Thompson, a spokeswoman for the Administrative Office of the Courts, announced the identities of the jurors would be withheld until the following Tuesday. Thompson told reporters a note that had been passed along to the judge three days into the trial threatened violence toward those involved in the trial. But Thompson declined to be specific as to the specific target of the threatened violence—whether it had been against the judge, jury, or prosecutors in the case.

Once the identities were finally made public, the jury selection questionnaires revealed that although none of the jurors claimed to be polygamists or even know anyone involved in plural marriage, three had polygamous ancestors and five were practicing Mormons. Because six of the eight jurors had lived in Utah at least twenty-five years, Tapestry attorney Douglas White saw the verdict as particularly significant. "There's a new generation of Utahans here. They've looked at us again and they've decided…that this is just not going to be tolerated anymore. People are tired of it."

Rowena Erickson agrees. "I think it's going to set a precedence in the future for the prosecution of polygamy and pave the way for more people to be prosecuted in polygamy."

Green and his family, however, remain defiant. "I think the leaders in Utah are the spineless, gutless ones who've turn their back on their own heritage, their own ancestors. And then they raise their children in a church that was started by immoral criminals who were polygamists. That's what's hypocritical to me." And despite facing up to twenty-five years in jail and a $25,000 fine at the June 27 sentencing hearing, Green put on a brave face. "There's been hundreds of good men in this state, who were the founding fathers of this state, who went to prison for the very same thing. It's an honor to go to prison for my beliefs, if I have to do that," he said, but added, "I hope I don't have to go to prison, though."

On Friday, August 24, Green was sentenced to up to five years in prison. He was also ordered to pay $78,868 in restitution to the state for welfare payments to his minor children.

The Fight to Illegalize Polygamy

Despite the successful prosecution of Green, it would seem the easiest solution in enforcing the intent of the bigamy statute would be to pass a law making polygamy illegal as well. The suggestion, however, was much too controversial for lawmakers to embrace. In January 2000, the Utah State House debated a proposed anti-polygamy law sponsored by Republican State Representative Ron Bigelow. The legislation would have provided the Utah Attorney General's office with $200,000 to fight crimes common among polygamous groups, including incest, sexual abuse, welfare and tax fraud, and failure to pay child support, as well as providing for a special prosecutor to fight these crimes. The House rejected the bill, claiming it singled out polygamists. Bigelow disagreed. "This is not about prosecuting polygamy."

The following month, State Senator Ron Allen reintroduced a bill that would give the state attorney general's office $500,000 to ferret out abuses and establish a telephone hotline and emergency shelter for women and children who sought to get out of polygamous families. Allen told *USA Today*, "I want all children to have a level playground on which to start their life. We are not going to stand by and let Utah take this black eye any longer."

One of the bill's supporters was Owen Allred, who seemed to be taking the tack that in order to save plural marriage, he had to acknowledge its ills. So he joined in a call for the state to investigate the clans, including his, "We've got some stinking problems....It is against the rules of our religion entirely to have intercourse with a woman who is not your wife. But, my gosh, there are so many of our people who will have intercourse with anyone. And even we've had problems with men being cruel to their wives and cruel to their children."

In 1999, Allen's bill died during a budget feud between the State House and the Attorney General. However, because the Olympics were not far off, the Representative had higher hopes of the bill passing. In the end, the Legislature approved $75,000 to look into abuses within plural communities and the Attorney General hired an investigator to probe "closed societies" crimes.

And as more attention was focused on polygamy, the estimated number of active participants seemed to keep growing. Brett Hill, editor of *Loving More*, a magazine for people with multiple partners, notes, "This is the same thing that happened with the gay movement, where a lot of people were gay but you just didn't know about it."

Dave Hutchison, who organized a Phoenix-based group called Liberated Christians, adds, "You have a lot of Christians feeling this way, then feeling guilty they're feeling this way, so they come to us and see the biblical basis. And all of a sudden they become liberated."

Not surprisingly, the Internet has become a lifeline for people across the country seeking to take the step into plural marriages. At least one website offers polygamous personal ads, where couples of plural families look for sister-wives.

Regardless of how blatant some polygamous families were, by November 2000, it seemed as if Utah politicians tacitly agreed to back off the direct issue of polygamy, perhaps hoping to turn it into a non-existent issue before the 2002 Winter Olympics swept into the state. The three candidates for Attorney General—Democrat Reed Richards, Republican Mark Shurtleff, and Libertarian Andrew McCullough—all agreed Utah's money was better spent elsewhere, although they stressed cracking down on domestic and child abuse and welfare fraud should be a prosecutorial priority. "I do not intend to have that office to become the prosecutor of bigamy across the state," Shurtleff, a Salt Lake County commissioner, said prior to the election. "There's a lot of other things that we're going after that are priorities."

Richards believed for the most part that prosecution of crimes related to polygamy should be left to local officials to prosecute, except in certain cases, such as that of Arvin Shreeve, leader of the Zion Society. In that 1992 case, the attorney general's earned convictions against Shreeve and several family members for ritualistic child abuse. Part of the evidence presented was videotape footage of underage women whom he forced to engage in sex acts with one another. McCullough, on the other hand, believed the state had no business interfering. "I don't see any point whatsoever in interfering with someone's religious beliefs." In the end, Shurtleff defeated Richards by a wide margin and in his victory speech, said he wanted to "reach out to ethnic groups, religious groups, communities…and bring everyone together."

The outgoing attorney general, Jan Graham, would admit that at no point in her career as attorney general could she say "we have done enough to help people in the polygamous community. The claim of religious freedom is no defense to the crimes of statutory rape, incest, unlawful sexual conduct with a minor, child abuse or cohabitant abuse." But then she added, "We have made great progress in terms of reporting abuse within these communities, making victims feel like they have the right to report abuse. We have made more progress in the past year than I ever thought we would make in ten years. So we're greatly encouraged. Things are changing."

But were the state's citizens and politicians prepared for the coming change and all it portended? Attorney Scott Berry sounded a warning. "By happenstance and culture and history and society, this is going to be a very traumatic issue for Utah to turn its face to," Berry said. "I'm not sure Utah is ready."

Chapter Twelve
EPILOGUE AS PROLOGUE

As the world looked forward to the dawning new millennium with both hopeful optimism and subtle concern, in many ways a significant portion on Utah's population remained firmly ensconced in the mindset of another century. Back in the early decades of the 1800s, America was undergoing a unique soul searching, the so-called Great Awakening that resulted in a spiritual and religious zeal not seen since the Puritans first stepped their conservative shoes on North American shores. Out of this zeitgeist arose the seeds of Joseph Smith's holy journey and the formation of his Church of Latter-Day Saints.

Although the majority of Mormons have found a way to reconcile their Church's prior teachings with modern societal values and laws, the fundamentalists who pursue plural marriage denounce any attempt to outlaw the principle as blasphemy and borderline genocide. Now that the world has become an ever-increasingly connected global village, it is harder for polygamists to live in anonymity and obscurity. As modern life closes in and begins to scrutinize, the clans grow more insular and isolated. The end of Utah's ambivalence about polygamy and the abuses that spring from it very well may mark the beginning of an abrupt change of lifestyle and force its practitioners deep underground. Irwin Altman, University of Utah psychology professor, argues that polygamous families are taking a place alongside other non-traditional households, from same-sex couples to single-parent homes, that have become fixtures of American life. "This movement," he says, "is here to stay."

For many, the Kingston trials have faded into yesterday's news and memory. But the clan still finds itself the object of media scrutiny and state investigators who are examining their business dealings and practices, as well as taking a more careful look at the near slum-lord conditions in which some of the clan raise their children. And in January 2001, law enforcement officials found themselves confronted with another possible criminal case against some clan members; a case in which church leader Paul Kingston finds himself possibly embroiled.

Details were still sketchy at the time of this writing but the general facts are these. A woman watching her own five children and baby-sitting an eighteen-month-old child, claimed the girl she was watching fell off a stool and hit her head on the floor. However, instead of immediately calling 911, according to police, the baby-sitter (whose name was being withheld) called her sister, and Paul Kingston, an attorney for the clan, and the child's mother.

Kingston allegedly attempted to administer first aid when he arrived at the apartment. At that point, authorities say the child was bleeding from her head, mouth, and nose. It was only after the toddler's heart stopped beating that someone called 911. A medical helicopter airlifted the child to Primary Children's Medical Center where she was listed in critical condition. According to news reports, doctors were unable to stop the bleeding and the little girl was not expected to live. The babysitter was arrested and booked into jail for negligent child abuse. As in the case of Andrea Johnson, detectives believe neither the baby-sitter, mother, nor Paul Kingston called the police because they didn't want their alleged polygamous family relationships to be exposed. Not surprisingly, the baby-sitter refused to identify the father of the injured child or the father of her own children.

Rob Parrish, deputy director of the National Center on Shaken Baby Syndrome, told the *Salt Lake Tribune*, "The injuries are not consistent with a simple fall." Parrish said he talked to doctors at the hospital "who believe something was used to hit the baby on the head or that she was slammed down against something." He went on to add, "Sometimes you'll hear doctors say injuries from abuse are the equivalent of injuries from a fall from two or three stories," Parrish said. "That's the type of force we are dealing with." What legal involvement Paul Kingston faces in relation to the incident remains to be seen.

In August, 2000, 3rd District Judge Stephen Henriod threw out Green's defamation lawsuit against Tapestry Against Polygamy. The suit was dismissed on the basis that Green failed to provide Tapestry's attorneys with information about his personal history "They wanted to know everyone I had sex with and how old they were when we had sex," Green said. "That flat-out had nothing to do with the court case and I thought it was irrelevant." The judge didn't, and also ordered the Greens to pay the group more than $10,000 to cover Tapestry's attorney fees. Green has appealed the dismissal.

Tapestry Against Polygamy continues its crusade. Although still a grassroots organization in size—with three board members, a couple of volunteers, and a small advisory board—the group continues to push for reforms while helping women start new lives. However, the group has recently undergone its own changes and growing pains. Two of the founding members, Laura Chapman and Carmen Thompson, are no longer with the group.

But Rowenna Erickson makes it clear Tapestry will continue to help women struggling to free themselves from the polygamous lifestyle. "People think it's going to die down, and it's not." She also asserted that for her, life was now a lovely place to call home. "I'm at peace," she says. "Some of those in our group haven't gotten there yet, but I am comfortable with who I am and every day is a joy."

Looking back and to the future, Erickson says she is convinced more than ever that plural marriage fundamentally does not work. "No, I don't think it ever works. You cannot live with polygamy, because that would mean ignoring the pain, abuse, neglect, and poverty." She recalls a friend commenting that in plural marriage, "spiritually speaking, you're going to be with him and have his children to populate other worlds, for eternity. Well what does it involve? He's going to have sex forever and ever and ever. And she's going to be pregnant forever and ever and ever. So this woman said, 'It's just one big eternal fuck.'"

Before leaving as Tapestry's director, Carmen Thompson sounded a warning that the issue of polygamy was no longer just Utah's secret. "We're now getting calls from the entire United States," she said. "Women are trying to leave polygamous relationships in Florida,

Ohio, Iowa, Michigan, Wisconsin. This is a national problem. It may be somewhat concentrated in the western United States but the entire nation needs to look at this."

Summing up her personal belief, and the feeling of many others, at the notion that polygamy is an expression of God's will, Thompson says, "If Christ walked through the streets of Salt Lake and saw all the women and children that are being used and abused and cast aside, I think he would be appalled."

BIBLIOGRAPHICAL AND REFERENCE SOURCES

In addition to court documents, press releases, media advisories, public records, personal interviews and historical documents, including affidavits in relation to the introduction of celestial and plural marriage on file in the historian's office in Salt Lake City, the following reference sources were used and/or reviewed in preparing the book.

20/20. "Man and Wives: A Look at Polygamous Marriages in the US." ABC News. 17 October 1997.

"A Flourishing Secret Society: Polygamy in Utah Thrives." *The Washington Post,* 18 August 1998. Reprinted from *Newsday.*

"A Polygamist Plea."*Salt Lake Observer,* 14-27 August 1998.

Abrahams, Israel. *Jewish Life in the Middle Ages.* New York: Macmillan & Co., 1917.

Adams, Brooke. *Salt Lake Observer,* 14-27 August 1998.

Affidavit of Lucy Walker Smith

"African Ivory Coast Struggles with Practice of Polygamy." *Morning Edition.* 22 August 1996.

"Analysis: Tom Green Found Guilty of Polygamy." *Weekend Edition.* 19 May 2001.

Anapol, Deborah. *Love Without Limits*. Internet Resource Center, 1992.

AP Wire Service. "Candidates Said Focus Would Be on Abuse, Fraud in Polygamist Communities." 18 September 2000.

AP Wire Service. "Panel OKs Bill to Boost Marriage age to 16." 21 January 1999.

AP Wire Service report. 16 June 1999.

AP Wire Service report. 7 February 1999.

AP Wire Service. "Report: North S.L. Drops Garbage firm." 5 December 1998.

Associated Press. "Polygamist Sentenced to Prison for Having Sex with Teenage Niece." *The Dallas Morning News*, 10 July 1999.

Associated Press. "Polygamist Takes Stand during Trial in Utah: Man Accused of Bigamy Testifies Without Emotion." *The Dallas Morning News*, 18 May 2001.

Barett, Greg. "Utah and its Polygamists Race Against Time to End Abuses." *USA Today*, 2 February 2000.

Becker, Gary. *Treatise on the Family*. Cambridge, Mass.: Harvard University Press, 1991.

Beiser, Vince. "The Perils of Polygamy: An Incest Case in Utah Highlights the Controversy over 'Plural Marriage.'" *Maclean's*, 26 July 1999, 32.

Berkes, Howard. "Profile: Massacre in 1857 of Arkansas Wagon Train by Mormon settlers in Utah." *Morning Edition*. 8 August 2000.

Berkes, Howard, Robert Siegel, and Linda Wertheimer. "Polygamy Flap." *All Things Considered*. 28 July 1998.

Booth, William. "Polygamist Is Found Guilty of Bigamy; Utah Traveling Salesman Flaunted His Lifestyle With 5 Wives, 29 Children." *The Washington Post*, 20 May 2001.

Brooks, Jaunita. *The Mountain Meadows Massacre*. Norman: University of Oklahoma Press, 1991.

Brunson, Arrin. "Should we Prosecute Polygamy?" *The Herald-Journal* (Logan, Utah), 24 April 1999.

Burton, Greg. "Polygamist Wants Separation of Rape, Bigamy Charges." *Salt Lake Tribune*, 3 May 2000.

Burton, Greg. "When Incest Becomes a Religious Tenet: Practice sets 100-member Kingston Clan Apart from Other Utah Polygamous Groups." *The Salt Lake Tribune*, 15 April 1999.

Burton, Greg. "Affidavits Give Peek into Secretive and Incestuous Polygamist Clan; Incest Prominent Feature of Kingston Polygamists." *Salt Lake Tribune*, 2 August 1998.

Byram, Cala. "Polygamy is Called Too Hard to Prosecute." *Deseret News*, 31 August 1998.

Byram, Cala "New Group Wants the State to Repeal Ban." *Deseret News*, 1 August 1998.

Carter, Melinda. "Panel Discusses Polygamy in Africa." Kansas State University. 24 Apr. 1995. Kansas State University. 22 Feb. 2000

Carter, Mike. "Polygamist Faces Trial in Daughter's Beating." AP Wire Service, 23 July 1998.

Chadwick, Alex. "Analysis: Polygamy Trial in Utah against Tom Green." *Morning Edition*. 16 May 2001.

Church of Jesus Christ of Latter-Day Saints, *General Conference Report*. 6 April 1904, 74–5.

Cloud, John. "Families: Henry & Mary & Janet &... Is Your Marriage a Little Dull? The 'Polyamorists' Say There's Another Way."*Time*, 15 November 1999, 90.

Compton, Todd. *In Sacred Loneliness—The Plural Wives of Joseph Smith*. Salt Lake City: Signature Books, 1997.

Dallas, Sandra. "Letter From Utah: Polygamy's Victims Find Their Voice."*Business Week International*, vol. 3698, 11 September 2000.

David, Mary Ben. *From a Woman's Place: The Case for Polygamy*. polygamy.com

Davidson, Ros. "Sins of the Father." Salon.com (July 29, 1998).

Deseret News, 14 November 1855.

Dillon, Lucinda. "Leavitt Clarifies Polygamy Stand." *Deseret News*, 1 August 1998.

Doctrine and Covenants, 107, 30.

Edwards, Bob. "Analysis: Polygamy Trial to Begin in Utah." *Morning Edition*. 14 May 2001.

Ellis, Peter Berresford. *Celtic Women: Women in Celtic Society and Literature*. Grand Rapids, Mich.: W.B. Eerdmans, 1996.

Emmett, Andrea Moore. "Only for Eternity." *Salt Lake City Weekly*, 1 February 1999.

Esshom, Frank Elwood. *Pioneers and Prominent Men of Utah*. Salt Lake City, Utah: Utah Poineers, 1913.

Evans, Bishop R.C. *Forty Years in the Mormon Church: Why I Left It*. 1920. Reprinted on www.biblebelievers.net.

Faux, Steven. "Genetic Self Interest and Mormon Polygyny." *Sunstone*, July-August, 38.

Foster, Shawn. "Baby Sitter Arrested after Delay in Calling 911 for Injured Child." *The Salt Lake Tribune*, 18 January 2001.

Frankel, Bruce, Cathy Free and Leslie Berestein. "Verdict: Lifting the Veil Ex-plural Wife Rowenna Erickson Attacks an Enduring Utah Institution: Polygamy." *People*, 21 June 1999.

Gallagher, Jennifer and Susan Snyder. "Scrutiny only Welds Bonds of Polygamous Group, They Say." *Standard-Examiner*, 14 Sunday 1999.

George Plimpton, edited By Richard O'Brien And Mark Mravic. "Scorecard."*Sports Illustrated*, 21 December 1998, 29+.

"Girl's Case Revives Polygamy Debate." *The Washington (DC) Times*, 22 April 1999.

Glasse, Cyril. *The Concise Encyclopedia of Islam*. San Francisco: Harper & Row, 1989.

Gurrister, Tim. "Faces Two Counts of Incest and One Count of Unlawful Sexual Conduct." *Standard Examiner*, 16 October 1998.

Gurrister, Tim. "Girl Bides Time." *Standard-Examiner*, 27 June 1999.

Gurrister, Tim and Goeffrey Fattah. "A Prosecutor Says Alleged Polygamist Didn't Receive Special Treatment." *Standard Examiner*, 30 June 1999.

Harrie, Dan. "House Nixes Bill to Fight Crimes by Polygamists." *Salt Lake Tribune*, 28 January 2000.

History of Utah, Vol. 2:380-1.

Hoekema, Anthony A. *The Four Major Cults*. Grand Rapids, Mich.: W. B. Eerdmans, 1963.

http://www.asnc.cam.ac.uk/Level3/reading.html

http://www.math.byu.edu/~smithw/Lds/LDS/History/History_of_the_Church/Vol_V

Hunt, Stephen. "Polygamy May Bring New Prosecutions" *Salt Lake Tribune*, 6 June 1999.

Idaho Statesman, 15 March 2000, page 5B.

"Inside Polygamy." *Investigative Reports*. A&E.

Johnson, Sonia. *From Housewife to Heretic*. Garden City, New York: Doubleday, 1981.

Jorgensen, Chris. "Polygamists Can Adopt Children, Rules Split Court." *Salt Lake Tribune*, 27 March 1991, B1.

Joseph the Prophet. *Journal of History*. October 1918, 746.

Joseph, Elizabeth. *Polygamy: The Ultimate Feminist Lifestyle*. From a speech given by Elizabeth Joseph at "Creating a Dialogue: Women Talking to Women," a conference organized by the Utah chapter of the National Organization for Women.

Journal of Discourse, Vol. 6, page 176.

Journal of Discourses, Vol. 11, page 239.

Journal of Discourses, Vol. 11, page 269.

Kelly, Dr. Fergus *A Guide to Early Irish Law*. Dublin: Dublin Institute for Advanced Studies, 1988.

Kilzer, Lou. "Polygamy and Profit. Utah Clan Builds Riches in Colorado, Elsewhere, While Growing Bigger through Intermarriage." *Denver Rocky Mountain News*, 13 February 2000.

Kilzer, Lou. "Leader: Group is Persecuted." *Denver Rocky Mountain News*, 13 February 2000.

Laake, Deborah. *Secret Ceremonies: A Mormon Woman's Intimate Diary of Marriage and Beyond*. New York: William Morrow, 1993.

Lay, Wilfrid. *A Plea for Monogamy*. New York: Don, Mead and Co., 1923.

Lessin, Sasha Ph.D. "Polyamory: More Love for All." *Loving More Magazine*, Summer 1999.

Llewellyn, John R. "State Is Afraid to Go After Polygamy's Kingpins." *Salt Lake Tribune*, 4 June 2000.

McConkie, Bruce R. *Mormon Doctrine*. Salt Lake City: Bookcraft Inc., 1966.

Meadow, James B. "Man and Wife and Man and...Monogamy Leave

You Wanting? Denver Household Tries Different Approach." *Denver Rocky Mountain News*, 30 March 1997, 14E.

Merson, Ben. *Ladies' Home Journal*, June 1967, 78

Messenger and Advocate, vol. 2, 475.

Messenger and Advocate, vols. 1 and 2.

Millennial Harbinger. *The Mormon Bible* Volume III, Number VI, June 1839.

Millennial Star, vol. 23, p. 754, 770, 816.

Moran, Hans S. "Kingston Case is Headed for Jury for First Time, Testimony on Group Allowed." *Deseret News*, 3 June 1999.

Moran, Hans S. "Polygamist's Lawyer Wants the Prosecutor Thrown Out." *Deseret News*, May 12 1999.

Moran, Hans S. "Kingston Faces Trial on Incest, Sex Counts." *Deseret News*, December 11, 1998.

Moran, Hans S. "Kingston Gets 28 weeks in Box Elder Jail; But Time Could Be Cut If He Apologizes to Daughter He Beat." *Deseret News*, 9 June 1999.

Moran, Hans S. "Kingston Seeks New Trial, Cites 'Highly Inflammatory' References to Polygamy; His New Lawyers Say the Comments Tainted the Jury." *Deseret News*, 15 June 1999.

Moran, Hans S. "Kingston Takes Plea Bargain But He Does Not Admit Belt-Whipping Daughter." *Deseret News*, 22 April 1999.

Moran, Hans S. "Kingston's Attorney Won't be Permitted to Depose Prosecutor." *Deseret News*, 21 May 1999.

Moran, Hans S. "Girl Testifies Against Kingston; Judge Tells All-Male Jury Case Is About Incest, Not Polygamy." *Deseret News* , 2 June 1999.

Mormon Church History http://www.byuh.edu/studentlife/scholar-ship/cannon.htm

Moulton, Kristen. "Courts Could Decide If Polygamy Protected." AP Wire Service, 20 June 1999.

Murr, Andrew. "Secrets In The Desert; Charges of Abuse and Polygamy Roil Utah." *Newsweek*, 10 August 1998.

Murr, Andrew. "Strange Days in Utah." *Newsweek*, 13 November 2000, 74.

Nauvoo Expositor, June 7, 1844

Nauvoo Neighbor, June 19, 1844.

Nearing, Ryam. *Loving More: The Polyfidelity Primer*. 1992.

Neary, Lynn. "Existence of Polygamy Today, its History in the Mormon Church and the Church's Views on the Practice." *Talk of the Nation*. 18 July 2000.

Nelson, James. "Prosecutor Concludes Utah Polygamy Case." *Reuters*, 16 May 2001.

Paddy, Burt. *My Struggles in a Mormon Hell: The Bizarre Rituals of Her*. Independent, 20 April 1994.

Partridge, Elizabeth. *Historical Record*, vol. 6, 240.

Pollitt, Katha. "Subject to Debate: Polymaritally Perverse."
    The Nation, vol. 269, 4 October 1999, 10.

"Polygamy Isn't Pretty." *Salt Lake Observer*, 14-27 August 1998, 20.

"Polygamy: An interview essay."
    netset.com/~khandi/polygamy.htm (22 February 2000).

"Polygamy and Its Aspects." http://collegian. ksu.edu/issues/v099B
    /sp/n143/campolygamy-carter.html

Price, Joyce. "Polygamy Could Help Moms Who Work,
    Says Utah's NOW." *Deseret News*, 12 August 1997.

Pugh, Jeremy. "Kingston Trial Attracting Attention." *Herald-Journal*,
    20 April 1999.

Quinn, D. Michael."Organizational Development and Social
    Origins of The Mormon Hierarchy, 1832-1932."
    (Master's thesis, University of Utah, August 1973), 69.

Revelation on the Eternity of the Marriage Covenant, Including
    Plurality of Wives, Given through Joseph, the Seer, in Nauvoo,
    Hancock County, Illinois, July 12th, 1843.

Rivera, Ray and Greg Burton. "Did Teen Mom Die Harboring a
    Secret?; Authorities May Reopen Case Involving Polygamous
    Clan, Allegations of Incest; Young Mother: Illness Long Went
    Untreated." *The Salt Lake Tribune*, 22 August 1998.

Rivera, Ray. "16-Year-Old Girl Testifies of Beating." *Salt Lake Tribune*,
    23 July 1998.

Rivera, Ray. "Kingston Gets Maximum Term, Lecture on Incest." *The Salt Lake Tribune*, 10 July 1999.

Rivera, Ray. "Utah Attorneys Key Figures in Polygamist Kingston Clan." *The Salt Lake Tribune*, 19 July 1998.

Rivera, Ray. "Church Makes Incest Doctrinal–Inbreeding Key to Doctrine of Keeping Bloodline Pure." *Salt Lake Tribune*, 25 April 1999.

Roberts, B. H. *A Comprehensive History of the Church of Jesus Christ of Latter-day Saints: Century 1*, 6 volumes, Salt Lake City, Deseret News Press, 1930.

Rogers, Paul. "Cash Cows." *San Jose Mercury News* 1999. http://www0.mercurycenter.com/nation/giveaway/holtz.htm

Salladay, Robert. "Mormons Now Target California." *San Francisco Examiner*, 7 April 1999, L1.

Sanchez, Jose Luis. "A-1 Disposal is Ordered to Halt Operations; Garbage Hauler has History of Safety-Related Accidents." *Deseret News*, 22 April 1999.

Sanchez, Jose Luis. "Garbage Firm Faces 6 Counts in Accident; Incident in North S.L. Hurt 4, Left Driver in Coma." *Deseret News*, 10 January 1999.

Schindler, Harold. *Orrin Porter Rockwell: Man of God, Son of Thunder*. Salt Lake City: University of Utah Press, 1966.

"Secrets in the Desert." *Newsweek*, 10 August 1998.

Sermon by Brigham Young, *Journal of Discourses*, vol. 4, 53–54. Also published in *Deseret News*, 1856, 235.

Sermon by President Brigham Young, delivered in the Mormon Tabernacle, 8 February 1857. Printed in *Deseret News*, 18 February 1857. Also reprinted in the *Journal of Discourses*, vol. 4, 219–20

Siegel, Lee. "U. Researchers Home In on Gene Defect." *The Salt Lake Tribune*, 12 October 1995.

Siegel, Robert. "Profile: Selection begins in Provo, Utah, for Polygamy Trial of Tom Green." *All Things Considered*. 14 May 2001.

Simon, Scott. "Profile: Tom Green's Polygamy Case Expected to Go to the Jury." *All Things Considered*. 18 May 2001.

Smith, Joseph F. *Journal of Discourses*, vol. 20, 31.

Smith, Joseph F. *Origin of Plural Marriage*. 82–3, 87, 92

Snowden, James H. *The Truth about Mormonism*. New York: George H. Doran Co., 1926.

Snyder, Susan. "Publicity Taking Toll on Polygamous Group, Ex-member Says." *Standard-Examiner* , 27 October 1998.

"South Africa Preparing to Officially Recognize Polygamy." *WIN News*, Autumn 1997.

Spencer, Herbert. *Principles of Sociology*. New York: D. Appleton and Co., 1899.

Stack, Peggy Fletcher. "Globally, Polygamy Is Commonplace." *The Salt Lake Tribune*, 20 September 1998.

Sterling, Terry Greene. "Secret Grief." Salon.com (27 October 2000).

Stewart, Kelly. "The Davis Enterprise." 20 June 1997.

Tanner, Gerald and Sandra, private letter written by a defector from the Kingston cult, Fall 1991.

Twyman, Gib. "Kingston's Trial Moved to Logan." *Deseret News*, 10 February 2000.

United States Reports, vol. 136, 1-68. The Late Corporation of the Church of Jesus Christ of Latter-Day Saints vs. United States, Nos. 1030, 1054.

"Unwelcome Buzz." *The Economist*, vol. 355, 29 April 2000.

"Utah Execution Draws Unwelcome Attention." *All Things Considered*. 25 January 1996.

"Utah Team Finds Gene for Rare Birth Defect; Discovery Provides Insight on Genesis of Limb Malformation." *The Salt Lake Tribune*, 27 June 1997.

Utah Const. art. III sec. 1 and www.le.state.utah.us.

"Vietnamese Polygamy King Said To Have 64 Children. So Far!" *Deutsche Presse-Agentu*, 9 March 1999.

Walker, Linda. "Child Protection Project." http://www.human-nature.com/science-as-culture/index.html

Wallace, C.G. "Kingston Trial Getting Under Way Defendant is Accused of Taking Niece as Wife." AP Wire Service, 1 June 1999.

Wallace, Irving. *The Twenty-seventh Wife*. New York: Simon and Schuster, 1961.

Weekly Tribune, Salt Lake City, August 4th, 1887

Westermarck, Edward. *History of Human Marriage*. London: Macmillan, 1901.

Wigmore, Barry. "I Was One of Tom's 8 Wives…and I Let My 2 Girls Marry Him." *Sunday Mirror*, 20 May 2001.

Wolfson, Hannah. "Christian Polygamists Cite Biblical Justification." Associated Press, 17 January 2000.

Wolfson, Hannah. "Is Kingston Trial About Polygamy? Prosecutors say case is about child abuse—that's all." 21 April 1999.

Woodruff, Wilford. "History of Wilford Woodruff." *Deseret News*, July–Aug. 1858.

Woodruff, Wilford. "The Autobiography of Wilford Woodruff." *Tullidge's Quarterly Magazinee*, October 1883-July 1884.

Woodruff, Wilford. *Wilford Woodruff's Journal, 1833-1898*. ed. Scott G. Kenny, typescript, 9 vols. Midvale, Utah: 1983-1984.

Zoellner, Tom. "A Man's Life: The Complete Instructions: How to Keep Your Wives Happy." *Men's Health*, 1 March 1999.

INDEX